Enjoying America's Gardens

Enjoying
America's Gardens

By JOAN PARRY DUTTON

REYNAL & COMPANY, NEW YORK

Other versions of some of the material in this book
have appeared in *House & Garden, The Christian
Science Monitor, Horticulture,* and *Pacific Discovery:
the Magazine of the California Academy of Sciences.*

Library of Congress catalog card number: 58-12945

Lithographed in the U. S. A.
by The Murray Printing Company
and bound by American Book–Stratford Press, Inc.

Contents

Enjoying America's Gardens

1      *Ice Age Survivors*

I CAME to see America by way of its gardens—a six-months' stay, perhaps. It was spring and I'd hoped to be home by Christmas. But it took me three years to work my way around the perimeter of the continent, and after a brief return to England one summer, I came back to explore five years more. America is that kind of country. And it still holds me.

I had written to Robert Pyle, a Pennsylvania rose grower at West Grove, Pennsylvania, near Philadelphia, enquiring for work. By a miracle of luck his reply came back over the Atlantic telephone: he offered sponsorship for my visa and work as his assistant in organizing an autumn congress of the American Horticultural Council.

I was off on a flying start, that was how he wanted it, so that I should arrive before the planting season began and he still had time to put me wise for my work. What compensation would the American dogwood—a world of dogwood—give me for the forfeit of an English spring? But the papers were signed, and the ticket bought. Almost before I knew it, the plane taxied slowly down the runway of London airport, the grass streamed beneath the wings, and we were air borne. Tomorrow was now inevitable: tomorrow was Pennsylvania without a cent in my pocket, without a single familiar face.

So my world changed overnight. So did my viewpoint. I found a country far more beautiful than I had imagined. The woods and streams, rolling hills and wide pasture lands, reminded me of England. But only the contour of the land was the same. The trees and the wild flowers, even the spring, all were different.

There is nothing reticent about the Pennsylvanian spring. It breaks with sudden violence, and passes with spendthrift speed. It allows one no time to watch the bud slowly unfold, and only a moment to know the flower before the wilting humidity of early summer begins.

A tide of bloom surged over the gardens of neighboring townships and spread fanwise across the outlying residential areas around Philadelphia. Redbud was a bold magenta splashed on the prevailing dogwood-white and green. Magnolias, more magnolias than I had ever seen, trees sometimes, eighty feet high, opened their wide blooms, white, rose-pink, or stained a claret-red. And all my preconceived ideas about American gardening exploded.

"America has no gardens such as we know them in England." That was the considered conclusion of Marion Cran, the English garden writer, after a tour of American gardens a quarter of a century ago. It is a catchword phrase that has been echoed ever since by English and Americans alike.

It all depends on where you stand, of course, and the view you see from there. In my first three months I did not go far beyond the state-line of Pennsylvania, but the pre-view was wide enough. Judging only by the miles of gardens that encircle Philadelphia, and by the outstanding gardens spread throughout eastern Pennsylvania, my guess was that eventually I should call down Mrs. Cran's remark as utterly absurd.

One surprise followed another. Everything was on a different scale. A world that was superficially the same was strange and new.

Corn, which brought to mind the European fields of wheat, oats, and barley, meant but one thing in the American scene: maize or Indian corn. And corn-planting time was when the oak leaf was as large as a squirrel's ear. My old gardener at home told me to wait to plant peas until the hawthorn leaf was as large as a mouse's ear.

"How long might the magnolias last?" I asked, dismayed to see the grass already white beneath the tall trees.

"As long as the wind allows. The seasons lasts about four weeks for magnolias in succession as against two months in England." And I took it that what held good for magnolias held good for all flowering plants in their season. Spring, that was more fleet than I had ever known, set the year's pace for every transient bloom.

Under Robert Pyle's tutelage, and through the mass of American Horticultural Council correspondence that came in from all over the country, the blueprint of a bird's eye view of American garden interests gradually emerged.

The blueprint revealed far more than garden-club activity.

It showed a bewildering array of gardens, from the small backyard gardens of home-owning men of moderate means to those of great estates; from nurserymen's enormous acreages to city parks, with botanical gardens and arboretums crowding the map.

And it was Robert Pyle's introductions first to nearby horticulturists, later to others far afield, that set the snowball pattern of garden-park-and-aboretum visits going. These made the blueprint come to life. Almost invariably one garden visit led to another, and in one respect there is one impression that stands out above all others. I was always surprised in the way people, even very busy people, put themselves out to make time to show me round. I was, after all, anonymous. I had no handle to my name. I was simply an amateur gardener come to look and learn.

I used to go sometimes to the little Quaker town of Swarthmore to see the campus planting at Swarthmore College—known officially as the Arthur Hoyt Scott Horticultural Foundation. Swarthmore, recognized as one of the outstanding horticultural foundations, is by intention a "People's Garden." The aim of the foundation is to display its five thousand different kinds of trees and shrubs and flowering plants in surroundings that the home-owner of average means can duplicate. The arboretum is in effect a 240-acre showcase of college campus and adjoining woodland planted with shrubs and flowers that are easy to grow, and which need no special care in the southeastern Pennsylvania climate.

John Wister, the arboretum director, and one-time Secretary of the Pennsylvania Horticultural Society, was one of the first garden personalities who pulled wool from my eyes. He shattered an illusion by telling me that the English flora is comparatively poor as compared with that of America.

For the first time he made me aware of the fact that the English garden had become long since thoroughly Americanized.

Most of the early plant collectors in North America were British. In two successive waves a century apart, they searched first the eastern seaboard and then the Pacific coast for plant material. The treasure they discovered was no less rich and varied than that brought back from Asia, the hunting ground of later and present-day collectors, and so better remembered in the public mind on that account.

The plant material introduced from the New World has now been cultivated and hybridized for so long in England that many North American wild flowers are thought of as the "old-fashioned" flowers of English cottage gardens. But the evening primrose shared the night with the American fireflies long before it opened its yellow bloom to the English dusk, and the Oswego Indians made a brew from the leaves of the shaggy-headed red bergamot centuries before it became a common old English garden flower. If the English garden had not been so Americanized, it would have no bergamot, no evening primrose, no red-flowering currant, no asters to speak of, and no goldenrod.

It was John Wister who gave me a foretaste of what was to prove the greatest thrill of all my garden sightseeing days: the thrill of discovering for myself, like the plant hunters before me, the ornamental trees and shrubs, the old familiar flowers of my English garden growing wild and untamed, often in an unbelievable profusion, in their native setting.

Philadelphia, John Wister told me, was from its beginning a base for plant collectors. Today it has a greater variety of trees planted around it than any other city. It lies not only on the Fall line climatically between north and south, but is within an area exceptionally rich in native plants and trees of horticultural value.

He solved the riddle of why the Pennsylvanian landscape was superficially so like England and why it was yet so different; why the elms and oaks were not the same; why magnolias did so well.

During the Ice Age, the climate and flora of Europe, the greater part of North America, and most of the world's surface, was changed. And not only was the flora—the old Tertiary flora as it was called—changed, but much of it was squeezed out of existence. In Europe, the Ice Age tree flora was reduced to about eighty-five species; in the western states of North America the hardwoods were largely driven out, and losses among wild flowers were equally great, probably greater.

But in southeastern North America and in eastern Asia, many of the old types of plants exceptionally survived; so many trees and plants native to this part of the United States are native nowhere else except in Asia, and the relationship of this plant life is generally much closer to that of Asia than to Europe. European plants, moreover, are not particularly well adapted to the climate of southeastern North America.

Even after learning all this, it was not easy to realize that not a single native species of tree is the same in Europe and America today. Europe has no tulip tree, no magnolia, no honey locust; no sweet, no sour gum; no catalpa, no native witch hazel, no native mulberry tree. The English sycamore, elm, walnut, and oak trees are in turn all different from the American species.

The heart of North America's great forest stronghold is in the Appalachian Mountains. The Appalachian flora extends from Canada to Florida, and borders the prairie states. The only other similar hardwood forests are the forests of China and Japan.

The Southern Appalachians mark the greatest concentration point of this rich flora—its members represent more flower families than there are in all of Europe. It, too, bears a strong resemblance to the flora of China and Japan. Trailing arbutus is native nowhere else except in Japan. The only other counterpart of the tulip tree is in central China; the only other native species of the Franklinia and its relation, the lobolly bay—both natives of the American south—grow in the warmer parts of Asia. So with Virginia creeper, the Carolina jessamine, the wild hydrangea, sassafras, with Dutchman's breeches, shooting star, and wisteria.

Wisteria? I did not confess my ignorance in knowing only the Asiatic wisteria. Instead I asked John Wister if it was true that the wisteria was named for his grandfather. He sighed.

"You bring up the same old question which crops up every few weeks or months. It's a story with wonderful variations. You'd hardly credit it, but occasionally I hear from someone who claims to have the original plant that Dr. Caspar Wistar (1760–1818) was said to have brought from Japan.

"Dr. Caspar Wistar was a very eminent man, but no direct relation of our family. The Wistars and Wisters stem from two brothers who came to America in 1718 and 1723 respectively. Neither of them spelled their names the way either of the families now spell it. Dr. Wistar taught Anatomy at the University of Pennsylvania, but as far as I know he never traveled outside Philadelphia, let alone out of the country. Nor, as far as anyone knows, had he any particular interest in plants."

It was Thomas Nuttall, the British botanist, who came to Philadelphia in 1807, who named the genus for Dr. Wistar. At the time he stated that he spelled wistaria with an "e" for euphony, not realizing that both branches of the family with two different spellings pronounced their names the same way.

"The old doctor would turn over in his grave," John Wister continued, "if he knew the plant was now spelled with an 'e,' but botanical rules require that plant spellings follow the original, even if the original be accidentally or deliberately mis-spelled. I think it's a ridiculous rule," he added, "and I notice that many botanists don't follow it. *Standardized Plant Names* spells Wistaria with an 'a' and in my opinion that is correct."

To make confusion worse confounded, Nuttall named the American wistaria, *Wistaria frutescens,* a native of Virginia southward to Florida, probably only a short time before John Reeves, who went to Canton, China in 1812, introduced the Asiatic wistaria into England. So the Asiatic plant bears to this day an American name.

2 　*Magnificent Longwood*

*Y*ou will never see another garden like it in America."
That is what people told me about Longwood, the garden
of the late Mr. Pierre S. du Pont, near Kennett Square, Pennsylvania and twelve miles from Wilmington, Delaware,
which for more than one hundred and fifty years has been
the Du Pont family seat in the United States. It was the first
garden that I saw in America, and it was no doubt Robert
Pyle's intention that Longwood should dispel at a glance
any misconception I might have of American gardens. And
though I privately discounted the inference of "in America"
as local pride, I do now say that Longwood is unique.

Since I first went to Longwood Mr. du Pont has died,
and the garden which in his lifetime was always open to the
public is continued under his endowment as the Longwood
Foundation—a "Horticultural display for the benefit and

13

enjoyment of the public." That is an exact description of Longwood; more than 335,000 people visit the great garden display yearly and enjoy it.

It was a cold, sunlit April day when I first went there. A boisterous wind chased the cloud shadows across the country-side. The wild cherry was in bloom along the woodland edge and spring beauty carpeted the banks of shaded streams; the ripening seed clusters of the swamp maple added vermilion to the tender browns and greens of spring. All was new. The countryside, at that moment, was upper-most in my mind. Longwood, I thought, though I had been forewarned, would at best undoubtedly prove a great garden, but it would be just another garden. But I always remember, even after many a return visit that never diminished that first impression, my amazement that spring day when Mr. John H. Marx, the superintendent, showed me round.

Longwood is magnificent: a thousand-acre tract of rolling hill and primeval forest land that William Penn granted to George Pierce in 1702. There George Pierce's son built his house in 1730, and around it he and his heirs added an arboretum of choice trees and shrubs.

In 1906 Mr. du Pont bought the Pierce estate. Around the old Pierce house, which he enlarged, and the arboretum, he created his fifty-acre garden; from 1915 Longwood was his country home.

Longwood Garden is a series of gardens that spread out and away from a vast indoor conservatory and the formal garden below it with its series of electrically controlled fountains. These are the two features which, to date, have made Longwood most famous.

Mr. Marx took me first to the conservatory. He opened the door. It was as a curtain raiser on a fabulous flower fantasy. In an instant we stepped from the fresh wind-swept out-of-doors into the still, heavy warmth of an exotic world.

The pillared hall of glass was massed with borders of bloom around a central square of lawn, making an all-year-round flower show that must rival the one-time lavishness of ancient Rome. From the north and the south, from the temperate and tropical zones, from season and out of season, flowers and fruit were gathered under approximately three acres of glass.

It was April, as I have said. Snapdragons and schizanthus, marigold and larkspur, petunias, delphiniums and canter-bury bells were in bloom beside the standard rose and fuchsia bushes. Orange and lemon trees were heavy with fruit. At the center of the lawn, a tree stretched its arms to the glass sky thirty feet high above.

Even if this main conservatory were considered alone, it would still without doubt be the most extraordinary private horticultural display in America. I thought of the old Dutch flower painters who waited patiently month by month to add one flower and then another in its season to their still-life paintings of fruit and flowers. What would they have thought of Longwood, where they could find in a day what they had waited a year to see?

But that was not all. We passed through a whole series of hot houses: there were pomegranates and the warm scent of ripening figs from southern Europe; bananas from Cuba; oranges and grapes from California; melons from the South-ern States; coffee from South America; one house of flower-ing peach and nectarine trees; another of carnations, of roses; a hall cool and deep with the earthy dampness of ferns, and an orchid collection which rates as the finest in America.

At the last we came to a hall massed with a gorgeous display of azalea bloom which, in turn, opened to the long ballroom where on Sunday afternoons organ recitals are given. Mrs. Pierre du Pont was partially deaf, and Mr. du Pont had the organ built that he himself might play to her in the evenings music that she could hear. It is a remarkable instrument, with more than 10,000 pipes, and occupies a space 63 feet long, 40 feet high, and 30 feet deep.

There were three crystal balls on a malacite table by the window. "Touch them," said Mr. Marx, waiting for my reaction. The two outer balls were warm to my touch—a synthetic triumph of the great Du Pont chemical company—though they appeared identical to the ice-cold pure crystal center ball. Was it only coincidence that they were, in a sense, symbolic of the gardens: synthetic for the artificial garden under its acreage of glass, pure crystal for the outdoor garden with the sky for ceiling?

The great Georgian-design conservatory, with a frontage of 650 feet and a structure that is mainly of bronze, faces south to the vast fountain garden below, which is as large as a city square. The conservatory and fountains took two years to build and were completed in 1931.

For those who have not seen Longwood, only photographs or film can picture the view from the conservatory terrace to the fountain garden below. A set of statistics in no way conveys the sense of the scene, but there is no other electrically operated, illuminated system of fountains anywhere in the world to equal it. On summer nights when the whole system is fully operated, when the fountains are put into play and the elaborate under-water lighting system turned on, a battery of red, blue, green, yellow, and white rocketing plumes light up the night sky. It is a sight that can only be compared with that of a king's garden, the garden of Louis XIV at Versailles, France, though at Longwood the fountains are more concentrated in their arrangement and design.

The construction of the whole scheme is an engineer's delight, and was carried out under Mr. du Pont's supervision by the Longwood construction and maintenance men, not by outside contractors.

Longwood is in itself an immaculate garden city. There are about one hundred houses available, and the population includes experts in all the building trades—electricians, plumbers, joiners, mechanics, painters, and the fire department personnel.

Approximately two hundred and fifty oil burners are used to heat the conservatory. Pipe lines deliver more than one million gallons of water monthly to feed the gigantic water tank, which is to say that Longwood gardens soak up in one month what an average family would use in ten years. When the fountains are in full play it takes about eighteen thousand gallons of water a minute to supply them, and the whole system needs a total of 650,000 gallons when the reservoirs are filled.

Beyond the main fountain garden are a formal rose garden and an all-green yew garden. Away to the east there is a whole series of gardens with massive flower borders, small boxwood enclosed gardens that stretch over flowering acres to the park-like outer boundaries.

At the extreme north-end of the woodland, beyond the lakes with the wide sweeping lawns, massed with daffodils and early spring bulbs, and the deep plantings of azaleas backed by broad-leaved rhododendrons, is a tree-enclosed water garden. Few people come so far, and most of those who find it stay but a moment as they pass by. Yet to my mind this is one of the most perfect separate gardens within all Longwood's planted acres.

This comparatively small water garden was laid out from a plan of the Villa Gamberaia, near Florence in Italy, which Mr. du Pont visited in 1925: four rectangular pools and fountains around a central fountain with a large oval fountain basin at the end. The four pools with fountains appear all the same size, but the two further pools are twenty feet longer to create the optical illusion of a garden of greater depth. There is no color here but green, no sound but the quiet drip of a fountain. But when the water is set in motion in the hot summer days, the place becomes a green and crystal outdoor room, light and gay and cool, the water flashing in the sun.

By description Longwood must inevitably sound opulent, and great by the sheer mechanics of its installations, its stone and brick pools and fountains, terraces, staircases and retaining walls, and its canals. But its true greatness, I think, is in the close, intimate, even simple relationship that existed between the plants and the two men who knew the garden best —Mr. Pierre du Pont and his superintendent, Mr. Marx.

The story is told of an old lady who traveled many miles to Longwood. She hadn't enough money for the bus to drop her at the entrance. She was footsore and weary after walking the last lap towards her goal. She stopped in the garden to tell one of the workmen, so she thought, about her troubles. He put down his spade, and went to fetch one of the bath-chairs available for just such tired old folk, and then the man wheeled her all around the paths. She never knew, because he did not want her to feel embarrassed, that the kind gardener was Mr. Pierre du Pont himself.

And I remember how Mr. Marx, in telling me he had

lost one of the old azaleas the previous winter, rather apologetically confessing "I felt as though I had lost a limb."
There can be very few gardeners whose love for individual
flowers, amid such a perfect galaxy of perennial bloom, remains so sensitive and single. Perhaps that is one of the
secrets that he and Mr. du Pont shared, what has made
Longwood a place of which it is true to say: "You will not
see another garden like it in America."

Mr. Pierre du Pont heavily endowed Longwood Garden
Foundation. The garden will grow and develop under the
wide terms of the endowment as the six trustees, all members
of the Du Pont family, think fit. The staff of about one hundred and eighty experts is under the directorship of Dr.
Russell J. Seibert; funds for plant collectors will be made
available; scientific work and plant hybridizing will be carried out.

Longwood is not an old garden, as gardens go, and as a
horticultural Foundation it is very young. But it will, as
Mr. du Pont intended, be not only a display for the enjoyment of the public but one of the great horticultural centers
of North America.

3 ℐ
🎀 *Live*

with

Roses

ℐ LIVED that first Pennsylvania summer through with roses although I did not work among them. I tried to grasp the history of a single rose from seed sowing of the Multiflora Japonica stock until, after their first winter of storage in underground cellars, the plants were set out in the fields to await the grafter's budding knife. The following season they carried the blooms of the new rose.

It was a late spring. They were still planting the young stock out in May, but made good the lost time. In two days alone twenty-three Puerto Ricans planted fifty-four thousand rose plants. I watched them, tough and wiry planters, going up and down the marked-out rows, bundles of the tiny bushes stuffed into their hip pockets as they bent under the broiling sun, planting roses by the thousand.

Robert Pyle was a great promoter of roses. Year after year

he went to Europe in search of winners—"Star Roses" by his trademark—that would bring him success. He believed in success, and he had some good stars.

Among his famous stars were Madame Henri Guillot and Madame Cochet-Cochet of France; Floridora from the hands of Tautau in Germany; the aristocratic and lovely Duquesa de Penaranda from Pedro Dot of Spain; Pixie, the first white miniature from De Vink of Holland, and Irene of Denmark which Swend Poulsen had originated and named for his own two-year-old granddaughter, not, as people generally think, for Denmark's Queen Irene.

Robert Pyle had a flair for launching his stars on their American careers. The beautiful tapestry-red Grande Duchesse that Ketten of Luxembourg had originated was named for Luxembourg's Grande Duchesse Charlotte. When, in World War II, she took refuge in America, Robert Pyle greeted her in October, 1940, with a bouquet of her own roses as token of America's welcome when she landed.

Happiness was christened in America. France sent the rose as symbol of friendship in the "Thank You" train she had loaded with luxuries in recognition of America's generosity during and after the war. And it was Robert Pyle who, at the request of French growers, presented sixty blooms of Happiness to Mrs. Truman at the White House.

The Peace Rose was Robert Pyle's proudest introduction, and he was able to introduce it at an extraordinarily appropriate moment. In 1945, when the forty-nine head delegates to the United Nations Peace Conference in San Francisco returned to their private hotel rooms, they found, set in a stem vase, a single bloom of a superb new rose presented to them by the American Rose Society. The late Jan Masaryk of Czechoslovakia, as he bent over the enormous yellow bloom, declared, "It is one of the most beautiful roses I have ever seen."

Has any other rose made its first public appearance in such distinguished company, among the statesmen of the world? Each delegate, in turn, acclaimed it as Jan Masaryk had done, as a rose of extraordinary beauty, and saw it as a symbol, as the American Rose Society intended. No one, however, could have foreseen such perfect timing for its presentation. It was the day when the name of the rose was repeated by millions of people the world over. It was VE Day, Victory in Europe, May 8, 1945, and the rose, the famous Peace Rose.

The story of the Peace Rose belongs in part to France, in part to America, to Pennsylvania and to California, and it is a story full of coincidence.

Francis Meilland of Lyons, France, a famous hybridizer, also a friend and collaborator of Robert Pyle, was its originator. Meilland, representative of the fourth generation of a family of rose breeders, had already introduced some fine roses: his first important creation was Golden State, a Gold Medal winner and the official rose of the World's Fair in San Francisco.

Few people recognize the hours, even the years, of intense application connected with producing new roses. A plant breeder learns to have infinite patience as well as keen judgement; he must accept disappointments. It takes a long time to produce and test new roses, and a genius for appraisal, first in selecting the parents, and then in recognizing, among thousands, the seedlings that have promise.

Francis Meilland and his wife raise some one hundred thousand seedlings each year, hybridizing among them some twenty-five thousand roses. After selection they retain about one thousand plants for the second year, and narrow the number down in the third year to a mere one hundred.

The history of the Peace Rose began in 1936. In that year Meilland grew around eight hundred small yellow-rose plants from the seeds of one of his many crosses. Among them he noticed just one variety which showed unusual foliage; he thought it worth further experimentation. In 1939 the plant bore splendid flowers.

It was a plant of such promise that in the fall of the following year, when Germany held northern France and unoccupied France was still free, Meilland described his new creation in a letter to Robert Pyle with great enthusiasm. He quoted the Duke of Windsor, then a near neighbor, who often visited Meilland's establishment: "I have never seen in my life such a marvelous rose."

And so the following spring Meilland sent plants of this marvelous rose on the long and then hazardous journey to America. The consignment was weeks on the way. Many plants died en route. But on May 1, 1941, the day after Germany threatened to sink all United States ships entering the war zone, the surviving plants were delivered to Robert Pyle.

The quality of the rose was immediately recognized. As 43R12 it was entered in the All-America rose trials as promptly as possible, and was sent out to fifteen test gardens to stand trial for two years.

The men who watched the rose during that time noted the handsome, dark green, shining foliage, the long straight stems holding the great blooms erect. They watched the golden buds open to the fresh and delicate coloring of the open flower, noted the color vary day to day and from one rose to another—from yellow to pale gold, from cream to ivory

—always with a flush of pink on the outer edges of the lightly ruffled petals.

For the Conard-Pyle Company this, the most long-lasting of all Hybrid Tea Roses, was the Star Rose of the Century. In July, 1944, experienced, keen judges voted 43R12 the highest score ever awarded in the history of the All-America Rose Selections, Inc.

What name should be chosen for this great rose? Many people were asked to make suggestions. Still, choice was difficult. Preferences differed. Finally it was decided that this greatest new rose of our time should be named for the world's greatest desire—Peace. In announcing the name, the Company said:

> "We believe that this rose is destined to live on and on as a classic, in our grandchildren's garden and for generations to come. We would use the name of Peace to preserve the knowledge that we have gained the hard way, that peace is increasingly essential to all mankind, to be treasured with greater wisdom, watchfulness and foresight than the human race has so far been able to maintain for any great length of time. Toward that end, with our hopes for the future, we plan to dedicate our best Rose as Peace."

Was it perhaps just a mere accident of history, or was it simply coincidence that the life-history dates of the Peace Rose are also those of our emergence from war to peace? For the Star Rose of the Century was christened at Pasadena Rose Show in 1945 just as Berlin fell to the Allies; as we have seen, it made its first public appearance on VE day in San Francisco. The date, set over a year before, for the announcement that the Peace Rose was the year's only All-American winner, turned out to be VJ Day. And the day the Secretary of the American Rose Society presented the Society's national gold medal—Peace was the first rose to win this award—was September 8, 1951, when the peace treaty with Japan was finally signed.

It was a great coming-out party, in San Francisco, that May day of 1945. Many of those who were there and who paid homage to the rose are gone, Jan Smuts of South Africa, Mackenzie King of Canada among them. But the rose remains as a symbol; the Peace Rose lives on.

One day Robert Pyle sent me out to make a set of color slides of individual rose blooms. I was pleased when the slides came back, pictures of gorgeous bloom. But Mr. Pyle saw them differently, and discarded them as useless. One slide showed a rose too full-blown; another, not quite so open, might have passed had there not been some flaw in petal or in leaf.

Unexpectedly he sent me out again, but this time with one of his staff, so that I might learn what a nurseryman would call a very good rose, if not a perfect one.

"What is the perfect rose from a rose-man's point of view?" I asked.

"Ah," he said smiling, with a little twist to his smile, "she is as rare as the woman who has both charm and virtue. You must look for carriage, for good foliage, for a shapely bud and a bloom with depth of color." And from my own amateur standpoint I added that indispensable virtue that the camera lens cannot record: for me a perfect rose must have perfume too.

Size and color seem to be the professional's first requirements, I suspect largely due to the craze for stylized flower arrangements; and in much of America's climate, carriage is of great importance. A rose must have sufficient stamina to hold up its head whatever the degree of heat and humidity. And nurserymen must meet the demand. Perhaps one day public opinion will clamour for fragrance again at the expense of size. I have never yet understood whether nurserymen raise the rose they think the public ought to have, or whether they raise the rose they think the public want. But a preference for one rose or another is certainly an entirely individual affair. I have never wholly admired the Peace Rose. I find her blousy and buxom, almost too coarse for a rose, but I know that popular acclaim would howl me down.

Helen Keller, the deaf and blind writer, came to the rose fields one day and was asked to describe her ideal rose.

"One that is rich, vivid in color," she replied, "vital in fragrance and velvety to touch." Armfuls of the most fragrant roses were gathered for her. "These," she said, "are the vivid moments among so many flat ones," as she bent down to enjoy the blooms.

It was one of those still, humid summer days on which the heat makes headline news, when I went out with my staff coach to the rose fields again. Still I was glad to be out and away from my desk where the ink blurred before it dried and my hands stuck to every piece of paper that I touched.

The long grass was cut and lay in long-patterned swathes across the unhedged acres. A tractor man, protected by a large sun umbrella, was hoeing up and down between the rows of roses, the only moving thing as far as eye could see. Thunder, rumbling away, added a menacing note to the sultry stillness.

Hatless, and intent on our search for the perfect rose, we spent the day like the tractor man, going up and down the rows. The scent of roses mingled with the hay. We would stop and admire a single rose in rank after rank of Charlotte Armstrongs, and search among the shining foliage of Mission Bells for a good nurseryman's rose.

I tried, for my own amusement, to decide among such a

selection which half-dozen roses I would name as my favorites, and found it as hard to answer as the choice of a half-dozen books I would take with me on a desert island. Crimson Glory, I told myself, I would put first, and another red rose, Ami Quinard, whose deep-red velvet petals turn dusty black as they fade without a trace of blue, retaining their velvet quality to the last, even when they are fallen in the dust. For white I would choose the climbing City of York. Certainly I would have that aristocrat, the Duzesa de Penaranda; Texas Centennial, Mme. Henri Guillot and Mrs. Sam McGreedy; also Sutter's Gold.

As other names and faces came crowding in, there was one old familiar rose I missed.

"Where's Madame Butterfly?"

"She's somewhere around. I think you are near her now; go three rows across."

"But . . . this isn't Madame Butterfly although it has her label." My companion came over and checked with me. Yes, it was Madame Butterfly, of course it was, he said. Not very good perhaps, but well . . .

The rose was not the Madame Butterfly I knew in England. I remembered there how her blooms loved to feel the dew without it being drawn from them before the sun was high; they loved to feel a cool breeze across their face. They loved fresh early summer mornings and the spider-webbed September days. But here, the hot sun of the eastern seaboard burnt the fair skin. The rose was only a shadow, no, not even a shadow of her real self. It was a shame to see her languish in that wilting heat. Perhaps, in another climate, in one or other of the forty-eight states, I should yet find Madame Butterfly.

At the long day's end, out of some three hundred thousand plants in two hundred fifty varieties. I had only fifteen photographs to my credit. Robert Pyle was pleased with the final results; quality, as well as a nurseryman's statistics, counted for him too.

Rose fields in bloom. That is a phrase that makes rose-growing sound so easy. But it takes courage and devotion to grow roses well in that part of the eastern seaboard. The bushes must be heavily protected in winter, and sprayed all through their flowering to protect them from the scourges of black spot and the Japanese beetle, a repulsive pest that chews a bloom to tatters. Also, the flower itself, the reward for months-long attention, is far more ephemeral than in a more temperate climate. The rose that opens with daylight is full at noon, and faded by nightfall. Only by picking roses early, before the sun is high, "stilling" them in the icebox and arranging them in the evening, will they open slowly and last one, even two days, indoors in full bloom.

Knowing this, it seemed all the more surprising that there were roses everywhere I went throughout eastern Pennsylvania; from miniature rose gardens tended like pot plants to those allowed to run wild and rampant, with roses along the wire fencing at the side of dirt roads; from two- to three-acre gardens to those that ranked among America's largest.

There was a rose garden at Reading, merely a few feet of concrete foundation, bastioned up from the sidewalk. Its owner had brought in the precious soil, scientifically fed and watered it. The roses were his sole reward, but what roses! The small place was a mass of bloom, and each individual rose, each individual bush as well-nigh perfection as any professional could wish.

In Harrisburg, the garden of another great rose man, Dr. Horace McFarland who died in 1948, was still maintained as one of the All-America Rose Test gardens with eight hundred varieties. By profession a master printer, specializing in

horticultural books and magazines, Dr. McFarland printed
Dr. Liberty Hyde Bailey's monumental *Cyclopedia of Horticulture.* He was also a pioneer in the development of modern color printing, and had made his own collection of plant
photographs numbering some fifty thousand. Many of them
were taken in his own garden where he grew, in addition to
his roses, plants from all over the world.

On the same day I saw Dr. McFarland's garden, I went
on to the nearby Hershey rose gardens, among America's
largest, containing some thirty-five thousand plants in wide
variety. I spent some time among the fine collection of old
roses and the bushes of Crested Moss, with the bud that
bears such a comic likeness to Napoleon's hat. I looked down
on a large planting of that incomparable single yellow rose,
Mermaid, which was used as a ground cover around the central pool, so that one could look down on the open yellow
saucers with their fine boss of stamens lying among the shiny
leaves, and not up at the underside of the flowers as is usually the case when Mermaid is allowed to follow her natural habit and climb. But I had already seen too many roses
that almost unbearably hot day. As the heavy, sickly scent
of chocolate from the Hershey chocolate factory drifted
across the valley and mingled incongruously with the rich
scent of the roses, I could look no more.

Next morning Robert Pyle's colored cook, Edna, put her
head round my door, waited to see if it was a good moment
to interrupt, and if I was in a listening mood. She needed
to talk.

"People!" she sniffed, and I gathered that someone had
earned her disapproval, "I don't know what people mean
when they talk about luck. I believe luck's in the Lord, and
the devil in the people."

She held some roses in her hand. She had brought them, I
guessed, as a good excuse to relieve her mind.

"Roses, pink and red, you take them. I saved them from
those fancy arrangements they were doing, stripping them
and all that sort of thing. I like the leaves as well as the rose,
they ought to let them be. Look how pretty they are." She
helped me arrange them to her satisfaction, leaves and thorns
intact.

That evening I went to see a flower-arrangement special-
ist, to find out what she thought about arranging roses.
Golden Rapture, known in Europe as Geheimrat Duisberg,
was her favorite rose for dinner arrangements, although she
much admired the intensely fragrant and long-stemmed rose,
Charles Mallerin, whose petals are even more velvety than
those of Ami Quinard.

How did she make her roses last. By cutting them the day
before she needed them, placing them overnight in cold
water with Floral Life preparation, she told me.

"I say to people," she added, "please do not take the
thorns from your rose stems if you want them to last. A rose
is beautiful with its thorns and with its leaves. Arrange your
roses the way they grow, so that you can see the stem and the
leaf. Appreciate the stem and the leaf and the thorn as much
as you appreciate the rose itself."

Edna would have approved wholly. And so, no doubt,
would have old Dean Hole. You must love your roses "well
and always," he wrote in his famous book on roses. Both
in and out of bloom, the year through you must love them.
Had not the rose pleaded with him in the depth of winter?
"I am no more the Rose, but cherish me, for we have dwelt
together."

Certainly, America cherishes the rose.

4

By Horseback, Boat and Foot

DRIVING through Fairmount Park in Philadelphia on my way to see John Bartram's garden, I stopped on the river road, and stared. Battalions of eight-foot-high dark-eyed sunflowers lifted their heads against the distant skyline. I stared so long that a policeman came to ask what I was looking at. "The sunflowers," I told him, nervous now that I had stopped too long.

Instead of reprimanding me for obstructing traffic, he crossed the road to pick a bunch of the flowers. Bringing them back he gave me a botany lesson, dissecting a flower-head to illustrate his points.

"If you go down to the naval dockyard you'll see them growing finer even than here," he said. "They like the soil there better."

I explained I was on my way to see Mr. Bartram's garden. He knew whom I meant. John Bartram is still a famous Philadelphian, though he died as long ago as 1777. And off I went with the policeman's directions and his sunflower gift.

John Bartram was one of the first Americans to travel his own country in search of flowers. On horseback, by boat, and on foot he ranged the forests from Canada to Florida, sometimes accompanied by his son William, but usually alone. He was in touch with almost all the well-known botanists in Europe. He sold or exchanged most of his finds with English plantsmen.

No one quite knows how many native plants John Bartram introduced into cultivation, but generally it is considered he contributed something like one hundred fifty to two hundred new species, among them tulip and magnolia trees, the dog's tooth violet, and the trailing arbutus. From the Shenandoah Valley in Virginia, "My Kashmir," he called it, he gathered the American cowslip, the trillium, and the silver bell.

William Bartram followed in his father's footsteps, but is best remembered by his book of *Travels through North and South Carolina, Georgia, East and West Florida.* He was not a great artist, but the Duchess of Portland commissioned him to paint her collection of sea shells and, even before he left school, he made drawings of American birds for the English ornithologist, George Edwards. These made ·him a forerunner in the American tradition of Wilson and Audubon.

Among all the Bartrams' treasures, the Franklinia tree was their greatest find; John and William discovered it together. On John Bartram's last long exploration, when he was nearly seventy years old and accompanied by William, he discovered the tree on October 1, 1765, growing along the banks of

the Altamaha River in Georgia. It was too late in the autumn for them to form any "opinion as to what class or tribe
it belonged," and neither the seed nor the wood was ripe
enough to gather. But John Bartram gave it a name, *Franklinia altamaha,* for the river where he found it and for his
friend Benjamin Franklin. Subsequently the tree was named
Gordonia altamaha or *Gordonia pubescens,* for its close resemblance to *Gordonia Lasianthus,* the Loblolly Bay, although both are distinct and separate species. But the tree is
still most commonly known as the Franklinia tree.

Three times William Bartram returned alone to the same
place along the Altamaha River, and found the Franklinia
again: in 1770 when he brought back the first slips for propagation; in 1773, and in 1777, when he saw the "new flowering shrub, . . . in perfect bloom, as well as bearing ripe
fruit."

The new flowering shrub is indisputably one of North
America's most beautiful trees, or more accurately a tree of
shrub-like growth that reaches a height of some thirty feet.
During July the buds form in close clusters; satin-smooth
and button-round, they grow more white day by day until
they break, one after another, into a ten days' profusion of
successive flowers. Franklinia is curiously punctual in its
flowering date. Over a long recording in and around Philadelphia, where it is probably most widely grown, the first
flowers invariably open on August first. The succeeding
blooms continue until the first frosts of fall, usually up to
November first.

Although a southerner, the Franklinia has withstood 50
degrees of frost in the Arnold Arboretum, Boston. Dr. Don
Wyman, director of the arboretum, told me that, together
with the Cedar of Lebanon and the Silk Tree of China, it is

one of the three trees that visitors most often ask to see. He himself considers the brilliant orange-red fall foliage of the Franklinia the most beautiful of all American trees.

William Bartram's own testimony to the beauty and discovery of the Franklinia is not to be found in his *Travels* but in the Museum of Natural History in London. There, together with his water-color drawing and the now dry spray he once picked from the living tree, is his manuscript note.

"This fine flowering Tree, was first observed growing wild near the River Altamaha in Georgia . . . its very large white fragrant flowers [three inches wide] embellish'd with a large tassel or crown of golden Stamens . . . produced from the boosoms of the leaves towards their extremities of its branches . . . Yet never saw This beautiful Tree growing wild but in one spot on the Altamaha about 30 miles from the Sea coast, neither has any other person that I know of ever seen or heard of it."

The note is dated 1788. In 1790 the Franklinia was found again. It was the last time anyone saw it growing wild.

Humphrey Marshall, John Bartram's cousin, owned a nursery business in Pennsylvania in partnership with his nephew Moses Marshall. In 1787 and 1789 they had received orders from the London firm of Grimwood, Hudson and Barrit, for considerable quantities of the Franklinia. In 1790 Moses Marshall, at the request of Sir Joseph Banks, went to Georgia and found the tree again at the same place on the Altamaha River. Nearly a century passed before there is any record of a further search. Since then, though collectors have continually searched, no one has again found Franklinia in the wild.

Was it the last stand of the tree that the Bartrams discovered? Did William and Moses Marshall between them strip it entirely? Or did it perish in the "Yazoo freshet" of 1796, or the cold Saturday of February 1835? Or was it destroyed by fire? No one knows.

But the Franklinia lives, not only in cultivation, but in the work of such artists as François Michaux, son of another famous plant collector, André Michaux, who brought the first camellias to America; and Audubon who, in 1834, set his Bachman's Warbler among its branches and described the Franklinia as "one of the most beautiful of our southern flowers."

The Franklinia and the Loblolly Bay are the only North American species of the Gordonia, named after James Gordon, an English nurseryman who died in 1780. The remaining eight species are from the warmer parts of Asia. Their relationship to the tea tribe, which includes the camellias and stewartias, is traceable in the leaf fragrance, and at times an infusion of the leaves has been used as tea.

The Loblolly Bay, *Gordonia Lasianthus,* which the Bartrams also discovered, differs from the Franklinia in being a more vigorous, though rather more tender tree, and reaches a height of seventy feet in the wild. Its myriad flowers are borne on long stems from July through September, and are smaller and more fragrant but otherwise similar to the almost stemless blooms of the Franklinia. The Loblolly Bay is also more nearly evergreen than other Gordonias, though it will lose its leaves in a severe winter. Generally, however, they pass through a whole gamut of brilliant color rarely seen in evergreens; gold, purple, and crimson in flaming contrast with the deep green of younger oncoming leaves.

William Bartram described the Loblolly Bay in what Thomas Carlyle, the historian, called the "wonderful kind of flundering eloquence" of Bartram's *Travels*; a book, he told Emerson, that "All American libraries ought to provide themselves with . . . and keep as a future biblical article."

William Wordsworth, his sister Dorothy, and Coleridge kept the book by them in just that way, for reference, even for pirating. The Loblolly Bay that William Bartram said "renewed its garments every morning through the year; and every day appears with unfading lustre," its leaves constantly changing color before they faded and fell, becomes in Wordsworth's verse translation:

> He spake of plants that hourly change
> Their blossoms, through a boundless range
> Of intermingling hues;
> With budding, fading, faded flowers.

There are strange echoes of the Altamaha River in Coleridge's *Lewti*—the Altamaha becomes "Tamaha's stream."

Wordsworth's *Ruth* and *The Prelude* are steeped in William Bartram's imagery. What Bartram wrote of the Altamaha with its winding banks and projecting promontories, "the air filled with the loud and shrill hooping of the wary sharp-sighted crane," and the "decayed, defoliated cypress tree, the solitary wood pelican, dejectedly perched upon its utmost elevated spire," became for Wordsworth:

> a domain
> For quiet things to wander in; a haunt
> In which the heron would delight to feed
> By the shy rivers, and the pelican
> Upon the cypress spire in lone thought
> Might sit and sun himself.

And Dorothy Wordsworth, whom brother William declared gave him his eyes and gave him ears, had the younger Bartram's words running in her head. She read of "roving beauties, strolling over the mossy, shelving, humid rocks . . . playing on the surface, some plunge their perfumed heads . . . in the silver stream, whilst others by the mountain breezes are tossed about." Was it merely coincidence that she wrote in her journal on April 15, 1802, that she had never seen the daffodils more beautiful: "They grew among the mossy stones. Some rested their heads upon these stones . . . and the rest tossed and reeled and danced, and seemed as if they verily laughed with the wind." So where did William Wordsworth find that well-worn line on "dancing daffodils?"

I liked to remember all this as I stood in Bartram's garden on the banks of the Schuylkill River: how he and William traveled in search of flowers, John striving for scientific accuracy in his description of them, William striving to put down on paper something of the beauty that he sought. The Bartram garden was the first botanical garden in America. The house that John built with his own hands still stands, the cypress tree he brought with him in his saddle-bag from Florida still lives, and the descendants of the flowers he discovered and distributed are now widespread in tens of thousands throughout the gardens of Europe and America. So, too, from the slips and seeds that William and his cousin Moses Marshall brought back, the Franklinia also lives.

It seems, perhaps, unfair that William Bartram's manuscripts, drawings, and herbarium specimens are housed in England. But it was English gardeners who largely supported the Bartrams' explorations. Financial support, however, measured little beside the hardships they endured in "travelling several thousands miles mostly amongst Indian Nations, which is not only difficult but Dangerous, besides suffering sickness cold and hunger." Neither did they expect, nor wish it to be otherwise. In the note accompanying the herbarium specimens which William Bartram collected for what he called the "inspection and amusement of the curious," he asked only a simple reward: "the bare mention of my being the discoverer."

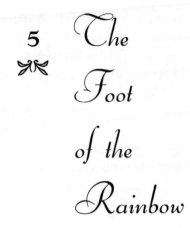

5

The

Foot

of the

Rainbow

𝓑EFORE I left West Grove in November, Robert Pyle suggested I call on Mrs. J. Norman Henry at Gladwyne, near Philadelphia, and provided the introduction. In reply to his written request for me to see her garden, he received this note: "Your young English friend can come here Monday afternoon for one hour at 3:30."

I arrived early, and waited outside in the car until it was exactly half-past three. If I had known what I learned by the time I left the house over three hours later, I think I should have been too diffident to ring the bell. That, no doubt, was why Robert Pyle had not given me his usual briefing.

Mrs. Henry is one of the great characters of American botanical history. Her sixteen-acre garden contains the finest collection of rare native American plants in the world, the

41

harvest from scores of her plant-hunting expeditions. The most remarkable fact of her story is that she did not start on her plant-collecting career until she had raised her five children, and was about forty-five years old.

I found her sorting some narcissi bulbs in the garden, a short, white-haired, and rather frail-looking woman. She looked up with a shy but reassuring smile. "If I had not forgotten you were coming," she said ruefully, "I would have had on proper socks and stockings, and have had the men move the tools and buckets."

We walked back up to the house together, and while Mrs. Henry went to wash her hands I waited in the tiny greenhouse adjoining the dining room. "I always wanted the place full of flowers," she said as I looked around, "but I know that will never be, for now I am purely an experimental botanist." It was not a show greenhouse certainly; instead of flowers there were labelled flats, necessary equipment for Mrs. Henry's work of breeding amaryllis, azaleas, geraniums, and lilies.

November is a crazy month to see any garden, but the time was in my favor. No one, Mrs. Henry guessed, would come to look unless they shared her thinking, that a garden has some beauty at every season of the year.

"My place is planted as a wild garden," Mrs. Henry said, as we went towards the shrub garden. "A visitor once paid me a compliment," she continued. "She asked if she could see the garden, and after a while came back disappointed, saying she could not find it though she had hunted all around. So I don't often show my garden to strangers, for so many come for idle curiosity, but I like doing it for people who know and appreciate plants."

There was another reason why November was a good time

for a first visit. I would learn more about Mrs. Henry herself, and less of the plants.

I could not see the scarlet yucca which in another season would bloom on the rocky scree above the house, nor the great-leaved magnolias in their pride of pale lemon flowers. I could not see those favorite natives: the rhododendrons, halesias, lilies, hymenocallis, trilliums, alliums, phlox, liatris, and penstemons in flower, nor the collection of hammelis-mollis which make that woodland a cloud of golden bloom in spring. But as we walked among the rare hollies, and the sour wood with its seeded panicles of flowers among the gold and crimson leaves, as Mrs. Henry picked a leaf here and there of the aromatics which she loves, and gave me a handful of brown husks that held the seed of the famous Franklinia tree, she told me something of some of her discoveries and expeditions.

"We Americans have been so busy importing flowers from other parts of the world that we've neglected our own beautiful native flowers," she said, "plants every bit as worthy of a garden place, and far more adaptable to the American climate than those from foreign shores."

The purpose of her expeditions has been to save rare plant species threatened with extinction; to share her treasure with growers who can, and will, propagate them, so that in time the plants may find their way into the gardens of America. How well she has succeeded in her purpose is proved by the record of her accomplishment.

Mrs. Henry has discovered hundreds of new plant species and varieties; more than one hundred have been placed in commercial hands. The Arnold Arboretum at Cambridge, Massachusetts, and the Royal Botanical Society of Edinburgh have received a generous proportion of the seeds and plants, while others have been widely distributed to other botanical gardens and the United States Department of Agriculture. She had made herbarium specimens of all the living plants that she has collected; of these, six thousand, all annotated, have been given to the Academy of Natural Sciences in Philadelphia.

Lilium iridollae, the only new native lily to be discovered on the Atlantic Coastal Plain in the last 105 years, is Mrs. Henry's greatest "find." Always an ardent lover of lilies, some ten varieties are named either for her or by her, though strangely *Lilium henryi* is not among them, and has no connection with her.

For a long time she searched far and wide for native lilies, bringing them back to grow in her wild garden, hoping always that one day she might chance upon some hitherto unknown and attractive species. October 15, 1940, was the day, though at the time she did not know it.

On that day she collected some lily seeds in Alabama and planted them out in a cold frame in her garden in February of the succeeding year. In 1945 they gave their first bloom.

Over the next six years after that October day, Mrs. Henry collected more specimens of the same lily, in seed and in bud, from the same area in Alabama. It was not until 1946, however, on a day of pouring rain, that she saw *Lilium iridollae* for the first time in bloom in its native Alabama home. She counts the sight of the beautiful yellow flowers, swaying gently on their slender stalks, as one of the "highlights of my life." Fragrant, of a rich yellow color, she likened the flower to a golden treasure. As the "pot of gold" at the foot of her rainbow, she recorded in *Bartonia,* "I am calling this new species *Lilium irodollae.*"

Plants of her own raising include the beautiful little rose-pink windowsill *Amaryllis henraye,* which was named for her by Dr. H. P. Traub, who hailed it as a miniature pink marvel, and as the most outstanding achievement in the entire history of the genus Amaryllis. And *Rhododendron gladyaense* with shell-pink flowers, one of her latest plant introductions, is possibly the finest of all summer-flowering shrubs, blooming in mid-July until early August.

Mary Gibson Henry comes of a plant-minded family, and was born in her Grandmother Pepper's house in Jenkintown, Pennsylvania. Her ancestors had come from England with William Penn. Her great grandfather, George Pepper, was a member of the first Council of the Pennsylvania Horticultural Society in 1828 and had the first greenhouse in Philadelphia. Lawrence Seckel, his brother-in-law, introduced the Seckel pear into America.

In 1909 Mary Gibson married Dr. John Norman Henry, who became Director of Public Health of Philadelphia from 1931 to 1935. During the years in the city, Mrs. Henry studied botanical books; among them William Bartram's *Travels* became an unending source of inspiration. The book later formed the basis for planning many of her own journeys, and one of the goals of her first trip was to collect a few specimens of *Rhododendron speciosum,* described so enthusiastically by Bartram, but no longer obtainable from either botanical or commercial collectors.

When their five children had grown up (there are now eleven grandchildren) Dr. Henry suggested that Mrs. Henry choose a site of whatever acreage she wished, with the one provision that it was within commuting distance of Philadelphia. The hillside at Gladwyne, ninety-five acres of farmland, was her choice. Soil and site were perfect. There the Henrys built their house, with a rocky piece of land behind it, and, below, the valley watered by four streams and sheltered by the tree-covered slopes beyond.

That is how Mrs. Henry, who had not left her home except for one night in all those nineteen years, came to create her garden. Free at last to come and go, she started on her long series of plant-hunting expeditions.

Dr. and Mrs. Henry led jointly the 1931 expedition, taking their children with them into the unmapped mountain wilderness of British Columbia. But Dr. Henry died in 1938, and on four long succeeding explorations in British Columbia one of their daughters, Josephine, went with her mother.

Ordinarily, however, Mrs. Henry is accompanied only by her head gardener and chauffeur, Ernest Perks, who has been with her on all the ninety-odd expeditions that she has undertaken in the United States. Her spade, a twenty-inch army trench spade which she bought second-hand for 29 cents a quarter of a century ago, can also be counted as a constant traveling companion. She refers to it as her side-partner, and many a time it has served her in a double role: as a plant-hunting tool, and as her chosen weapon for killing rattlesnakes.

About twenty trips have been made to the northeastern states; more than sixty to the Southern States: ranging up and down the Atlantic Coastal Plain to Florida; to the Piedmont Plateau, the Appalachian Mountains, and the mountains of eastern Tennessee and Alabama; to Mississippi, northern Louisiana, and the Ozark region in Oklahoma and Arkansas.

In the west, eleven seasons have been spent in the Rocky Mountains, from southern New Mexico to northern British Columbia. The Far Northland, with its miles of great blue meadows, and its mountains clear-cut against a dazzling sky, is Mrs. Henry's favorite hunting ground—"I would rather go there than anywhere else in the world."

Here she is remembered not only by plant names but by place names on the Far North map. Mount Mary Henry in British Columbia is named for her. And her own maps of the trail-blazing expedition of 1935, when, with six guides and twenty-nine horses, the party trekked across a thousand unmapped miles, were later used in charting the Alaska Highway northwards.

It is hard to imagine, standing by Mrs. Henry, who measures no more than five feet one inch, that she is as intrepid an explorer as any plant collector of old. She will admit that time and time again she has risked her life in her search for flowers, though she declares that "the flowers have done far more for me than I have done for them."

Nothing seems to have daunted or intimidated her. She has traveled thousands of miles on horse or on foot. She has crossed rivers by raft, and on the backs of swimming horses; she has slept in below-zero temperatures on snow.

There have been bad moments, and startling encounters. Wolves have howled round the camp tents, and once in the isolated Georgia mountains she found herself staring into the muzzles of moonshiners' guns. But always she has stood her ground, and she is herself a good shot. Both she and Josephine like to hunt; they once provided one three-month expedition with all the meat required, in variety of bear, deer, grouse, sheep and mountain goat.

She does not think of herself as courageous, because she is not afraid, believing that animals do not ordinarily attack unless provoked. Rabbits, moles, and mice make her more fearful than either wolf or bear, for they are the garden enemies who prey on her plants and seeds. Nor does she feel a stranger in the unmapped wilderness, which is safer to her than the crossing of a Philadelphia street. Yet, parodoxically, above everything else she prefers the privacy of her own ninety-five-acre estate.

To those who ask why she goes afield to invite privation, Mrs. Henry makes much the same reply as did other plant-hunters before her. "To one who loves the Northland there are few hardships, and any discomfort just goes to show that the best in life is only to be had by contrast, and we enjoy good times a hundredfold when hard work brings them to us."

With her, the words "hard work" mean just that. Mrs. Henry is as indefatigable when not exploring as she is in her plant collecting. Her work as what she terms an experimental botanist can claim only part of her time. She is a Research Associate in Botany at the Academy of Natural Sciences of Philadelphia, and a consultant to the United States and Canadian Departments of Agriculture. She lectures not only in America but to the Royal Horticultural Society in England, the Botanic Garden of Edinburgh, and the Royal Scottish Geographical Society in Scotland. Additionally, she contributes articles to many papers, so that it is hardly surprising that she discourages idle curiosity.

Her garden is now a permanent one, endowed and named by her as The Henry Foundation for Botanical Research. Any profit that she realizes from new plant introductions or nursery sales goes to further botanical research either at the Academy of Sciences or at the Henry Foundation. But although there has been no personal monetary gain, reward has come to her in full measure. The Canadian Government has named the sub-Arctic peak, Mount Mary Henry, in her honor, and she is remembered in the names of a legion of flowers, among them the pink Scotch Broom cytisus *Mrs.*

Norman Henry, a pink iris *Mary Gibson,* a paintbrush *Castilleja Henryae,* and *Phlox Henraye.*

As one of America's most distinguished living horticulturists, Mrs. Henry has far exceeded her family's botanical tradition, following in remarkable fashion the life pattern of America's first famous botanist, the eighteenth-century plant collector John Bartram. Both were Pennsylvanian-born; both started their plant-collecting lives comparatively late and with no previous training. Both have contributed as much to horticultural knowledge as any of their contemporaries, as plant collectors and experimentalists, sharing their discoveries with American and British botanists alike.

Mrs. Henry's garden is as notable today as was Bartram's garden on the banks of the Schuylkill River in his day, and it is planted with the same kind of materials, newly found rarities. And as Bartram, who ordinarily traveled alone, was sometimes accompanied by his son William, nature artist and author of the famous *Travels,* so Mrs. Henry is sometimes accompanied by her daughter Josephine, also a naturalist and a top-ranking illustrator of nature by photography.

King's Botanist, as Bartram was called, is a title that no longer exists. There are others, however, that botanists and horticulturists value equally, if not higher. Over the years Mrs. Henry has received the Herbert Medal, awarded by the American Plant Society; the Schaffer Gold Medal, presented by the Pennsylvania Horticultural Society for notable contributions to horticulture; the Mungo Park Medal award of the Royal Scottish Geographical Society for exploration in Northern British Columbia, and the Silver Medal of the Massachusetts Horticultural Society. Her place in horticultural history is no less than that established by the great John Bartram.

6 Flowers
or
Weeds?

$\mathcal{E}$MERSON defined a weed as a plant whose virtues have not been discovered. Asters and goldenrod prove his point. English gardeners generally count these flowers as among the glories of the autumn border, but in America, where they grow widespread and rank, they are still generally regarded as weeds. Asters are only now beginning to appear, in their modern hybridized forms, in American gardens, but goldenrod is rarely if ever seen.

It is hard to put a finger on the subtle distinction between a weed and a wildflower. Some beautiful plants are never rated more than weeds, a somewhat disparaging noun. And though many regard asters and goldenrod as weeds, a few have sung their praise and hailed them as beautiful wildflowers in their native land.

The famous Dr. Bailey counted them "amongst the glories

of the American autumn," commenting on the way they compliment each other. And the English gardener, in growing them so often side by side in his border, has but followed their natural planting. Both plants have also the virtue of long-lasting bloom, both in the border and as cut flowers in the house, lasting fresh almost as long as chrysanthemums.

Donald Culross Peattie gave asters their due. I needed to confirm for myself what he said:

> Europe has no asters at which an American would look twice. In this our Western world the asters stand all through autumn, shoulder to shoulder in forest, on prairie, from the Atlantic to California, climbing up to the snows of Shasta, creeping out upon the salt marshes of Delaware. Here some call the white ones frost flower, for they come as the silver rime of chill flowering in the old age of the year. In the southern mountains they are hailed as 'farewell summer.'

Europe has very few native asters. But those of old did not go without notice. The Greeks named them asters for stars; thus the word disaster comes from unlucky or ill-omened star. Virgil in his *Georgics* first mentioned the Italian staarworte, *Aster Amellus*. As such John Gerarde, the Elizabethan herbalist, grew it in his London garden, and it goes under the same name to this day.

Captain John Smith, when he returned to New England after the disgrace of his days at Jamestown, Virginia, gave the New England aster, *A. Novae Angliae*, its name. And it was John Tradescant, gardener to Queen Henrietta Maria and son of John Tradescant the Elder, who introduced *Aster Tradescantii* into England, the first aster to be called a Michaelmas Daisy.

The majority of aster garden hybrids so widely grown

today in England owe their parentage chiefly to *Aster leavis* and the New York aster, *A. Novi Belgii.* English gardeners have grown the New York aster since 1710. But it was earlier, in 1687, that aster seed gathered from the land on which New York now stands was sent to a German botanist, a Professor of Botany at Leiden in Holland. One of the resultant seedlings attracted his attention, and he named it *Novi Belgii,* being no doubt the nearest equivalent to New Netherland, since at that time the territory was colonized by the Dutch. But when Charles II of England ordered an officer to take possession of the province in the name of his brother, the Duke of York, New Netherland became New York, and the aster likewise became known as the New York aster, though the original improvised Latin name, *Novi Belgii,* was retained.

Peattie was right, of course. Europe has no native asters that can compare with those of North America. But the hybrids that the English developed have produced a race of flowers that are as beautiful in their gardens as are the wild asters in their native setting. And I confess I would not include the New England aster in my garden. It is one of the most colorful, its blues and purples and pinks are the most noticeable of all wild aster bloom. But it is too stiff in habit. It tends to lose its lower leaves, and as a cut flower it is a disappointment. It closes its petals at night and when gathered does not, like the unpicked flower, open again with the morning.

William Cobbett, the fiery pamphleteer and writer who spent some years in America as a refugee from debt and political unpopularity at home, wrote of the goldenrod in his *American Gardener,* 1819. He described goldenrod as the torment of the neighboring farmer, who regarded it as "That

accursed stinking thing, with a yellow flower, called the
'Plain-Weed.' " He spoke of Americans' amazement that it
had above all the plants in the world been chosen as the
most conspicuous ornament of the front of the King of
England's grandest palace, that of Hampton Court, where,
growing in a rich soil to the height of five or six feet, "under
the name of 'Golden Rod,' it nods over the whole length
of the edge of a walk, three quarters of a mile long and perhaps thirty feet wide—the most magnificent border, perhaps,
in Europe." How delighted Cobbett was to find the corn-
poppy, a pernicious weed to the European farmer, growing
as a choice flower in American gardens!

One day I heard a twentieth-century echo of Cobbett's
words. A friend, just back from visiting England, came to
tell me of her visit to Hampton Court. "It can't be," she had
thought to herself, straining her eyes to the long border,
"they can't have planted goldenrod there surely?" Pulling
her companion by the arm they had advanced together towards the long herbaceous border to find goldenrod planted
there as it was planted years ago. Thus rarity sets the value
on flowers as it sets the price on all the world's commodities.

Sneeze-weed is a common accusing name in America for
goldenrod, if you blame it for hayfever; pestilent weed if it
invades your pasture land, or just plain weed if it is too
common to have any significance for you. But the children
of Alabama loved it well enough to choose goldenrod as the
state flower; Nebraska and Kentucky also namé it as their
state symbol.

The Romans treasured goldenrod, calling it solidago or
"makes whole" plant, for its supposed healing powers. And
so Elizabethan England valued it, importing large quantities to be sold in powdered form in the London markets at

half a crown a pound. Twentieth-century America has also discovered some virtue in the plant. The chemists extract some three to five pounds of oil from 150 to 250 pounds of bloom of sweet-scented goldenrod to flavor chewing gum and candy. The oil resembles oil of anise, the conventional liquorice flavoring. And from the same sweet-scented goldenrod some brew themselves a refreshing drink.

The first time I saw the white-faced Hereford cattle grazing among goldenrod on a Pennsylvania hillside, for a split second I was back at home, thinking someone had left the gate open, and they were out on the herbaceous border. Since then I have seen the wild plant growing east and west across the continent, gold against the blue of the Atlantic and the Pacific oceans; in the Blue Mountains of Virginia, in the Rocky Mountain West, and in the Far Northwest. It grows in every state of North America, in every terrain from the shoreline to the foothills, and the foothills to the mountains.

Always the sight of it brings to mind my mother's garden, and the glorious arrangements she made with the gold sprays and Michaelmas daisies that she set in a copper bowl on an old oak chest. I like it for the way it nods its head among the flowers of English poetry and prose. W. H. Hudson, the naturalist, bound it to his memory of a downland valley, and the peasant poet John Clare to the memory of his childhood days. I love it for its own sake too. For the way it took its place, plumed and alien like the Roman centurion along the English border, until, after centuries of planting, it has become part and parcel of the English scene, another North American native that is also an old-fashioned English flower.

That first fall in Pennsylvania I watched the aster-goldenrod season through. Already that August there had been a few fore-running autumn days: when a dog's bark struck more clearly on the air; the harsh bronze color of the landscape was tempered gold, and one single branch in a still green-leafed tree turned scarlet before its time. The insect hum that had for so long been the undertone of summer days grew thin and erratic until towards the end of the month it diminished and dwindled away. On cold nights, the tree or temperature cricket fell silent. "A touch of fall in the air" was the sidewalk greeting.

"Where shall I see the asters?" I asked, determined not to miss them. "Everywhere," was the reply.

And then a stir of anticipation, and those last-minute whispers before the curtain goes up: "Is the color really more brilliant than at home?" I asked an Englishman. "Wait," I was told, see for myself, then I should wonder why I had asked the question.

There was, in the autumn rhythm, none of the urgency, none of the impetuosity of spring. Rather, there was a reluctance, a hesitancy in the general tempo.

Goldenrod was everywhere, in one variety or another it had been in bloom weeks before it reached the slow zenith of its flowering at the beginning of September. I found a few of the hundred and eighty-five varieties among literally acres of gold. The early plume was the first and last to bloom. Sweet-scented goldenrod yielded an anise-like sweetness. The Canada goldenrod, the most common and the most rank in growth, was the most splendid of all, with its great spreading head of densely flowered, recurving sprays that at times reached the height of a tall man. And once I found the seaside goldenrod among the sand dunes of New

Jersey growing within spray-reach of the sea, bending its arching stems to the ocean breeze.

A hint in the name *Solidago ulimfolia,* the elm-leaved goldenrod, led to a discovery that it is not only elm-leaved and elm-branched. A hillside yellow with this goldenrod is as a forest of elm trees, but that is not all, for the individual beauty of a tree is lost in the forest as the identity of a face is lost in a crowd. To see but one miniature elm in autumn gold, I bent down and looked up at the sky through the branches of one single plant, one stem of goldenrod. And I saw the same up-pouring branches and the same spread arms that crown the eastern elm, a golden rocket spangled against the blue autumn sky.

The goldfinch came to the mauve-headed thistles; the butterflies and bees hovered over the wild mint and the ironweed, thronged to aster and goldenrod alike, for by September the asters, like the goldenrod, were everywhere.

Evening after evening, all through September, I searched for different asters and wondered, even with the help of my botanist friend Marianna and Dr. Bailey's *Encyclopedia,* how I could ever hope to name all I saw.

I love the autumn, and September best of all, and asters are September flowers, to which their English name bears witness; they reach the peak of their flowering around Michaelmas Day, September 29. But Marianna did not share my enthusiasm for asters. They held no association for her as they do for me. They are plants, she declared, that you had to meet halfway.

One evening I went up the porch steps of her house with a big bunch of asters in my hand. I'm sure Marianna sighed, but if she did it was so lightly I did not hear.

"See," I waved my flowers, and quoted: "Every Aster in my hand goes home loaded with a thought.' "

"Nonsense," she said.

"It's Emerson's nonsense, not mine."

"Emerson's nonsense then. How many thousands of flowers do you think you've got in your hand?"

Sobered, I took out the heavy encyclopedia. Marianna's passion for reason tore the starred heads to tatters. I read out loud to her, never pausing for the interruption which I knew would pounce the moment I stopped for breath.

" 'The native asters are amongst the very best plants for borders and roadsides. . . .' "

Marianna could bear it no longer. She seized the book from me. "If you look at his opening sentence on the aster tribe you will see that Bailey says they are 'botanically confused.' And having described innumerable varieties, more than you would ever remember, he ends on the same note, 'The species are much confused.' "

I never dared to bring any more asters back for naming after that. I had identified those I most wished to find; the white wood aster and blue heart-leaved were abundant in the woods; the golden-headed aster and the mauve seaside aster in the sandy New Jersey soil, and the swamp aster that bent under the weight of its six-foot spray of lavender heads.

Most common and most dense in growth were the acres of white and pale misty-blue field asters, *A. paniculatus and A. cordifolius,* that bloomed wherever low-lying marshland gave them room. They covered whole stretches of country as an autumn morning mist. The floor of the valley where I had gone most often to find my flowers was a solid mass of aster bloom.

By the end of the first week of October, when the rain had

battened down the great tall sprays and drained the color from the flowers, only the upland asters remained, the white-wreathed or starry aster and the heath-like aster, *A. erico-ides*.

Aster ericoides was the last of all to linger. It came, as Peattie said, a silver rime of chill flowering in the old age of the year. I stood with it about me as I looked across the valley. September's flowers were spent. Only this frost flower remained. "Farewell summer." I spoke its name, by which the country people know it best, aloud.

There was only a momentary pause before the hills were swept with exultant shouting color. Green turned to yellow in the tulip tree, in maple, hickory, and beech. The dogwood leaf was pure shotsilk, half-green and half dusky purple-red. Tupelo, the black or sour gum, turned sepia-green before it deepened to smoulder at the last blood-red and darkest green like the heart of a bloodstone. All the yellow of the daffodils and flowers of spring went into the bright sunlit yellow radiance the black-limbed Norway maple out-poured to the sky. All the golds of sunflower and goldenrod were in the leaves of sassafras.

The October equinox came through the woods with a great sweep of sound. It blew the smouldering colors into flame. The woods were on fire. An immense bonfire lit up the sky. The dogwood and the tupelo burnt a clear and brilliant red at the last. Sumac licked the hillsides with its flames. The scarlet oak, the swamp and sugar maples, flowered into a last flamboyance.

And the wind passed; the leaves were fallen and the fire died down. Here and there the huge mahogany leaves of the black oak hung like purple shadows. November mists hung above the woodland like the smoke of dying forest fires.

7
⊰⊱
The
Gentian's
Secret

O<small>NE</small> weekend in October, at a moment's notice, I went
up to New York on an urgent errand for Robert Pyle. If
there was time he also wanted me to see Mr. Clarence Lewis
in Northern New Jersey. "His place," he told me, "is called
Skylands. You'll find it all right; you can learn something
of its whereabouts in New York." These were the only directions he gave me. He added, "He has a very fine garden, you
might get a glimpse of that too."

Where did he want me to stay while in New York, I asked.
"The Secretary of the New York Horticultural Society says
you can stay in the library there, at Essex House. There is
a couch, a kitchen and bath they have for emergency use."

On Sunday evening I settled myself in the Society's library. Sunday evening in a big city can be a trifle lonely.
What traveling gardener had ever slept here, I wondered;
then I turned to the books for company.

There were many old friends, explorers and adventurers almost all of them. Some had been in the New World before me, the old herbalists and old gardeners. Their hands were gone but they had left the wisdom of their green and flower-loving fingers between the old worn bindings of these books. I touched them as I ran my eye along the shelves: Hill's *British Herbal,* Parkinson's *Paradissus,* and Gerard's *Great Herbal.* I opened a volume of Ray's letters and read how, on April 1, 1885, he was telling Mr. William Robinson that he could expect one ounce of sugar from a gallon of liquor drawn from the Great Maple. I turned over the pages of a book on wild flowers. There was a colored plate of the fringed gentian *G. crinita,* one of the most prized and rare of all American wild flowers.

The flowering dates for the gentian were given rigidedly: September 15 to October 15. Monday, I realized, was October 15, and there was no recorded date of it ever being found later than that day. Well, maybe I should find it another year.

Monday stretched before me in a vista of miles. By noon, I had finished the work in New York; only the Skylands visit remained, if there was time. I decided to go.

I drove up the West Side Highway thrilled with the prospect of driving at last over the immense but slender grey span of the George Washington Bridge. As I moved up the ramp I only once dared to glance back at the city skyline; I had no time to lose. I had at least fifty miles ahead of me due north, and the whole long way back to West Grove afterwards.

I had my first real direction from a roadside milk-bar attendant by four that afternoon. "You'll find the place up there in the hills—over Eagle Mountain."

The late afternoon sun slanted across the wooded country road as I turned off into the hills. The reddening dogwood and scarlet oak were incredibly brilliant in the cross light, the beech and maple of every shade from pale yellow to old gold. So I came to Skylands, as I might have expected, set in a ring of hills.

I rang the bell. Mr. Lewis, the maid said, was somewhere in the garden; he might be a long way away. The maid could not help, and I didn't think I could stay long. I looked away and mumbled that it would have been nice to see the garden.

Away in the distance a woman was advancing. She waved her hand, and we waited.

"Come in," she invited, as she scraped her shoes at the door after her afternoon gardening. "We'll have tea now. I'm Mrs. Fitzpatrick."

"The young lady said she would like to see the garden." The maid spoke for me. Mrs. Fitzpatrick looked up from her shoe cleaning, gallantly postponed her tea, and started off to show me what she could in the fading light, picking a boutonniere of the fragrant dark red rose Rome Glory for me on the way.

We went down a long grass sward and through a double alley of sweet bay magnolias, on through the peony garden and the azalea garden, past the massed lilac bushes. How beautiful the place must be in spring, I thought, as we went on and on, downhill and through an avenue of ornamental pink Japanese crabs.

I could hear the drip of a wall fountain, and traced it to a canal where water lilies were still in bloom. Beauty berry was laden with white and mauve berried sprays; firethorn glowed with its deep orange-berried fruit. But the woods had not yet reached their peak of color; that was still some three weeks ahead Mrs. Fitzpatrick said, although there was already enough color to please even the dullest eye.

There was a small octagonal garden, a secret garden, inhabited by small lead cupids with clematis trailing round their ears and over their shoulders. One turned his head away from the fluffy seeded spray that fell over his shoulder and slipped underneath his right arm; for him there was just one single pale lilac-colored bloom.

On we went still, down to the lake and the deer-haunted woods, down to the wild garden where we found Mr. Clarence Lewis, peering intently in the rough grass at his feet. He straightened himself to greet me, and then in answer to my unspoken question as I glanced down to see what he had seen: "Fringed gentian . . . the seed . . ." he said, but the rest of the sentence was lost to me.

Mrs. Fitzpatrick caught my arm as she, too, bent down. "It's almost dark, still you can see enough. Look; here's the last bloom!" and she picked the half-closed bud and blew the petals wide for me to see the rare blue of the open flower.

Mr. Lewis had wanted to see if any seed was already set, for this would be gathered, according to his custom, to send to other gardeners and botanical gardens. Apparently the fringed gentian was notoriously difficult to tame and grow in cultivation. Even in the Edinburgh Botanical Garden all attempts to establish it had failed, Mr. Lewis said, although on several occasions he had sent seed.

"It may be that the plant needs some symbiosis which may be provided by its growing in a particular grass sod, or it may need some inoculation in the soil," he said. "Or," he continued, smiling and shrugging his shoulders, "but I could go on guessing and guessing, and come nowhere near exhausting the possibilities of why it won't cooperate with a gardener who wants to grow it. It is not only Edinburgh," he went on, "that has had this difficulty, but many gardeners here, and to such an extent that anyone who does succeed can hardly question that his particular success is due to his having had the luck to stumble on the right place or the right method, rather than to his possessing any special skill.

"It's been my luck," he said, as he peered down again, "to have this natural stand here in this wild garden, and the most Mrs. Fitzpatrick and I have done in connection with these particular gentians is to encourage their spreading by a very long continued process of scattering the seeds each year where they might have a chance of taking hold and increasing their natural spread."

That, then, was the gentian's secret. "As you see," Mrs. Fitzpatrick said, quoting Reginald Farrer as we went up through the garden and back to the house for tea, "what company they keep; coarse weed neighbors there among the grass, for if planted by themselves they simply will not grow."

Indoors, I had the impression of being in an English country house. There was a bowl of colored leaves in the hall; another of firethorn in the library; books and *Country Life* magazines on the table. We sat down there for a leisurely late tea, a white tablecloth spread with plates of buttered scones and white iced cakes before us. I can remember our exclamations as Mr. Lewis came in and put down on the immaculate tablecloth a rusty label he had found under a lilac tree.

It was after six o'clock; it was always time to go. They marked out the map and came to see me on my way. As I turned the car into the darkness ahead I saw them wave, standing in the square of light by the open door. Mr. Lewis had the offending lilac label in his hand.

I had a hundred and sixty miles to go. "Keep the track clear," Robert Pyle used to say to me when I had much to do and far to go. I had no more to do, except to get myself back, but I could not keep the track of my mind clear. I still saw the fringed gentian; still saw the lead cupids with the clematis about their heads; still saw that glorious garden set high among the hills and the color of the leaves against the setting sun as I came up over Eagle Mountain on the road through the woods.

All the way the leaves were falling as snowflakes fall; not the white goose feathers of winter snow, but the red and yellow flakes of autumn leaves. I remembered: it was October 15. I had found the last bloom of the last gentian on the last day and in the last hour of daylight.

8 *Back*

✧

to

Ol' Virginia

Sometimes at home in England I used to look up against the light at the under-veining of the young Virginia creeper leaves outside my bedroom window. The word "Virginia" had meant nothing more than a label then. I did not even associate the name with the state of Virginia! But my second spring and summer in America I worked as an editorial associate with Colonial Williamsburg, as the Rockefeller Foundation is known which restored and reconstructed Williamsburg to its original eighteenth century beauty as the early capital city of Virginia. Soon the words "Virginica" and "Virginiana" were a ringing refrain in my head.

Mentally I stepped straight back into the eighteenth century. My work involved copious research among the early plant collectors, and most of their discoveries bore the now familiar tag. Spring beauty, Claytonia, was *Claytonia vir-*

ginica; witch hazel and fringe tree, the wild clematis and the sweet bay magnolia were all stamped with the same latinized version of the name Virginia.

But merely learning about plants such as William Bartram had gathered for the "inspection and amusement of the curious" was not enough. Nor was the "bare mention" of a plant discoverer's name. I wanted to know about the plant-men themselves as well as discover for myself the plants they found. It was not always easy to stay desk-tied when the New World of which I read was all about me out-of-doors.

"When will spring come to the Tidewater?" I asked, though it was still January. "It won't come with a rush," I was told, "it seems always on the verge of happening, advancing and then retreating. The temperature will drop and the birds vanish, the frogs go silent, and in the gardens the pansies freeze solid where they stand. The only thing you may be sure of is spring's uncertainty."

So I found it. January, according to the temperature of 80 degrees, was June. A magnolia which should have waited for April unfolded its buds too trustingly; by the first week of February frost had seared the open blooms, and by the end of the month there was a blanket of snow.

I had had a foretaste of the Virginian spring. I brushed the snow from a bank in the woods and found the trailing arbutus snug among the dry leaves of oak and beech, already breaking into flower. I wondered whether John Bartram would agree with those who say that the dusty pollen fragrance alone is worth a spring. And I went back to my desk, and kept close company with the manuscripts and books of early Virginia.

The eighteenth century was a tremendously exciting age. The century, the greatest century in garden history, came in traditionally, predominately green; the New World was still very new and, apart from the Atlantic States, was virtually unexplored. When the century ended gardens were a smother of bloom, and Lewis and Clark were planning their 1804–1806 expedition, the first overland travelers to reach the Pacific Coast.

It was an age when from all over the world, from the Near and the Far East, from the newly discovered continents of Australia and Africa, from the Indies, from New Zealand, men brought back to Europe a strange and beautiful assortment of new plant material. The Tzar of Russia and the crowned heads of Europe vied with each other in stocking their botanical collections and pleasure grounds with everything that was new and rare. When the New World revealed its great wealth of flowers it became the plantsmen's Eldorado.

Of some eight thousands plants which make up the flora of eastern North America, only a bare half dozen were in cultivation before 1600. By the beginning of the eighteenth century the number was increased to about one hundred and fifty plants. At the time of the Revolutionary War of 1775–1781, the number had increased to some six hundred plants.

The red and blue lobelias were early finds. The colonists at Jamestown, Virginia, sent home the red lobelia in 1629. Parkinson in his *Paradisus* called it "the rich crimson Cardinal's flowers," for their likeness to the crimson of a Cardinal's robes.

John Tradescant the Elder was sent out to the New World in 1657 by Lord Burleigh, to collect plants for his fine garden at Hatfield. Tradescant was the first to find the Virginia creeper, the cone flowers, the columbine, asters, lupines, and phlox. He was also the first to find bee-balm or bergamot, though, for some reason or other, bergamot was lost to cultivation for a hundred years.

Tradescant is now remembered by the spiderwort, *Tradescantia virginiana,* though present-day Virginia is not necessarily where he found his namesake. In Tradescant's day Virginia extended far beyond its present boundaries—as far west as the Mississippi, and "Virginiana" denotes a far wider range for the plant than today's boundary lines.

Bishops, like ministers of state, had an eye on their gardens in choosing emissary priests for the new colony. Bishop Compton of London, who later became second President of the College of William and Mary at Williamsburg, and who had a famous garden at Fulham, sent John Banister to Virginia in the dual role of priest and plant collector; in 1678 he published John Banister's catalogue, the first known catalogue of Virginia plants.

Mark Catesby, who came from Suffolk, discovered the catalpa, the yellow-berried hawthorn, the Carolina ash and the scarlet-flowered acacia. His great two-volume work, a *Natural History of Carolina, Florida and the Bahama Islands,* proved to be the most sumptuous book of the period—a copy is in the Governor's Palace at Williamsburg, where a fresh page is turned over every day.

Against Catesby's illustration of the eastern dogwood, *Cornus florida,* he wrote *Cornus mas virginiana,* and as such I like to think of it still, for flowering dogwood is Virginia's own state flower. He also illustrated the pink dogwood, and sent specimens back to England, but it was not in general cultivation until about one hundred and fifty years later. For a long time there was some doubt as to whether the pink dogwood even existed, yet there it was all the time faithfully recorded in Catesby's book to prove the point.

Most of the early plantsmen were British, but not all of them. France sent André Michaux, botanist to Louis XIV, one of the most important collectors, and later Peter Kalm the Finn, a favorite pupil of Linneaus, came as the master's emissary, though his *Travels into North America* was not published until 1812. But the two most remarkable collectors were the Americans, John and William Bartram.

John Bartram, the Pennsylvanian ploughman who left his farm in search of flowers, was born at the turn of the great century in March, 1699. His life spanned the whole first era of North American plant discovery, almost the whole period that Williamsburg was Virginia's capital city. He lived plant collecting almost to the last, and died in 1777, the year Linneaus also died.

John Bartram, as noted previously, contributed something like two hundred new species to the ever-growing tide of color. For more than thirty-eight years of his long life, he corresponded with Peter Collinson, a Quaker merchant in London with a famous garden at Mill Hill. Collinson obtained for Bartram the support of wealthy European collectors with whom he exchanged and sold his plants, and it was Collinson who finally obtained for him the title of King's Botanist to George III, with a salary of fifty pounds a year.

The merchant and the ploughman, between them, corresponded with all the influential garden-minded men of their day; not only botanists and plant collectors but the then rich nobility. In England, among a coterie of influential men there was Sir Joseph Banks, who instigated the search for breadfruit that ended in the mutiny on the

Bounty; Philip Miller, author of *The Gardeners' Dictionary* and curator of the Apothecaries' Garden in Chelsea and the Royal Garden at Kew; and Sir Hans Sloan, whose collections later became the basis of the British Museum, and who once gave John Bartram a silver cup—rather a poor exchange for Bartram's flowers. In every sense Peter Collinson and John Bartram were the king-pins of the European and eastern North American plant exchange.

William Bartram, known for his *Travels* and his drawings, is somewhat overshadowed as a plant collector by his father's fame. But William was the first explorer to penetrate the southern and highest end of the Appalachians, and it is claimed for him that he brought out of it as many treasures as his father ever brought from his own favorite hunting ground, the Shenandoah.

But traffic in plant material was by no means a one-way affair. Very soon the early gardeners in America were just as eager to acquire the familiar plants from the Old World as Europeans to obtain what was new and rare. And if the exchange was uneven in quantity, the quality was good.

By some fortunate incidence the supply and demand of European and American plant material strikes a convenient balance. For it is a curious fact that the Old World has provided most of the spring flowers, and the New World, the western world, has provided most of the autumn flowers.

From Europe came the daffodils that tradition says the wives of the Jamestown colonists brought over in their aprons. There are the common and grape hyacinths, the English daisy and the English primrose, foxgloves and hollyhocks, lilac and Canterbury bells. And there was box, the perennial favorite of Virginia gardens for its extraordinary adaptability to a climate that proved far less favorable, for gardeners, than that of England.

André Michaux of France paid his debt to the southern states by introducing the pink-flowered Albizzia, commonly called mimosa, the chinaberry, the tea plant, and the camellia. Philip Miller included in a small packet of seed he sent to Georgia some cotton seed, and from that packet four-fifths of the world's cotton is grown today.

But this is no place to make out even a partial list of who was who in the American garden world of the eighteenth century. When the time came to close the books, push back my chair and go out into the Virginia woods, I had met enough of the old plantsmen to accompany me on my rounds. The snow had gone and spring had come.

I found the bloodroot that gave the Indians the red dye for their war paint: at first a round flower bud in a folded leaf, as a pearl within the oyster shell, before the single white blooms starred the forest floor. The shadblow or service tree, *Amelancier canadensis,* was white before the dogwood bloomed, flowering so they say when the shad come up the river. Bird's foot violet made wide pools of blue along the roadside, and the wild columbine that Tradescant found was pale coral beneath the deeper coral honeysuckle trailing overhead.

There was Spring Beauty, which some call simply Claytonia for John Clayton who came to Virginia as a young man, and who for fifty-one years served as Clerk to Gloucester County. He spent his long leisure hours botanizing and writing his *Flora Virginica* which the Dutch botanist Grovonius, as joint author, published at Leyden in 1739. When I bent down to catch the faint fragrance of the tiny white-starred Partridge Berry, whose fruit the bobwhites love so well, I would hear John Mitchell whisper *Mitchella repens*, reminding me of his slim flora of Virginia published in 1742.

I remembered John Banister when I looked up through the white filagree bloom of the fringe tree; when at last I found the sweet bay magnolia flowering at the edge of the forest; laurel magnolia or swamp laurel, *magnolia glauca,* it is now variously called. The colonists called it also beaver tree, and finding that beavers loved it, used it as an appetizing bait for their traps. But the old names, sweet bay, magnolia virginiana, as Banister called it, suit it best. Whatever the name, you can, as Peter Kalm declared, detect the sweet bay by its sweetness three-quarters of a mile away, if the wind is right.

Peter Kalm himself I remembered by the mountain laurel, which Linneaus named for him, *Kalmia latifolia*. Its folk name, Calico flower, describes it to perfection, and gives that instant picture of old cotton prints that the print bonnet-shaped flowers suggest. Peter Collinson loved the flower. "I have a sprig of the Kalmia in water," he wrote coaxingly to John Bartram, "and it stares me in the face all the while I am writing, saying or seeming to say, 'As you are so fond of me, tell my friend, John Bartram, who sent it me, to send more to keep me company.' "

It is, perhaps, inevitable that the old name Virginiana or Virginica was in time discarded in favor of other names that allowed for clearer identity and classification. Rarely, however, did the new name compare with the old. *Magnolia glauca* is positively ugly; *Stewartia malachondendron* for *Stewartia virginica* is a cumbersome name for such a delicate flower, which John Clayton sent to his friend Mark Catesby, and which Catesby in turn named for his patron, John Stuart, the Earl of Bute, though the name spellings differ.

Even the common names of plants soon differed, even in those early days, from one locality to another. The zephyr or fairy lilies, *Zephyranthes atamasco,* are peculiarly restricted in Virginia to the Tidewater land around Jamestown, and are commonly called Jamestown lilies. In the southern states they grow abundantly all through the low-lying savannah land, and Fraser's lily is their southern name. No one could tell me why. But doubtless the name is for John Fraser, the Scotchman, one-time nurseryman of Kings Road, Chelsea, London, who collected in the Carolinas around 1790, or perhaps in honor of his son, John Fraser, Jr., who sometimes accompanied him.

Some years before Bartram gathered the lilies, Mark Catesby found them growing as thick as the cowslips and wild orchids in his Suffolk meadows. Peter Collinson used the Indian name, Atamasco Lily, when in 1740 he wrote to John Bartram: "Thee sent me what we call the Atamasco Lily, from its shape. It has a blush of purple before the flower opens; is white within. It is properly a Lilio Narciss: the leaves of the last and the flower of the first. If, in thy rambles, thee happens on this flower, pray send a root or two."

"Rambles indeed!" Bartram might have muttered, for rambles as applied to Bartram's immense and hazardous journeys must surely be the outstanding example of English understatement in all garden writing. Nor were the roots easy to dig, for they grow deep down in low-lying land.

No understatement of name has rivaled the simplicity of the common names of Calycanthus, the Carolina Allspice. It was, in fact, once so familiar that it has the distinction of being the only shrub listed in an encyclopedia as "merely shrub." Taylor's *Garden Encyclopedia,* under Sweet Shrub, or strawberry shrub, so called for its fragrance, adds after strawberry shrub, "called sometimes merely shrub."

Only a well-loved flower can be so simply distinguished. The flower itself is not attractive, a ragged, strange, and rather dull maroon-colored flower, but its whole essence is in the half-aromatic, half fruit-like fragrance that most nearly resembles the tropical fruit smell of sun-warmed strawberries. But no one can say just what the fragance, contained also in the crushed leaf and in the broken stem, really brings to mind. When country children used to walk to school, they picked the flowers and put them in their handkerchiefs so that they could pinch the flower cluster and sniff its sweetness through their lessons. It is a nostalgic fragrance. Like Southernwood, only far sweeter, the shrub conjures up the past and recaptures happy childhood days.

By the end of May the woods were out of bounds. The undergrowth was rank, and full of ticks. Certainly I had been warned, but I had chosen to forget. One day I laid down flat on the ground to look closely at the yellow lady slipper, in a bank of maidenhair fern, that I might see her fully, face to face. That night when I got into my bath I discovered that the ticks had me at last. "Lazy beggars, they don't even earn their keep. If they have got under the skin you'd best burn them out with a cigarette end or a lighted match," was all the sympathy I got.

From that time on I spent my leisure time rambling, as Collinson might have fairly said, through the old plantation gardens. By the middle of the eighteenth century, the colonists and their sons' sons shared in the European garden craze; besides they, too, were gardeners at heart.

Capital cities had become garden cities. Plantation owners,

like English landowners, planned their estates on the grand country house and garden scale. Gardening had become the pleasure of Governors and Presidents as well as of Kings and Queens.

9
✎

Greenest of Them All

$\mathcal{T}$HE formal design of gardening was fashionable in America long after it had been replaced in Europe by the informal landscape craze of the second half of the eighteenth century. And for a very good reason. The colonists wanted their gardens to remind them of home, and as they were surrounded on all sides by virgin country, they had no need to copy nature by creating shrubberies and wildernesses in their gardens.

Accordingly, early Virginian gardens were designed within a framework of semi-permanent material, of stone and brick, of evergreen and water. They depended for their effect on pattern and texture, and on light and shade rather than color, which was used far less lavishly then than it is today. The modern gardener, in using color for his effect, works with a far more transient material. And he forgoes, to a

large extent, that quality of permanence which belongs
where green is dominant.

Yet for all their English influence, early Virginian gardens
were essentially Virginian. They developed distinct characteristics. The service quarters; the cook house, wash house,
dairy and smoke houses, were built outside the dwelling
house and were distinct, separate features of the over-all
house and garden plan. Shade was a prime necessity in summer, contrary to the English need for light and sun. Arbors
and shaded walks served as outdoor retreats; large, closely
spaced trees were planted immediately around the house to
form canopies of shade.

Climate was also a determining factor for all plant material. John Custis of Williamsburg spoke for Virginia gardeners in general when he complained that three or four
hard winters followed by hot dry summers had "demolished
all my flowers, and a great many of my best greens, so that
I am out of heart of endeavouring anything but what is
hardy and Virginia proof."

Ground covers, such as periwinkle, sometimes replaced
turf, and, after the spring bulbs had withered, were often
used to cover the flower beds with a green carpet which
remained fresh the year round. But box was the Virginian
gardener's best evergreen friend.

Box is the first thing that comes to mind in thinking of
Virginia gardens. There was always box. Common box with
its bitter fragrance that suited the gardener's every need. It
withstood winter-kill and summer-burn; it was, indeed,
hardy and Virginia proof. Common box and its two varieties,
the dwarf or edging box, and tree box which sometimes
attains a height of thirty to forty feet, became the main
feature of almost every garden, as it was once the main

feature of Pliny's favorite villa in Tuscany. Nothing has ever replaced the supreme suitability of box in the Virginia garden.

Old Virginia gardens make their appeal today not simply because they are old or very green, but for their spacious quiet ease, their sense of continuity, their repose. They are, in effect, green architectural gardens, although the severe formality of clipped box is often missing. The box is rarely clipped and shaped strictly to classical lines, but allowed to grow free and untrimmed instead. In the lush Virginia climate it grows with such abundance that the angle lines become softened and fill out into irregular curves, and the box in time becomes billowing mounds of undulating green.

These gardens, for all their predominance of green, are not devoid of some color almost the year round; and the green serves to heighten what color there is. Flowering native shrubs light up the shade. The native wistaria, *Wistaria frutescens,* puts out its leaves before the flowers and in this respect differs from its oriental counterpart. The sweet pepper bush *Clethra alnifolia* not only bears spikes of very fragrant white flowers but also carries attractive seed heads in the fall. The redbud, the witch-hazel and stewartia; the sweet bay, the fringe tree and flowering dogwood light up the green gardens and the forest alike. And there is always the Great Laurel Magnolia, the supreme ornamental tree of the Southern states, that opens its ivory blooms in summer and studs its upright cones with scarlet seeds in fall.

Pomegranate and crepe-myrtle trees have proved themselves hardy and Virginia proof, and bloom all through the hot dry summer months. Crepe myrtle is so widely planted as to be almost as characteristic of Virginia gardens as the scuppernong grape trailing over an arbor and a row of fig trees along a fence.

Once every year for a short spring, color takes precedence over green. It comes first with the daffodils, a thread of gold that spreads and widens with the days, until it covers whole acres of land on old plantations, where the bulbs have spread and colonized with the same abandon as the box. By the third week in April, usually chosen as Virginia's garden week, the spring bulbs and early summer perennials give the gardens their maximum of color. Thereafter the green comes surging back, and color is again a secondary theme.

When people speak of Virginian gardens it is the green gardens of old plantation houses, in particular the James River plantations, that come to mind. They are as old as the Old Dominion's history, but they have grown with the years. Something, perhaps, has gone from many of them since they were first laid out; something has been lost and something added by their successive owners. But they still retain the fundamental quality for which they are famous, and they are as much a part of the fabric of Virginia as the stately homes to which they belong.

The gardens of Williamsburg are an exception. They were restored or reconstructed as nearly as possible to their original design, and are maintained accordingly. It follows naturally enough that such gardens, which neither gain nor lose through the years, and show none of the individuality of successive owners, are by nature static. Gardens such as these, the museum pieces of garden art, you may see in Williamsburg. In fact so strictly are these gardens kept within their authentic eighteenth centuryism that only flowers known to the colonists at that period may be grown in the restored gardens. If a tenant has a love for petunias, for instance, that were introduced later, he is just out of luck.

The Governor's Palace Garden is as far removed from the other gardens in Williamsburg as Hampton Court Garden from its surrounding suburban gardens. And although the Governor's Palace Garden does not approach Hampton Court in size, it does contain a great many features of the English palace garden.

William III of England, for whom Williamsburg was named, was homesick for his native Holland, and like the early colonists wanted his garden to remind him of home. The Governor of Virginia, in his turn, wanted his palace garden to be as nearly like the king's palace garden as the colony's finances would allow. And though he was chided for his extravagances, he did very well. William III would have felt very much at home, walking the arbors and the parterres, admiring the topiary, and threading his way through the maze, which is an exact replica of the maze at Hampton Court.

The reconstructed garden of the Governor's Palace at Williamsburg is one of the very few remaining examples of the perfect eighteenth-century garden; in fact its only counterpart is the reconstructed garden at Villandry in Touraine, France. Other eighteenth century-gardens have been altered, new styles and new plant material added, but in the Palace garden everything is as it was; not a flower, not a single feature, nothing has been added that was not known and in current use in its own period.

The Palace garden is a great outdoor museum. Here you may see what fashion has retained and what discarded. Mazes and mounts have long since disappeared from garden design, and only in Holland does elaborate topiary survive as a thriving art in a fantasy of squares, of pyramids, cylinders, and balls and bells. But the most simple form of topiary, the hedge, survives; and the lawn, the most simple of all parterres, remains.

Elsewhere in Williamsburg the gardens are far less ambitious in scope and design, and are well worth the present-day gardener's study. Along the Duke of Gloucester Street the houses are located directly on the sidewalk so that all space within the half-acre lot, which was originally established by statute, could be fully utilized. The service dependencies, the coach-house, garden and orchard space, in addition to the dwelling house, were all included without any sense of over-crowding, so that these gardens are still valuable examples of good small-lot planning for those who want to design small city gardens today. Although the gardens are uniform in size, they show an infinite variety of design, and stand as testimony to those past gardeners who planned them for beauty as well as utility, and who succeeded so admirably in both.

Carter's Grove, an hour's drive from Williamsburg, is the most stately of all the fine old James River plantation houses, and claims to have the finest pine paneling in the world. I have seen it at dead of winter when snow lay on the ground, and at the height of summer when the netted strawberry patch was bright with fruit. I remember it best as I saw it first, on a cold February afternoon when the sun was setting, a ball of red across the churlish muddy river. The willow oaks and locust trees were etched in black tracery against the winter sky, the tulip trees on the river side towered behind the steep-pitched roof. It was a dramatic picture, finely drawn with an economy of line and color that would later be a trifle blurred by summer's greenness.

I had thought the snow-covered box might appear formless. Contrarily, the snow enhanced its architectural value. It outlined the soft undulating groups planted in the grass beneath the trees so that they appeared moulded by a sculptor's hand rather than by the free-flowing lines of nature's choosing.

Brandon, another of the James River plantation houses, I remember as the evergreen heart of Virginia gardens. It is the greenest of them all. If I had had my choice, I should have gone to Brandon in the old way, by the ancient river highway in a long canoe, with the Negro paddlers singing as they swung their oars. That is still open but untraveled, and the highway now runs through the woods and across stretches of farmland, invaded the May day I went there by acre upon acre of white ox-daisies and yellow ragwort.

Brandon, forty-five miles east of Richmond, on the south side of the James River, was granted in 1616 to John Martin, companion of Captain John Smith on his first voyage to Virginia. After a brief ownership, Martin sold the land to Nathaniel Harrison, who named it Brandon after the English town. For more than two centuries his descendants established Brandon as a famous name.

Brandon welcomes the stranger with the colonies' traditional emblem of hospitality, the pineapple. Pineapples carved in stone decorate the gate piers at the entrance, and passing into the long tree-shaded approach, a large oval parterre planted with evergreen ground cover, you see the pineapple again on the roof of the house.

The main garden lies on the north or front side of the house, built to face the river highway. There the greenest of all gardens waits to receive you. I say "receive you" with deliberation, for you cannot fail to be instantly aware of a sense of ease, of its waiting to receive.

You see the garden first as an immense square of sward surrounded by tier upon tier of green: not a monotony of green, but green of every shade and texture. The old box planted along the house front and enclosing the three sides of the lawn has long since grown together into billowing masses that dip and curve in green waves around the wide open green space. And behind the box, crepe myrtles and southern magnolia trees reach up to the tall tulip trees that bring sound and movement to the place, the river breeze forever fluttering their leaves.

A long central turfed path leads from the open green, through the tree-shaded lower garden to the broad brown James River beyond. You do not see, as you go, the two parallel paths that mark symmetrically the outer boundaries, nor the fine vegetable and cut-flower gardens, the swimming pool and play area on either side of the original garden. Instead, you see a whole series of galleried gardens between their ramparts of enclosing box and flowering shrubs.

The spring flowers were over. It was the day of the Sweet William and the dwarf azalea, narrow hem-like borders of brilliant color embroidering the green. There were foxgloves in the shade of a giant pecan tree, twenty-two feet in girth and three hundred years old.

Hedges of mock orange, deutzie, and the native stewartia were thick in rampant bloom. But the stewartia's white camellia-like blooms with their boss of white stamens and purpled anthers exact a penalty for their beauty: the flowers fade in a day when picked for cut-flower bloom.

It is a happy thought that John Martin's descendants

now own Brandon, that under their care it is still a great garden. It is old, ripe, and fully mature, with no hint of decay, which is the test of all great gardens, young or old. Beautifully ordered and softened in outline, you know instinctively that some green-fingered hand is forever at its pulse: you will recognize Brandon as the living illustration of Andrew Marvell's "green thought in a green shade."

10 Where Great Men Walked

I KNEW William Byrd II of Westover by his books, and always when I think of him I think of the blue bird too, because I saw both indigo bunting and Westover for the first time on the same day.

It was full summer when I went to the old plantation on the James River, about twenty-five miles south of Richmond. The sun shimmered over the wheat fields and thick green woodlands. From somewhere a bird was singing and I stopped to listen. There, on an old bare bough of a roadside bush, in the hot noontide hour, the indigo bunting poured out his song. His brilliant sapphire plumage was no whit lessened by the bright blue sky above, or the dusky purple vetch that spread itself below. It was a living Audubon print, a startling patch of color on the Virginian greenness. William Byrd would have stood and marveled at just such

a sight and such a song, noting down in his diary that the
bird was "exceptionally beautiful" and having a "voice,
which is very lovely to hear."

William Byrd's mother and father had come to Virginia
from England four years before he was born in 1674, near
the falls of the James River, at the place where Richmond, the
city he named and founded, now stands. When he was seven
years old he was sent to England for his education, and only
returned for a few months until in 1705, at the age of
twenty-four, he succeeded to his father's estate of some
twenty-six thousand acres and his office as Receiver General
of the Colony's revenues. From then on, although he visited
England from time to time, William Byrd II spent most of
his life in Virginia.

He was one of the great men of his time, and typified the
cultured Virginia landowner at his best. He was a member of
the exclusive Council of Virginia, and of the Royal Society of
England, and counted among his friends such men as Charles
Boyle and Sir Hans Sloan.

Westover, the house he built in 1730, is an exceptionally
beautiful Georgian plantation house that looks out over a
wide sweep of lawn sloping down to the river's edge, and
planted with enormous tulip trees. At Westover he collected
what was, by repute, the finest library in Virginia and, although he was neither plant collector nor botanist, he was
a connoisseur. His gardens were famous and what he grew
in them he grew well.

The *Secret Diary* which Byrd wrote, like Pepys, in short-
hand, is full of reference to country matters; his *Natural
History of Virginia* records what he saw through eyes accustomed to the English countryside. It was he who told me
through his books that the jack snipe was the only bird he

knew that in no way differed from the European species;
that the Indians obtained an oil as sweet as olive oil from
the green live-oak, that from the acorns they made chocolate
which he considered no whit inferior to that obtained from
cocoa. He named the sweet gum as the most beautiful wood
for furniture; the sugar maple as the most useful tree in the
world for the wine, spirits, vinegar, honey and sugar that
might be made from the maple syrup. But best of all, I think,
he loved the tall tulip trees that he planted between the house
and the river.

His was the appraising eye that delighted in that "miracle
of nature," the humming bird; that noted the "whitish yellow" plumage of the crane whose quill he found "fine for
writing." And it was, no doubt, with such a quill that he
wrote of the animals and birds, the trees "and still many
other flowers unknown in Europe . . . which please travel-
lers with their beauty."

East of the house lies the walled garden, and a series of
small box-enclosed gardens. Here William Byrd grew the
fruit that was his speciality; the cherries it was his pleasure
to send to the Governor at Williamsburg; the promegranates
that Catesby, the English botanist, recalled, growing "in
great perfection" there.

The wide sweep of lawn with the tall tulip poplars between the house and the river is, undoubtedly, much as William Byrd knew it. But the walled garden which must once
have been so trim is now a wilderness, and the great bushes of
sweet shrub and syringa trail their branches to the ground. I
heard children laughing as they ran beneath the arching
sprays thickset with bloom, playing hide and seek along the
paths that all lead to the small central square where the
Black Swan, as William Byrd was called, is buried in his

tomb. I do not know. The place seemed alive with his presence.

I used to stand under those enormous tulip trees that are forever restless in the river breeze, and think of the conflicts which beset William Byrd. His life was spent in public service among the offices of state, though he was at heart a true countryman. He was by birth and environment a man who belonged to two countries. Perhaps at times he felt he belonged wholly to neither one nor the other of them. When he heard the quail call in the Virginian evenings he would be reminded of the partridge calling in the English twilight; when he heard the snipe drumming in an English watermeadow he would remember them in the marshland of Virginia.

The Black Swan loved Virginia, where his responsibilities caused him to make his home. And he loved England where he spent his youth. He had intended finally to sell his Virginia property and spend the remainder of his days in England where, among the friends of his boyhood, he hoped to live out his later years. But Virginia, that had claimed most of his life and much of his service, claimed him also at the last.

Thomas Jefferson, Governor of Virginia and third President of the United States, was not, like William Byrd, torn between his love for two countries; he was whole-heartedly American. But both followed a life of public service; both had in common a love of gardening, an eager curiosity, and, fortunately, the habit of keeping voluminous diaries. Yet to know either of them by their writings alone is to know them only in part. It is as true of Thomas Jefferson as it is of William Byrd, that however well you may think you know them through their own and other people's writing, you still will not know them unless you have been to Westover and to Monticello.

At Monticello you will see about you the reality of Thomas Jefferson's dreams, and how his cunning hand matched his inventive brain. And it is here that you look out over the great expanse of Virginian country that he served and loved so well. Away to the north the Blue Ridge Mountains rise above and beyond Charlottesville, a massive rampart of incredible blue for all its forest greenness. To the east lies the foothill country around Tufton, and southward in the valley the flat woods of Albemarle stretch away as far as the eye can see. Westward, the garden merges into the gently sloping hillside that was once planted with vineyard and orchard.

At Monticello, Jefferson's home, as at the University of Virginia at Charlottesville, which he founded, and the State Capitol at Richmond, you will see Jefferson's handiwork as one of the foremost architects of his day. On the surrounding land and in the garden you will understand something of his work as scientific farmer and fine gardener. A portion of the five thousand acres of the original estate, together with the house and garden, now belong to the Thomas Jefferson Memorial Foundation, and are open to the public, maintained as nearly as possible as they were in Jefferson's lifetime.

Monticello was begun in 1769, and was a long time in the making. Jefferson might say that it was still unfinished for he was ever forward-looking and change-loving. Wherever you turn you will see the individual stamp of his versatile hand and brain. There is the dumb-waiter for the wine bottles on either side of the dining-room mantelpiece, and the

swivel chair, both of which he invented, also the folding
doors similar to those used in street cars today.

Most intriguing of all are the clock and weathervane. He
could tell the time of day and the day of the week, both inside and outside the house, by the cannon ball weights and
pulleys that operated the clock. He could tell the way the
wind blew by glancing from the reception room to the compass he set in the eastern portico ceiling and connected to
the weathervane on his rooftop.

Similarly the garden reflects Jefferson's individual taste
and preference for the open landscape rather than the traditionally formal design. And Jefferson himself is your best
guide to his estate and garden. His *Garden Notebook,* 1766–
1824, ranges over the whole field of agriculture, forestry and
horticulture, and is packed with his observations at home
and abroad.

You may walk with Jefferson along the serpentine, flower-
bordered paths that lead round the whole oval stretch of
lawn. If it is April, you will note with him that his sweet
williams have "begun to open"; if it is July you will see the
garden gay with snapweed or *Impatiens,* and the brilliant
small mauve, red, and yellow pincushion heads of globe
amaranth, *Gomprena globosa.* If you dine with him on July
fifteenth you will share his "Cucumbers" that "came to
table," and hear that he has planted a "patch of peas for the
Fall."

He will tell you of the contour ploughing he introduced
on his estate, of his experiments with growing benne, which
flavors the candy and cakes they make in Charleston today.
He will tell you of the plants he has raised from seed collected by Lewis and Clark, whose expedition to the Northwest Pacific he ordered.

Jefferson counted his introduction of the olive tree and dry rice into South Carolina, together with the writing of the Declaration of Independence, as among his most important services. "No occupation," he wrote in 1811, "is so delightful to me as the culture of the earth, and no culture comparable to that of the garden," adding with the humility characteristics of great men, "But though an old man, I am but a young gardener."

It has been said that you can tell a man by his flower border, and it is true that gardens reflect, as much as the furnishings and atmosphere of a house, the individuality of their owners. No one who visits Monticello should fail to see Ash Lawn, the house that Jefferson built for his friend, James Monroe, the fifth President of the United States. You come to it along a narrow brick path closely hedged with box and shadowed by trees. On the south a small flower-bordered lawn commands the view over the countryside and across the valley to Monticello two miles away.

It is strange that two places so intimately bound together should be so entirely different in atmosphere. Ash Lawn is redolent of the past, it broods as James Monroe must sometimes have brooded in frustrated disappointment. It looks back on the past, as Monroe's wife, broken in health and withdrawn into retirement, must have looked back to the day she, an eighteen-year–old belle of New York, married Monroe, and to the years she spent in the glitter of European courts when he was Minister to Britain, France, and Spain.

However it may be, Ash Lawn is of the past and Monticello is of the present. And there, at Monticello, in the long, leisured, sunlit afternoons you may imagine Jefferson still looking forward to fresh invention, still enjoying his garden, an old, perhaps, but always a young gardener.

11 *Choose Your Beauty*

$\mathcal{I}$T was early March when I went to Charleston, South Carolina, a name that is synonymous with flowers. Hardly anyone was astir when I woke but the flower women, walking slowly along the streets with their rush baskets, full of white swamp lilies, on their arms. Only the mocking birds, calling from the city's housetops, broke the stillness of the spring morning.

For a long time I had wanted to see Magnolia Garden, named for the fine *Magnolia Grandiflora* that grow there but famous for the camellias and immense plantings of azaleas among the cypress swamps of the Carolina Low Country. The Rev. Grimke-Drayton, who began the garden about 1830, planted there some thirteen years later the first *Azalea Indica* to be imported into America, together with many varieties of the *Camellia Japonica*. Now, and for many

99

years past, thousands take the fifteen-mile–long road out of
Charleston to see these plants in their height of bloom.

In pre-war editions, Baedecker named Magnolia as one of
the three great sights of America, together with Niagara
Falls and the Grand Canyon. John Galsworthy, who traveled
the same road thirty years ago, put Magnolia at the top of
his garden list. "I specialize in gardens," he wrote, and he
had seen a number of the world's famous gardens, including
the Boboli at Florence, the Cinnamon Gardens at Colombo,
Conception at Malaga, La Mortala in Italy, the Generaliffe
at Granada, and nearer home, Versailles in France and his
own Hampton Court. Yet he declared, in speaking of Magnolia, "that none in the world is so beautiful as this."

> Nothing so free and gracious, so lovely and wistful, nothing so
> richly colored, yet so ghost-like, exists, planted by the sons of
> man. It is a kind of paradise which has wandered down, a mi-
> raculously enchanted wilderness.

Nearly ten years later he said again: "To this day I have seen
no garden so beautiful as Magnolia."

No wonder I woke expectantly. But by the time I stopped
at the entrance gate, I had a sudden wish to go no further.
It was tempting providence. What if the garden proved disappointing? Should I, as some had warned me, find it too
opulent, too colorful? Should I not let Galsworthy's description stand, let the garden remain forever an enchanted wilderness in my mind? The friend who had come with me
from Virginia had come a long way. She was having no such
nonsense. "It's poppycock," she said. "Come along." And we
went in together.

I asked for Mr. Norwood Hastie, the present owner of
Magnolia and direct descendant of the Grimke-Drayton who
planted the garden. I gave him, for introduction, the name

of a mutual garden-friend. "If you'll wait a minute I will show you round, and then you can wander about by yourself for as long as you like afterwards."

As we went along the paths which were in reality avenues of tall camellia bushes, past the long swathe-like borders of azaleas, Mr. Hastie told me that the original house was burned shortly after the Revolution, nothing but the old steps remained; that the second mansion was destroyed by the Northern troops in the Civil War, but the garden has always remained. The fame of the azaleas and the number of people who come to see them has spread with their own increase. Mr. Hastie proudly reminded me of a notice at Kew Gardens in England which read: "Azaleas in their highest glory are to be found in Magnolia Gardens, near Charleston, South Carolina, U.S.A."

There was less color that year than usual, and though Mr. Hastie spoke of it regretfully I was glad of some contrasting green. Fearful of talking superlatives that he must tire of hearing, I asked him questions instead. I learned that half a dozen gardeners cared for the twenty-five acre garden, that they kept the azaleas thoroughly mulched, spraying them three times a week: that neither the soil nor the swamp water gave the azaleas such intense color, a misconception that is widely held.

I stayed in the garden a long time after Mr. Hastie went indoors, walking among the tall camellia bushes which are his favorites, and the drifts of azaleas massed along the lawns and edges of the swamp. I came to a white bridge arched over the swamp waterway, like the bridge Monet so often painted in his water garden. From there my eye traveled the long view either way of swamp and cypress trees, upwards to the Cherokee roses climbing among the trees, and higher still above them where the wistaria and the lovely yellow fragrant Carolina jasmine wreathed toward the sky.

Gradually the sense of the place came to me. It was quite windless. Not a whisper stirred the long pendants of Spanish moss, not a breath ruffled the surface of the water where the vivid imperial color of banked azaleas was reflected in the ebony blackness as a wreath of flowers on a black lacquer tray, so that it was hard to tell where the living color ceased and where the reflection began. I had a feeling that if I called aloud my voice would shiver the silence as though a mirror cracked, and there would be but a stifling echo answering out of the wilderness.

It must have been the first Grimke-Drayton's sense of the dramatic to plant such strident color against the somber monotones of the Low Country landscape, and set the azalea flaming in the stagnant swamp where the gray and ghostlike shrouding moss feeds upon the live oaks, and the bald cypress make their last stand. For the bald cypress are relics from the ancient past, the southern coastal swamps their only foothold in the world. Aloof, already remote in their antiquity, there is an air of impending doom about them as they rise from the dark water, straight and solemn as the aisled pillars of a cathedral, their delicate fern-like foliage making a traceried canopy overhead.

Magnolia: the place is well named. Magnolia is an exotic word. Whoever named the magnolia for Pierre Magnol, the seventeenth-century director of the Montpelier Botanic Garden in France, had a flair for words. It was near genius to add two letters to Magnol's name to make such a memorable word. Magnolia is a name that people remember. And Magnolia Garden, once you have seen it, is a garden you will always remember too; an enchanted wilderness, a place of wild tranquility.

But I do not, as Galsworthy did, associate the word "free" with a place that by its enchantment holds you spellbound. Nor would I "freely assert," as Galsworthy, that no garden "in the world is so beautiful as this." One garden above all others may make the most appeal to one pair of eyes, but you cannot match one beauty against another beauty where there is perfection either way. Francis Bacon, the Elizabethan, who wrote that masterpiece *Of Gardens*, came nearer to the truth in saying there is no excellent beauty that has not some strangeness too.

As I walked back through the garden once more I found a few swamp lilies. The sight of them, white and frail along the margin of the water, gave me a sense of relief, the refreshment of a summer breeze. They were the same lilies, *Zephyranthes atamasco*, that the flower women gather to sell in the city streets, that people in the Virginia Tidewater call Jamestown lilies, but which here in the South are called Fraser's lilies.

Azaleas and camellias had no place in the original color scheme; only Fraser's lilies, the Great Southern Magnolia, and the Carolina jasmine were truly native. Even the Cherokee rose is probably a naturalized immigrant for all its Indian name. No one knows how it got into Georgia, where it was first noticed by André Michaux, for it was found to be identical to the Three Leaved Chinese Rose, *Rosa laevigata*. The best guess at an unsolved mystery is that Fraser, who crossed and recrossed the Atlantic between his plant-hunting expeditions, introduced it in part exchange for the southern flowers he found.

No place offers a greater contrast to Magnolia than Middleton nearby. A similar history of house spoliation during the Civil War is the only thing they have in common. Between the two gardens there is the same sharp contrast as between the pure and the synthetic crystal.

Middleton is the oldest landscaped garden in America. It was designed for Henry Middleton, Governor of South Carolina and friend of the botanist, André Michaux, by a pupil of the great Le Notre who created the garden of Versailles in France. It took a hundred slaves nine years, from 1741 to 1750, to complete the formal terraces, the walks and artificial lakes, and the long vistas to the river and the savannah land beyond.

Here André Michaux brought the first *Camellia Japonicas* to be planted in America, and three of the original bushes still bear bloom. All along the camellia walk the sprays have long since formed an archway overhead.

Henry Middleton's son William, once Minister to Russia, added to his inheritance by planting a fine collection of *Azalea Indica* which his neighbor at Magnolia had been the first to introduce. Today they make a magnificent stretch of color across the reflection lake and beneath the massive oaks on the woodland slope above. But neither camellia nor azalea predominate, they are but incidental to the over-all impression of wide green spaciousness. There is no shut-in-ness; nothing impedes the view across the garden to the superb line of magnolia trees that form a rampart of shining leaves along one side of the oblong canal.

The eighteenth-century formality of the garden has long since been softened. The once trim terraces are now smooth contoured curves of mown grass leading down to the "butterfly" lakes, man-made in the shape of a butterfly's wings. There is nothing to mark a line where the garden ends and the savannah begins. And over the savannah there is a wistfulness that hangs over all the Low Country of the Carolinas, a naked loneliness of rice fields, lying deserted. At Middleton the old rice mill is idle, and the water in the surrounding pool is still.

If the garden had a voice it might say "All is never lost." Though Middleton is undeniably sad, it does not impose its sadness on you. There is nothing mysterious, nothing secret, no spellbinding enchantment in this garden that, in contrast, lies open under the wide skies. And though Middleton is robbed of its original splendor, its natural beauty remains unimpaired.

12 ❦ New Orleans and Texas

New Orleans, in Louisiana; Houston, San Antonio, Dallas, and Fort Worth in Texas; so the itinerary ran. The cities were way-stops in my working journey. I saw them in the hottest months of the year, when the Southern states swelter in semi-tropical humidity.

Harry Daunoy and his wife Maria, rose lovers and soil experts both, were my New Orleans' guides. Maria's definition of the word Creole gave me some sense of the city from the start. The Creoles, she said, are descendants of New Orleans' first proud settlers, Americans who are of pure French or Spanish extraction, or half French and half Spanish. Creole cuisine, like New Orleans itself, is part Spanish, part American, more French than either; a combination of good things, seasoned with the local "Mississippi flavor"—the city is wedded to the mighty river that is at its door. The gardens, contrariwise, are more Spanish than anything else.

It takes days to explore the gardens of the French quarter alone, to cross from one side of a balcony shadowed street to the other, to climb the spiral staircase, to trespass along the narrow passages leading to the side carriage entrances and the gardens at the back of the old mansions. But even at a cursory glance the influence of Spain is unmistakable.

There are the patios and the sky gardens of Spain, the courtyards enclosed by fence or wall for privacy, and overlooked by balconies filled with potted plants. The famous black wrought-iron used with lace-like lavishness for balconies and fences is the touch of Mississippi flavor here, and the influence of that touch is now nation-wide.

In gardens all over America, you may find cast-iron chairs and tables that are copies of the furniture introduced by the Creoles in their gardens. Leading magazines advertise the "rich ante-bellum" patterns of "the decorative Grape & Leaf design with ornamental apron on settee and matching Chairs." Shops offer for sale the "Louisiana Chair" that comes in white, Bermuda Blue, Creole Pink, and Antique Green, a rather far cry from New Orleans unpretentious black. Other patterns of vine leaves, oak leaves and acorns, and roses, are repeated a thousand times, but in New Orleans itself the most beautiful example of Creole taste in ironwork is an old green weather-worn "cornstalk" fence with its corn cobs and leaves, butterflies and morning glory, of which there are today only two examples extant.

Old New Orleans inherited the Spanish love of fragrance. The "night-time" garden, where the Moon Vine opened from dusk to dawn and the night-blooming jasmine poured out its vanilla sweetness, was an essential part of every Creole home.

In contrast to the old French Quarter, the beautiful antebellum—meaning before the Civil War—and colonial mansions of the Garden District and the fashionable Uptown District are surrounded by open and unfenced gardens. The Creole influence, however, persists in the love of fragrant flowers. A local touch is added by the choice of shrubs and trees. As in the courts and plazas of the old part of the city, large-leaved tropical plants, banana trees, and palms grow side by side with the native magnolia grandiflora and massive oak trees.

Camellias, azaleas, and oleanders are New Orleans' favorite shrubs, but the gardens are not simply spring gardens as might be supposed by the climate. In spite of the oppressive late summer heat, I found the gardens lush and green, bright with flowers.

"How do you manage it?" I asked the owners of one garden as we sat indoors briefly to rest, sipping iced tea and fanning ourselves with old Victorian fans.

"We *are* proud of our gardens," they said, "and work on them very hard. The worst of our climate is that it lacks the spice of variety; the plants have no rest period, almost all our trees stay evergreen. In Virginia people make a great effort for garden week, and then seem to sit back and wilt, but here we continue to work all through the hottest months. Even now in September you see what flowers we have." And the fans came into play again.

Roses and hibiscus and the lovely, intensely fragrant Butterfly lily, *Hadychicuum coronarium,* were in bloom. Cassia or Senna was a shower of gold; plumbago with its phlox-like sky-blue flowers was rampant everywhere. Mauve lantana and the pink Rosa of Montana trailed over the fences. The Japanese plum, *Mespolus,* trained espalier fashion was a splendid decoration on outside walls. Kumquat, with its beautiful olive-green foliage, was widely grown, and its green fruit used for table decorations at Thanksgiving and Christmas; the sweet rind and sour pulp, so Maria Daunoy told me, made an excellent preserve.

The old roses, especially the Louis Phillipe rose grown as a hedge in the City Park, the noisettes and tea roses bloom almost the year round, Harry Daunoy said. The modern roses, however, are comparative failures. They lack the stamina of the older varieties, and have no constitution to resist disease, especially black spot. Many people are unaware of this and incorrectly blame the soil condition for the difficulty in growing the new roses.

Climate is not the only thing that makes New Orleans' gardeners work hard. There is a very good reason for most people thinking that the soil condition rather than the lack of stamina is the cause of difficult rose growing. New Orleans is seven feet below sea level, and though the drainage now goes as deep as thirty feet in places, it is still a gardener's concern.

To New Orleans water is a city problem in reverse. Water tax is, in effect, a drainage tax. Every drop of rain water which falls has to be pumped away, and the city operates the largest water purification plant in the world. And that is why New Orleans, before deep drainage was installed, buried its dead above ground.

The old graveyards with their monumental tombs, the cities within the city, as they are called, affect the cut-flower trade. For Catholic New Orleans, All Saints' Day is second only in importance to the festival of Mardi Gras. The custom of decking the graves with flowers makes chrysanthemums one of the great local commercial flower crops.

Of all the gardens I saw, the most distinctive was also the

smallest, a miniature patio garden extending directly from the living room down a short flight of steps. It was a skilful modern adaption of the old-time patio, entirely refurbished in the fashion of today but retaining the essential character-istics of the true patio. The white-walled garden-room was enclosed by high walls on three sides and open only to the sky. In one corner was an orange tree bright with fruit and a tumbled mass of plumbago below it. In another corner a spiral stairway led up through the branches of a cocullus tree to the small potting shed on the flat roof above, entirely hidden from below. Fig trees were espaliered on the walls, but the wall opposite the house steps contained a wall foun-tain. A simple ground cover made a small octagonal ever-green carpet around the central shallow basin fountain. The small room was alive with the sound of tinkling water.

Within such a framework city gardens are adaptable to every climate. I could imagine the place roofed with glass and massed with bloom, serving as a hot conservatory in a cold climate. Or in a tropical area it could be a fountain room. As it was I saw it as unmistakably New Orleans; a Spanish patio with the "Mississippi flavor."

The evening the Daunoys came to see me off at midnight, we wiled away the waiting hour sitting in the French market, drinking the traditional black coffee and little square sugar-coated doughnuts at the French market. They forewarned me of the size of Texas, an empire in itself, with an area three times that of Great Britain; that everything in Texas was bigger than anywhere else. Long before I was to cross the state line I realized that only a Texan-born can ever claim *to know* that vast and varied territory.

I think of Houston as one of the most public-garden–minded of cities with magnificent landscaped grounds sur-

rounding hospitals and public buildings. It may well hold
the record number of garden clubs; in 1950 there were two
hundred fifty clubs, and today there may be thrice that many,
each twice as big. In Houston, time moved so fast the very
ground seemed to move under my feet; after long sightseeing garden days I laid half-awake at night and saw imaginary
pictures of vast flowing rivers of oil, with new houses and
great apartment blocks rising along the banks as I watched.
Even now the city leaves me dazed with an impression of
mighty things in my head.

Few will deny that Houston is one of the most robustly
American of all American cities, and that San Antonio is
one of the cleanest. San Antonio is less Spanish in character
than it used to be, the rapidly growing metropolis over-
laying the old influence. However, the little green-bordered
river that runs through the heart of the city still preserves
an oasis-like character, and the garden at The Alamo is still
an old-time Spanish garden transplanted from the Old
World to the New.

Standing and talking to the gardener there, in the dry sear-
ing temperature over a hundred degrees, I looked around
at the pink and mauve thunbergia, the amaranthus or cocks-
combe in wide variety, the pink oleander bushes, the carnations and pinks. And then gratefully I turned toward the
fountain at the center of the courtyard, sprinkling down over
the fragrant water lilies.

For those who know the old gardens of Spain, in particular
the gardens of the Alhambra and the Generaliffe, this garden
at The Alamo serves as a reminder of what too many gardeners in the Southwest and California have forgotten—and
thus foregone—in their adaptation of the Spanish patio garden. They have forgotten what the Spanish padres taught

them when they laid out the old Mission gardens: that the over-all color of a garden can be green without a blade of grass; that irrigation methods can enhance and not detract from the beauty of a pleasure ground.

In arid country such as Spain and the desert lands of the American West, the color green and water are two of the most precious commodities. Spain, perhaps more than any other country, has expressed a love of green, especially in textiles, superbly well, and the artist El Greco used green almost exclusively in his cloaks and draperies. It follows naturally enough that the Spanish gardener, for all his love of the brilliant color of geranium and carnation, amaranthus, zinnia, and petunia, makes green the dominant color in his garden, and he achieves this without growing a blade of grass. He knows that in desert climates grass is the most impracticable of all plant material.

Brick and patterned stone are used for walks and courtyards and leaf-green is the foil and background for the bright-hued flowers and flowering shrubs: green in the yellow green of lemon trees, the dark shining green of magnolia leaves, the black green of the sharp pointed cypresses, the olive-green of olives, and the quiet, aromatic green of myrtle and box. By contrast the American gardeners of the Southwest for the most part achieve their green effect by grass, and employ millions of ugly sprinklers and mile after mile of hose to do it.

The Spanish gardener employs water for a three-fold use. Without any of the easy devices used today, of old he engineered intricate irrigating systems that provided life for his flowers, fruit, and trees, refreshment in the noon-day heat, and embellishment for the garden in the form of fountains, canals and pools.

The garden at The Alamo is a good place to remember these things. Above all, in that garden courtyard, with the sound of water gently splashing, one might remember what Hilaire Belloc wrote of fountains. A fountain, he said, makes alive in a special way all the leaves and branches of the place, all the air. "No other work of man," he claimed, "is so simple and so single, so satisfying, so complete, so full and so successful a challenge to the shadow of mortality and to the burden of change. For though the fountain is ever in movement, it is ever one in strength and character: young when we were young and still young when we are grown old." He exhorted: "Go you, therefore, and make fountains about your gardens . . . if you can afford to have a garden at all you can surely afford to have a fountain which shall baptize it continually and give it perennial grace."

American gardeners, especially those who tread in Spanish footprints, well might heed.

Dallas, fashionable Dallas, derives its wealth, like Houston, from oil, and it affords magnificent gardens. Its gardeners have chosen the most luxuriant grass I have ever walked across; they could, I think, also have afforded fountains. There plants grow Texan-fashion: crinum lilies seven feet tall fill the gardens with their gardenia-like scent; dahlias from Oregon bear great heads of brilliant bloom standing on nine-foot stems. The zinnias blaze; the lawns are superb.

The grass, the caladiums, and the immaculate grooming are my over-riding impressions of Dallas gardens. Caladiums grow by their thousands under the filtered sunlight and protection of the great oak trees. To walk over the chunky St. Augustine grass is like walking over a deep rich pile-carpet. But the gardens, ever uniform in design and planting, are to my eyes too brushed and combed. They are outside drawing rooms, tended by outside hired help; gardens for show but not for fun.

That opinion merely reflects my own taste, and is not criticism. What I best remember of the city, above any one single garden, is the view one evening when I left for nearby Fort Worth. I looked back across the prairie land and saw the city as a sentinel-towered skyline rising out of the illimitable ochre-colored plain, pointing high to the wide western sky. Fashionable Dallas has probably the most beautiful profile of any American city.

The citizens of Dallas call their neighboring city Cow Town but, so it was explained to me, Fort Worth doesn't really mind. Rather Fort Worth is proud of the fact that her wealth has come from hoof and horn. By the huge signboard of a Hereford Bull with the words COW TOWN written large and bold underneath, and the sculptured cattle heads on the main city bridge and atop the Post Office pillars, she proudly acknowledges her debt.

It was to Mrs. Lake, a Park Commissioner of Fort Worth, that I owe my introduction to that part of the great Texan empire. I like to recall the day we went to Weatherford, about an hour's driving from Fort Worth. We talked of Texas, of course, without a mention of whom or what we were going to see. It was just "one garden I must take you to." As we drove along Mrs. Lake reminded me of Robert Pyle, drawing on her encyclopedic fund of information.

"Over in the east part of the state," she waved her hand as we sped along, "there are two-million acres of cross-timber land still untouched. The rest of Texas in on the move. Fort Worth is the capital of the Grand Prairie region of Texas, flanked by the eastern and western cross-timbers. They say that at the end of the twentieth century Houston will be . . ."

"What are cross-timbers?" I had to pop my questions in as I could.

"Oh, stretches of a distinct type of lumberland; the four chief trees are post oak, used for posts and boundary marking, cedar elm, live oak and hackberries."

"Where does the West begin?" I asked then.

Mrs. Lake hesitated. I believe she wanted to say Fort Worth, when abruptly and none too politely, I asked her to stop the car. She did, asking if anything was wrong. No, absolutely nothing, I assured her.

But there on either side of us were great rolling stretches of downland country, like the Sussex Weald, with immense cloud shadows chasing across the land. It was a moment of extraordinary soft opalescent light, haze-blue and high white cloud, the land colored with yellow broomhead and heather-like drifts of purple thistle; with the long spikes of blazing star and millions of fairy dusters forever nodding their white heads atop their slender stalks. I had not thought the plain would be so gentle nor have so soft a color.

We did not stop again until we had entered a private drive and pulled up at the entrance to the house. Only then did I learn that it was the home of English-born Douglas Chandor, the artist, and that the garden had been fourteen years in the making out of raw prairie land.

A tall, lithe man came over the arching bridge across the pool. "My hands are dirty. I've just come in from the garden," Douglas Chandor said apologetically. I noticed that his shirt was wet with sweat.

The garden proved to be a series of gardens; a boxwood garden, a sunken green garden of lawns and shrubs, peach-covered espaliered alleys with deep red verbenas either side to the rock and water garden. He turned suddenly with a short laugh. "How strange, how very strange to hear an English voice—here."

"It isn't all one chunk of rock, you know," he pointed to what appeared a natural outcrop of stone. "I brought it in piece by piece, and I painted the moss and the cracks. That boat you see down there. It never sails; it's made of stone."

From every stand-point there was a view at the end of the long terraced alleyways, usually of some definite single feature. Chinese dogs of stone guarded the grey garden from the top of gate pillars which was, I think, the most individual feature in a remarkable garden. There was lavender and santolina, the native salvia and the rain bush which bursts into pale lavender flowers just before and just after a rainfall. Varying tones of grey that matched the predominating color grey of native trees and plants gave the garden a sense of belonging to its setting of prairie land.

Following along a whole alley of gardenias, past espaliered apricots and pears, we came to another pool with an oblong central fountain. "If you look closely along the waterline," said our host, "you will see the base is made from coca-cola bottles; only the dogs—Chinese porcelain—were bought off Third Avenue in New York. The rest is my own manufacture. . . ."

As I looked across the pool to the opposite bank at the wistaria trained as an overhead canopy, Douglas Chandor answered my unspoken comment. "It's a lovely sight in spring; a sky of wistaria of all varieties, and underneath we've planted a mass of narcissi; I adore narcissi.

I asked if he could grow primroses. "No, they won't do here at all," he answered regretfully. "The only flower whose

fragrance makes me think of them is the star magnolia. I
have to be content with that. I haven't seen a primrose for
years."

When I think back to that garden now I always remember
Douglas Chandor's hands, and then I think of his portrait of
Mrs. Roosevelt. I marveled that he could handle rocks and
garden so hard, and still keep his own long-fingered hands
so immaculate and so steady. Before we left he showed us his
portrait of Mrs. Roosevelt, and told us she had only con-
sented to sit if she could do something with her hands. So
she had sat for him, knitting, and along the bottom margin
of the portrait there is a set of hand-studies which he made
as he was working out the portrait in his head.

13 "You'll like Colorado"

I HAD almost lost account of time when I set off for Denver, capital and leading city of Colorado, by way of Santa Fe, New Mexico. Mile after mile of arid plain and mesa was a golden landscape where the rabbitbrush or golden bush, *Chrysothamus,* was in bloom. Always there was distance.

A lumberjack who sat beside me in the bus was sure, he said, that I'd like Colorado. "You're going just about the right time. You'll see the aspen all gold. You'll find the air good too; it's so dry in winter you won't feel the cold." As he got off the bus with a violin under his arm, protecting it from the rainstorm by a large paper bag, he called in parting: "You'll like Colorado."

Past Santa Fe and Taos the wasted, corrugated land fell away as we climbed up to a 9,000-feet pass where the aspen, as the lumberjack had promised, were shimmering and shining in moving clouds of gold. I could never say where the West begins. But when we crossed the state line into Colorado at the summit of the Raton Pass, and looked across the autumn-tinted foothills to the mesas and the snow-capped Sangre de Cristo range, I knew I was already way beyond the rim, and that I was in the West at last.

In Denver, George Kelly had work waiting for me at Horticulture House. At the time George was horticulturist to the Colorado Forestry and Horticulture Association, and editor of its magazine *The Green Thumb,* and I had met him at the Horticultural Congress in New York.

Horticulture House was the hub of Denver's gardening. The library room served as a club house for professionals and amateurs alike; they all brought their problems and their garden gossip to George.

On rare occasions I could answer a question for him. One day a truck driver rushed in for the address of the English Royal Horticultural Society.

"I want to grow English roses," he explained emphatically. "I've got a piece of land up near Seattle, and I'm going to grow them there." He was specific. "I want them from England where they graft them on the native stock, the English wild rose, and not as they do here on the Japanese Multiflora japonica." He repeated; "I want the old roses, English roses" and added with sudden disdain: "They think of them here as they do of cigarettes and soap powder."

There goes another echo of Mrs. Cran, I thought, and I remembered too the prized roses in Pennsylvania and the work that went into their growing. "You see," the truck driver confided, "my people came from Scotland. I've never been over, but I'm British, all through."

People would stop to talk a moment when they came by.

From the commercial growers I learned that carnations are Denver's floral pride. Other states grow more, but no other single city raises as many as Denver's three and one-quarter million plants a year.

From people in trouble with their trees I learned that in Denver every householder is responsible for the street trees in front of his house. They must be kept watered and healthy, and none may be felled or planted without the City Forester's permission. As chlorosis was enemy number one, it was a costly business to keep trees in good shape.

Mr. S. R. DeBoer, the landscape architect, one of whose books has been translated into Japanese, asked me one day what impressed me most about Denver. "Its greenness," I told him unhesitatingly, "the lawns and tree-lined streets."

"What about the blue of our sky?" he asked. "There is no blue like it except in the Engagdine Valley in Switzerland, and in Persia. When you've been in the West for a year, or maybe two years, you will never want the grey skies of Europe again, not permanently." He went on: "Grey, not green, is the predominating color of our native plant material. Blue and grey are the desert colors."

George Kelly maintained that the terrain and climate of Colorado, with the dry air and restricted rainfall, erratic springs and parched summers, most closely resemble those of the Gobi desert in Central Asia. "About the same conditions hold good for the whole Rocky Mountain Plains area," he used to say. "It's the largest single area of one type in the United States, and horticulturally it's a forgotten country."

Colorado is not so much a horticulturally forgotten country as it is a less well-known area outside the boundaries of the Rocky Mountain Empire. It is hard to imagine that this garden-loving city was, barely more than half a century ago, a stretch of arid desert country where cottonwood and willow were the only native deciduous trees. And even these, for the most part, hugged the water courses in the valleys. On higher ground little more than sagebrush and yucca withstood the hot, dry climate where the sun shines on an average of 304 days in the year, and the rainfall, correspondingly meager, measures no more than ten to fourteen inches a year.

Denver, like New Orleans, works and spends hard for its gardens. But mile-high Denver, unlike below sea-level New Orleans, where every drop of rainwater must be pumped away, has to conserve every drop of rain that falls, and has to depend largely on the winter snowpack for its water supply.

In a sense Denver is at the crossroads of two distinct garden influences, and though many of its gardens are long established, none are, obviously, really old. But this in no way detracts from their beauty. The Spanish-type garden spread north and northeast from California and Santa Fe, and the English garden influence spread westwards from the east. To date, the English influence has proved the stronger of the two. No doubt the large number of English who settled Colorado Springs, and the Cornish miners who came to search for silver and Colorado tin, were responsible for the widespread use of grass lawns. Grass and trees reminded them of home, and predominating green gardens challenged the natural desert grey.

Judging by the new-style houses and gardens being built and laid out in rapid succession, Denver is going to resolve its two conflicting influences by the western ranch-type layout of house and garden. Gardeners are relying more on brick and stone instead of grass which is so costly to maintain, and are making more use of grey-leaved plants, not only Colorado natives but Asiatics, finding that such trees as the Ginella maple, the Siberian pear and the Russian olive do uniformly well. Denver's Garden Center will undoubtedly be responsible for much of the new trend.

Aside from gardens, plant collectors are well aware that Colorado has a rich foothill and mountain flora. There are those who claim that, because of the dry climate and the variety in altitude, the Colorado flora is more varied than that of the Pacific Northwest.

Even at its lowest Colorado is high country, the roof of the continent with 51 peaks over 14,000 feet, and more than 1,500 peaks over 10,000 feet.

A plantsman would count on going to the foothills in June, and to the subalpine zone around 11,500 feet in July to see the slopes carpeted with a procession of flowers. In August, higher still, the sky's his limit for the true alpines.

Irish-born Mrs. G. R. Marriage of Colorado Springs has probably done more than anyone else to make the Colorado Rockies' alpine flowers better known. Although in self-depreciation she calls herself a horticulturist rather than a botanist, she has a knowledge of the native plants around her that many a professional botanist might envy. She has also introduced into cultivation plants which, though previously discovered, had never been "in the trade" before.

It was the sight of alpine flowers in all their mountain glory, and the wish to make them thrive in her garden, that set Mrs. Marriage on her collecting way, she told me when I spent a weekend with her. After years of trial and error in growing them herself, mostly error she will say, and when at last she found the best conditions to make them thrive in captivity, she distributed both plants and seeds to other alpine enthusiasts.

It then became her goal in the years of collecting and growing to introduce the most suitable Rocky Mountain natives to gardens; she contends that North America alpines attract attention as being greater novelties than do those known for many years in the mountains of Europe and Asia.

There are still, she declares, many plants in the Colorado Rockies awaiting their introduction to the horticultural world, and content to wait for some are shy, others, like *Primula Parryi,* are apt to be homesick; while several, like the alpine phloxes, are not eager to reproduce their kind either by seeds or by cuttings, and are reluctant to leave home.

"No wonder they are content," she added, "they live in a climatic paradise. Tucked in under a thick blanket of snow all winter, they wake in late spring to the bluest skies and clearest air with bright sunshine above, and a cool trickle of melting snow at their roots all summer."

Among the twenty-five or so plants which Mrs. Marriage has put into cultivation she counts as the best three sub-alpine phloxes, *Phlox condensata, P. multiflora, P. bryoides; Pentstemon crandalli* and *Boykinia jamesi,* which won an award at the Royal Horticultural Society's Chelsea Show in London some years ago. And she has a great thrill in seeing plants from the Colorado Rockies growing lustily in the gardens of her friends in England.

Year after year, in the climatic paradise she has made her home, Mrs. Marriage has gone up to the mountains in the late spring in search of flowers. With an air mattress, a sleeping bag, a box of good food and a station wagon to sleep in if it rains or snows, she has persuaded many a timid visiting member of the English Alpine Society that there is even a cosiness in living the high mountain days.

"When I've found a plant I have been looking for at the very end of the day," she told me, "it is so much easier to stay by it, and have it by me first thing in the morning. And when my daughter comes with me, there is nothing better than to wake up on the mountain side and smell the coffee she is brewing, and the bacon and eggs." Her enthusiasm is infectious. Her eyes sparkle. "Oh boy," she exclaims, "it's good!"

Ordinarily her meetings in the high mountains with the sheep-herders and miners are pleasant, although sometimes they are suspicious of her poaching on their preserves, prospecting perhaps for uranium or gold. Once a big burly fellow found her daughter digging near the foot of a fourteen thousand-foot peak and asked about the permit. For reply she referred him to her mother, and led him over the crags to where Mrs. Marriage was, as she described it, hanging on by an eyebrow, trying to photograph a gorgeous cascade of *Boykinia jamesi.*

"Where's your per-r-r-mit?" he asked.

"What part of County Cork are you from?" she countered. He put out his huge hand for her to shake, and they were friends at once.

Another time, on Silver Shoes Mountain, she stopped to talk to a woman who lived there, and who told her why the mountain was called Silver Shoes. Once it was mined for silver and there had been a mining camp there. Eventually, following the men, the "fancy ladies" came, but when smallpox broke out they left one by one until only one woman was left. She, who wore silver-heeled shoes, stayed and nursed

the men until she, too, died. The men in gratitude named
the mountain for her, Silver Shoes.

It was on Silver Shoes Mountain that Mrs. Marriage
helped the well-known botanist Dr. Wherry to solve a botanical mystery. He had noticed a fern in a northern herbarium labeled as found in Colorado. Yet, apart from that
one herbarium specimen, the fern was known only as a native
of the Arctic Circle.

Mrs. Marriage found the fern near Fairlight, and sent Dr.
Wherry a spray. He was traveling at the time, but altered
his journey and sent off a wire. Mrs. Marriage drove him a
hundred miles to find the plant with her again. Seeing was
believing; Dr. Wherry verified the herbarium specimen was
correctly labeled.

Some time later, when Mrs. Marriage's son was working on
a project of road-cutting through the mountain, he too
found the fern. Under the top eighteen inches of soil in
which the fern was growing, there was a seven-feet layer of
solid ice. The mystery of the plant being native to both Colorado and the Arctic Circle was solved; the Colorado soil
where the fern was growing rested on perpetual ice.

Those who know Mrs. Marriage's lively writing on the
use of native Rocky Mountain plants and shrubs must hope
that one day this will be gathered within the covers of a
book. As it is, her writing is scattered through various horticultural magazines. Heavy demands on her time, as Chair-
man of the City Park Board and landscape architect, make it
impossible for her to write but shortly and with a specific
purpose: to describe the lesser-known plants, encourage their
use, and so make known to other garden designers the avail-
ability of a greater variety of worthwhile plant material.

It is native material which, naturally, stands most chance

of meeting her own requirements. It must be "test-sure hardy" in Colorado Springs.

"If you come eastward in late June or early July," Mrs. Marriage said as I left, "you ought to come through here to see the mountain flowers. I could take you to a field of evening primrose; to mountain meadows where the blue columbine grows among the aspen. You'll see masses of flowers blooming their heads off at once if you come in early June."

That was a promise for some future day. I knew already that I could never hope to see each area of the North American continent at its most splendid moment of the year. I had set my sights on Colorado when the aspens turned gold in the fall; on the Cascades of the Pacific Northwest at the time those mountains were in flower.

Although the flowers were over I went, every weekend of the golden Indian summer, into the mountains. I knew the tree steps up the foothills: first the Ponderosa pines, the Douglas firs and the Blue spruce, up past the Englemann spruce until I was among the quaking aspens' autumn gold. The mountains ran with gold between the evergreens where the aspen grew in wide-spaced drifts between the lodgepole pines.

Before I left Denver, George Kelly gave me a glimpse of the Colorado wilderness from the roof of the continent. We spent a whole long day 11,500 feet up at timber line, photographing a strange conglomeration of fallen trees, whittled by wind and weather into a ghostly company of twisted and contorted skeletons.

We ate our lunch high up on Mount Goliath, above Echo Lake. Far in the distance, beyond the mass of blue mountains, a thread of color lay like a sandbar across the horizon. George pointed, cheese sandwich in hand, as he talked.

"Over there, due east you can just see the eastern plains. Back of us it's mesa country, stretching towards the sage flats along the Utah boundary. That is the wilderness, harsh and inhospitable to some, but to others a landscape of magnificent beauty. You get a taste of it here."

I looked across to Mount Evans. "Do you think we might get up there today?"

"If the road is open we'll have a try."

About four o'clock George decided to pack up. The light was no longer strong enough to photograph. He said: "If you're going out to dinner tonight, and we have to get to the top of Mount Evans we had better be going now."

Echo Lake was half frozen over; there were a few flurries of snow. Cold air whistled through the old car, numbing our knees. The road to the top was open, and up we went, curling round hairpin bends until we were within four hundred feet of the 14,250 feet summit. From there on it was leg power.

"You still want to go to the top?" George asked.

Those four hundred feet were tough going. We spoke only when we paused to rest a moment, sparing our breath as we braced ourselves to reach the summit while there was light enough to see the view.

"You can't do much in this altitude." George spoke to give me time and encouragement to catch my breath. "A man can only swing a pick four times and then rest before he does another four." I nodded. Even to say "Yes," would be an extra effort.

The sun set just as we reached the top. It was very cold. Echo Lake lay far below. Around and beyond us was a world of mountains.

"Odd . . ." I was still short of breath. "I suppose, . . . only a short time ago all this country . . . was something which had to be fought and invaded. Now you are trying to preserve it. One would think that man could never make even a dent in country like this."

"Wait until you see Boulder Dam, then you'll see what man has done, and can do. But we can't afford to go on losing any more of our wilderness."

We turned to go. "It's a quick drop." George warned, and it was. In two hours we dropped nine thousands feet down to Denver.

14 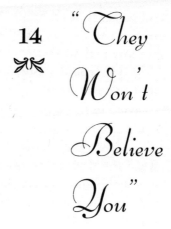 "They
Won't
Believe
You"

ONE hour after I was back in Denver from the mountains
I was a guest at a dinner party where I knew no one, not
even the hostess. The invitation had come by telephone, and
there I was. Sitting at the table, looking at the foothill snow-
berry trailing down the tall centerpiece dishes, I noticed how
lovely this native shrub looked in the candlelight among
the glass and silver. It was nice to see it so well appreciated.

"What do you think of Colorado?"

The question brought me back from the mountains with
a jerk. It was an impossible but common question. Colorado,
twice the size of England, and what had I seen of it? I tried
my best:

"I think of it as meaning color, light, and crystal air. It
is painter's country; I'm told that no one has yet recorded
on paper either the quality of light or the color of the

landscape, though Frank Mechau has painted it better than anyone has written of it in words. But I've seen so little to give any real answer."

"If you could paint," someone persisted, "what picture would you choose?"

I tried to think back. The fluttering leaves of golden aspen would be too familiar to them. They might not see the grey mist which the leafless trees throw over the foothills between the dark green pines; it would not be bright enough. Nor, I thought, would the wilderness appeal.

Then I remembered the afternoon when I had gone to Boulder—the Colorado city, not the dam—along the strip of rich farming land that lies between the eastern desert country and the mountains to the west. The light, soft but clear, lent a dream-like quality to the valley, and the cottonwoods lifted up their great yellow heads against the mountain blue.

The light had been going as we turned back. We passed a herd of goats, and there was a flock of geese along the road. Where the crops had been cleared, the pale stubble land had been cut by long furrows, so that there were dark contrasting strips of freshly-turned red earth.

"It was coming back from Boulder," I said. "It was a stark picture, poster-like, devoid of detail. I only saw it in outline. The mountains shouldered the sky: great massive curves of solid color. They changed, as I watched, from blue to deep violet, and all at once it seemed there was nothing but violet black against a vermilion sky."

"Go on," they urged.

"I cannot tell you more than that," I said, "for just then I turned my back. The man in the car said, 'Look, oh just look, isn't it wonderful, what do you think of that for color, for our sunsets and our mountains?' But I had already looked, and I wanted to remember it as I saw it then, and I felt that I could look no longer. 'I have looked,' I answered him. 'It can't be more beautiful than just at this moment. I won't look any more if you don't mind.' "

I glanced round the table. "They told me that in New England people would judge me according to my brains"; I said, "that in New York it would be by the dollars in my pocket, and in Virginia by the blue blood in my veins. They told me the West would take me as I was. Before tonight I had not met the owner of the house; I was asked on the telephone to come. It seems you extend your hospitality to people even when you haven't seen them. You accept them blindfold."

My hostess smiled. "But they must not be blindfold to our glory, which is color."

"No one ever quite believes in the color of Colorado unless they have seen it," someone said. "A while ago there was a London showing of Colorado landscapes, of the tawny plains and the hyacinthine distance deepening into the tremendous blues. The critics howled at the exaggerated color, as they called it."

I knew this to be true. How could a man, as he looks across an English valley, visualize for one moment the Colorado scene if he had never seen it with his own eyes?

"When you go back home, it will be like the pictures, you know," the speaker went on. "They won't believe you —they won't even want to know. You mustn't be hurt if they are far more eager to talk than listen, to tell you who has been born and who has died while you've been away. They won't want to hear about these things here. There will be a gap between your thought and their's; that is one of the penalties of travel. I adore England, but I know I only want

to live here now." She was a Canadian speaking. "No one
who has lived long with this landscape seems to want it otherwise."

That was the first I heard that phrase: no one who has
lived long with this landscape seems to want it otherwise.
I was to hear it repeated again and again all through the
West.

"Where does the West begin?" I asked.

"That depends where you ask the question. In the East
they will tell you it begins not far from Boston or New
York. Go a little further and it might be Chicago. Parts of
Texas might be west, but central and eastern Texas are
much more the Middle West. Really I suppose the eight
states: Montana, Idaho, Wyoming, Utah, Nevada, New
Mexico, Arizona, and Colorado make up the real West, the
Mountain West or the Rocky Mountain Empire as you'll
hear it called."

The guest continued: "The West Coast is something else
again. California, Washington, and Oregon are as a country set apart. Californians and Coloradans distinguish clearly
between the Coast and the West: Californians talk about
going West, Coloradans about going out to the Coast.

"Actually it's hard to set geographical boundaries for the
West, or anywhere else for that matter. The West is immensity and movement, color too. It's as much a tradition
as it is an area. You'll find it also means a different outlook
and a different point of view. I'll be surprised if you don't
feel the West get a hold over you. It doesn't take long."

In Barrie's *Dear Brutus,* Lob warned his guests that if
they went into the wood they would be under the spell. Now
I felt like one of Lob's guests. I had been warned. I was on
the threshold of the West.

"It's a legend, and it's a way of life and a symbol . . . No one who has lived long with this landscape . . ."

My days in Colorado were as much a milestone in my thinking as the geographical dividing line of the Continental Divide. Nothing could diminish my love for such old gardens as Brandon and Westover in Virginia, or Middleton in South Carolina, but from now on the wild gardens in their stupendous natural settings of the West were to have more appeal for me than the carefully tended cultivation gardens.

I knew this one day when I visited a garden which afforded a view that stretched across the plain to the foothills of the Rockies, and the snow-capped front range that stretched one hundred and fifty miles from Pike's Peak to the south, and Long's Peak to the north. The owner was not at home. I left a note. "Thank you for letting me see your garden when you weren't here. I've stolen a grape from your vine."

I did not pick that wrinkled grape on sudden impulse, nor in idle curiosity to taste its sweetness. I picked it because the roots of the vine were deep in Colorado soil, and because the fruit had ripened in the western sun under the high blue Colorado sky. I had had no chance to work the soil but now something of Colorado was part of me. I had no doubt that the owner of that garden would understand.

The last weekend I went up to Rampart Range. It was a crystal day. The kinnikinik was full of berries; I found a bear's mark in the snow. It was hot, but though the temperature was in the 80's, the sun at that altitude was deceptive. My face would be sunburned but my back in shadow was like a sheet of ice. Already there was a lot of snow on the higher ground though I could still see the alpine meadows and the grey mist of the leafless aspen between the lodge-pole pines.

Two days later a furious November storm howled out of the northern Rockies, to snarl transportation and bury Denver under an eight-inch fall of snow. The people who had been wishing for snow, complaining that the air had become so dry, now had their wish. Traffic on the icy streets came to a standstill; on the sidewalk the snow squeaked underfoot, a sure sign of hard weather. In one hour the temperature plummeted 20 degrees and fell below zero during the night. Except for skiers, the Colorado wilderness would now be inviolate in a winding sheet of snow.

By luck I had my next travel jump at just the right time. In five whirlwind sightseeing days I traveled out to the Coast, as Coloradans say, to the sun of southern California.

The road I took has been traveled and described often and the journey itself had nothing whatsoever to do with gardens as we usually think of them. But all the vast wide spaces of the West were now, in their season, a series of wild natural gardens.

A few hours after leaving Denver the bus driver stopped at the summit of Loveland Pass after a grueling two hours driving through a snowstorm. I asked him to let me outside a moment.

"Do you really want to get out, it's very cold; there's nothing to see?" he discouraged.

Of course he thought me mad. What was the Continental Divide to him who crossed it so frequently? But he gave me my moment, and the passengers shivered as he opened the door. I stood on the ice-capped road in the swirling blizzard, on the great ridgepole of the continent midway between Canada and Mexico, between the Mississippi River and the Pacific Ocean.

I spent a day and a night in Salt Lake City, a spartan place of wide and windswept streets, high up with its back to the northern mountain wall, then swung south through the Mormon state. Utah made me shudder. I'd seen nothing comparable; nothing so vast, nothing so wild and savage, nothing so inhospitable. There were but few cultivated patches of land, almost no sign of human habitation in all that tremendous landscape where great shadowed blocks of mesas stood sphinx-like and inscrutable. One immense rampart of rock, fluted and furrowed along the base by some monster-handed sculptor, stretched for miles and miles into the faint distance of plain and sky. As I look back on it now, the everwidening valleys and the ever vaster plains were all a natural approach to the staggeringly titanic country round Boulder Dam in Nevada.

It defies description. How can one measure the immeasurable? Enormous black and violet-shadowed mesas rose up from the desert plain. An endless array of mountain peaks towered into the long distance, terrifyingly beautiful, satanically hostile and hateful. I was appalled yet fascinated. Yet here, man had had the audacity to create one of the world's greatest engineering feats. He matched his skill on a scale which befits the landscape, and the great hydroelectric plant there was his answer, a monument of sanity and stability in a chaotic landscape.

I should not have seen Boulder Dam so closely before the Grand Canyon of the Colorado, which I saw in adjoining Arizona. Not that there is anything comparable in the two, but to approach the Canyon the mind should be clear, like a slate wiped clean. One of the extraordinary things about it is that you approach through a quiet-toned hill country of pine and sagebrush—it gives no hint whatsoever of what lies ahead. Then suddenly you find yourself at the Canyon's edge, and as you stand at the very rim of the abyss the stupendous spectacle is all before you. Without warning, there it is!

Some find it shockingly grotesque, others sublimely beautiful. Either way it is chaotic and disturbing. But there is, at that moment, no turning back. You have to stand and face the Grand Canyon of the Colorado.

I could not, even if I stood there now, ever begin to comprehend, much less say what I saw. The first sight makes a sudden impact on the mind, a stunned, surprised bewilderment. The immensity of the Canyon is not that of Utah's savage wilderness and far-reaching horizons, but the immensity of an immeasurable timelessness and tremendous depth. It is almost meaningless to convey the sense of the place by saying it is a mile deep, ten miles across and I don't know how many miles long.

You cannot measure the Canyon any more than you can measure Boulder Dam—or time. What you see and sense there is timelessness and silence, a livid silence which wells up and flows into you out of that bottomless pit where, a mile below, the Colorado River appears as a thin and muddy line. Not a sound comes up from the churning water as the river pounds its way to the sea.

Ten miles across this vast pilation of colored rock, the northern rim is a thin straight line on the horizon. And all between are corroded, soaring pinnacles of crimson sandstone; weathered walls that no human foot has ever trod; jagged peaks and crags that no mountaineer has ever climbed.

It is not only size and sculpture, but also a cataract of color. One moment a "rose-red city half as old as time" or a painted desert, or a dawn or sunset that might be earth or sky. It changes every moment, as you watch. Islands of crimson rise out of the blue depths, to change to grey and green.

The garnet will turn sullen, and the ruby glow wine-red. The purple will turn to pale amethyst or porphyry. There is nothing but an indescribably wild splendor, a changing kaleidoscope of color, and the silence.

The realization came to me that the Grand Canyon of the Colorado was but one of the West's vast and natural landscaped gardens. The place, inhospitable to man, was home for thousands of wild flowers. The name that Colorado coined for one of its spectacular settings—the Garden of the Gods—applied equally to the Grand Canyon, and probably to countless other scenic wonders of the West.

I turned my back. I saw little more of that journey through the wide grazing valley and the pine-covered mountain ranges, across the desert, past date farms and grapefruit groves of the Coachella Valley of California, to the warm sands of Cabrillo Beach washed by the Pacific tides.

Around Los Angeles oil derricks made strange forests across the hills, but it is like a forest blackened by fire where only the skeletons remain. Almost always I found the smell of oil was there.

Beyond the huge, sprawling city there were groves of avocado and oranges heavy with fruit under the December sun; sometimes the scent of orange blossom mingled with the half-acid, half-aromatic rind scent of burning eucalyptus leaves in ranch-house yards.

In Hollywood, that part of Los Angeles once called Holly Wood for the abundance of red-berried California holly growing across its hills, there was a jeweled thoroughfare of Christmas light, and along Christmas Tree Lane colored lights spangled the tall Himalayan deodar trees with stars.

Christmas amid the orange groves, the scents of fruit—and oil! My mind was bedeviled by it all.

15 *Plantsmen*
🎀
Pioneers

$\mathcal{A}$NY plantsman who comes to the Pacific Coast must, sooner or later, inevitably question the origin of plant names. He will notice a scattering of Spanish, English, German, and Russian names. He will understand such descriptive terms as *occidentalis* and *californica,* as in the East he will understand *Canada* and *Virginiana;* but others will baffle him: constantly recurring words that are used sometimes as the family or generic name of a plant, most frequently as the adjective or specific name—*Menziesii, Douglasii, Scouleri, Jeffreyi, Tolmiea, Coulteri, Lewisii, Clarkia, Fremontia.*

Among these are familiar names: Lewis and Clark, and Fremont, who pioneered the land routes to the West, and with other plantsmen discovered the plant wealth of the western world. But it was Captain James Cook's third sea voyage that attracted world attention to the North Pacific

Coast; and it was ships, not wagon wheels, that launched
pioneer plantsmen on the second wave of North American
plant discovery. The flora of the Northwest rings with their
names.

The story of Captain Cook's voyage was as electrifying as
Elizabethan stories of the Spanish Main. Spain, England,
Russia, France, and America from that time on sent out expedition after expedition to charter the coast, trade in furs,
stake territorial claims and seek a navigable passage between
the North Pacific and Atlantic oceans. And early botanical
exploration, which reached its height during the first half of
the nineteenth century, developed as part of this world movement to the Pacific Northwest.

Britain claimed the lion's share, but not the monopoly, of
West Coast plant discoveries. And the plant explorers themselves were now reinforced by collaborators. There were the
systematic botanists Asa Gray, John Torrey, Frederick Pursh,
Sir Joseph and William J. Hooker, who, though they never
set foot in the Northwest, completed the work of the collectors by identifying, classifying and naming the specimens
brought back to them.

The Spaniards were the first in the field. Long before
Drake claimed New Albion, Spanish explorers and con-
querors noted and named certain plants. They called the
California poppy *Copa de Oro,* cup of gold, and *Dormidera*
after its habit of closing at sundown, or on sunless days. They
called the California coastline *Le Tierra del Fuego*—land of
fire or conflagration—for its seemingly limitless poppy fields
that stretched mile upon flaming mile; in swaths twenty
miles long by ten miles wide, visible from forty miles away.
No wonder that the sun-filled cup is now California's state
flower.

The French, hard on the heels of Captain Cook, made important finds. Collignon, gardener-botanist on the La Pérouse Expedition took back to Paris seed of the rose-colored Sand Verbena that he collected at Monterey in September 1786; to him goes the honor of introducing the first California plant to flower in Europe.

Then came Archibald Menzies, forerunner in date and achievement of that Physician-Trader-Naturalist group sent out from Britain to search specifically for plants. Menzies, a surgeon as well as a botanist, was the first serious plant collector on the West Coast. The Indians remembered him as "the red-faced man who cut off the limbs of men, and gathered grass."

Menzies came of a family of Scottish gardeners, graduating at Edinburgh in both botany and medicine, and served his first assignment as a surgeon in the Navy at Halifax, Nova Scotia. On his return to England he signed up under Captain Colnett, who was about to sail for the North Pacific on a three-year round-the-world fur-trading and exploration voyage.

At the time England was in dispute with Spain. Although some of Menzies' seeds, plants, and drawings from the early part of the voyage were sent to England, the later material was lost. When the ships sailed into Nootka Sound, off the Canadian coast of Vancouver Island in 1787, the Spanish, who held the harbor then, confiscated the Captain's papers together with the rest of Menzies' material. But it was here, on the shores of Nootka Sound, that Menzies first found the flowering red currant *Ribes sanguineum,* and other plants named specifically after the place: *Rosa nutkans, Lupinus nootkatensis,* and the raspberry *Rubus nutkanus.*

On his return to England, Menzies immediately sought

further travel, and through Sir Joseph Banks secured the post of fulltime naturalist on Captain George Vancouver's famous voyage in the ship *Discovery*. The purpose of this five-year enterprise was to safeguard the British colony in the Nootka Sound area; to charter the California coastline north to Alaska, and to seek some navigable passage between the North Pacific and Atlantic oceans.

Vancouver never wrote with any enthusiasm of Menzies. His comment on the appointment was terse. He resented, perhaps, the somewhat extraordinary measures he had to take to assist a botanist. "Mr. Archibald Menzies," he wrote in his Journal, was "appointed for the specific purpose of making such researches; and had, doubtless, given sufficient proof of his abilities, to qualify him for the station it was intended he should fill. For the purpose of preserving such new or uncommon plants as he might deem worthy of a place amongst His Majesty's very valuable collection of exotics at Kew, a glazed frame was erected on the after part of the quarter-deck, for the reception of those he might have an opportunity of collecting."

Discovery reached the Puget Sound area in 1792. On May first, Vancouver's men made their first landing at Port Discovery, where Menzies was immediately attracted by "a small species of wild Valerican with reddish colored flowers growing behind the beaches in large thick patches."

The following day he recorded, and first described in his Journal, the tree by which he is forever remembered, "the Oriental Strawberry Tree" as he called it, noting that it grows to a small tree and "at this time is a peculiar ornament to the Forest by its large clusters of whitish flowers and evergreen leaves, but its peculiar smooth bark of a reddish brown color will at all times attract the notice of the most superficial observer."

The "great flowering dogwood," and the large pink-flowered rhododendrum *R. occidentalis* were in bloom. Along Hood's Canal, on the Olympic Peninsula, he saw with equal delight "a beautiful new species of Vaccinium with evergreen leaves in full bloom," adding that though he had seen it before in several places since they came into "the Straghts," nowhere had he seen it in such perfection as here. And still today I doubt whether there is any other place in which the evergreen huckleberry grows so abundantly.

In three successive years Menzies visited the American coast, coming from the Sandwich Islands in the spring, spending the summer northward, and passing south again in the autumn. In California, Bodega, San Francisco Bay, Santa Clara and Monterey were all known to him, as well as several places along the coast from Santa Cruz southward, including the islands below Santa Barbara.

Menzies undertook the work of ship's surgeon in addition to that of botanist when the appointed officer was ill and finally sent home from Nootka in 1792. Although Vancouver afterwards complimented him by stating that not a life had been lost by sickness during the voyage, matters were not over-easy between them. Vancouver, with senior rank, could and did over-rule Menzies when he wished. He assigned the man who cared for Menzies' plants in the glass cage to other work. And on the ship's second visit to San Francisco Bay, when the expedition was not so well received, ordered Menzies to remain on board. Nor was Vancouver apparently impressed by Menzies' finds. He remarked at the end of a long descriptive paragraph in his Journal on the trees and plants he himself had noted, and added that "Amongst the more

minute productions, Mr. Menzies found constant amusement; and, I believe, was enabled to make some addition to
the catalogue of plants."

"Some addition!" Botanists who later checked Vancouver's reckoning credited Menzies with three hundred species
from the Northwest. Among the "more minute productions,"
Menzies was the first to collect the Coast Redwood which he
found at Santa Cruz; the Douglas Spruce which he found on
the shores of Nootka Sound in 1792; the Nootka Cypress, the
Oregon Cedar, and the Hemlock Spruce; the White Fir,
Abies grandis, and at Sitka, the Sitka Spruce.

On the shore of San Francisco Bay, Menzies was also to
collect the California Laurel, *Umbellularia californica,*
which Oregonians insist on claiming as exclusively native to
Oregon, naming it Oregon myrtle. He was also the first to
find the fuchsia-flowered gooseberry, the rosy-flowered bramble, the salmon-berry and the yellow bush lupine, *L. arboreus.*

On his return to England, Menzies apparently forgot that
as a Navy man he should turn over to the Secretary of State
all the material he had gathered. Consequently it was sixty
years before the government at last checked, described, and
published his finds. This, in part, accounts for the fact that
many of Menzies' plant discoveries were credited to other
men, and often named by or for them. The Pacific dogwood
is one of these, but that is another story. The great redwood
is still another. After Menzies' discovery, Lambert described
the tree; David Douglas thought it gave the mountains "a
most peculiar, I was almost going to say, awful appearance—
something that plainly tells you we are not in Europe" but
it was not until several years after Douglas' day that it was
introduced to Europe. As it is, there are lupines, penstemon,

Phacelia, Ribes, and the snake root which carry the name Menziesii.

It was the American botanist, Frederick Pursh, who finally gave Archibald Menzies his due. More than a hundred years after Menzies found his "Oriental Strawberry Tree"—the early Spanish explorers called it the Madrono after the classic arbutus, *Arbutus Unedo* of the poets and Southern Europe —Pursh named it scientifically *Arbutus Menzieii*. And it is by this arbutus, one of the world's most beautiful ornamental trees, that Menzies is best and most proudly remembered.

The Madrone, as it is simply called in the Northwest, and Madrona in California, is as Menzies prophesied a tree that even the most superficial observer could not, at all times, fail to notice. It is a tree of year-round beauty. The color and the satin smoothness of the trunk and limbs are the tree's most distinctive characteristic; deep-mahogany bark splits in late summer and reveals the pure apple-green of the new on-coming bark; this turns a deeper green to suntan cinnamon, deepens again from blood-red back to the old deep mahogany. Long panicles of small wax-like bells hang down, a mass of bloom, in spring; clusters of bright red berries burst from their rough orange-brown husks in the fall.

W. L. Jepson, famous California botanist, in an address on the Twenty-fifth Anniversary of the California Botanical Society in 1938 explained that the name Madrono had been chosen for the Society's Journal because

> it is the name associated with the (California) region; because, most of all, it is the name of the native tree which has great biological and forestal significance.

Jepson continued that there is no other tree in the western woods "more marked by sylvan beauty, by flowers and fruits beyond compare." He likened the flower to sculptured ivory urns and the fruits to etched carnelian globes.

However, Menzies' arbutus is no more confined to California than the California laurel to Oregon. Its range includes British Columbia, Western Washington, and Oregon, and it is in the Northwest, where Menzies found it first, that it grows to its most magnificent stature. There, on fertile, well-drained soil, near salt water and in a climate with heavy rainfall and penetrating fogs, the madrone at its best attains a height of some one hundred twenty-five feet, with a trunk four feet across.

The first settlers in the area of Puget Sound named Magnolia Bluff for the madrones they found along the shores of that great inland sea, mistaking the trees for magnolias. Nor were they far wrong. The madrone, though specifically distinct. is related to the magnolia, and bears a strong resemblance to it, especially in the glossy leaves.

Jepson associated the tree with the California region, but Seattle is the city above all others that gives the madrone pride of place in the public parks, by the margins of its lakes, and along the streets of residential district. There are even a few great stands of trees still left, untouched by modern building, on the high precipitous bluffs above the Sound.

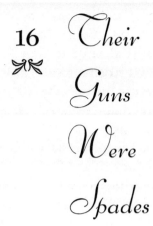

16 *Their Guns Were Spades*

*T*HE nineteenth century opened with the American overland expedition of 1804–1806, led by the two soldiers Captains Meriwether Lewis and William Clark, the first white men to make the continental crossing from east to west. There was no botanist, no Menzies along, but Lewis and Clark were under orders of their Commander-in-Chief, President Jefferson, to botanize as best they could. Their best proved very good.

For Lewis, the more botanically minded of the two, the bitter root *Lewisii rediviva* is named, also the lovely ephemeral blue flax, the pink mimulus, and the western mock orange *Philadelphus Lewisii*. And William Clark is best remembered by *Clarkia pulchella,* pulchella the beautiful, which lay unnoticed in the herbarium until David Douglas rediscovered it.

The Russians' turn came next. An expedition was sent out in 1815 under Captain Otto von Kotzebue with two scientists aboard, Johann Frederich Eschscoltz, an entomologist, and Adelbert von Chamisso, poet as well as botanist. Their finds include the California lilac, *Ceanothus thyrisiflorus;* the California sage, *Artemesia californica,* and the California poppy.

Few plants have ever suffered such international mixedupedness as the Spaniard's cup of gold. Menzies had gathered a withered poppy bloom in winter, and mistook it for an English celandine! And so it fell, by luckless chance, to Chamisso, who was of French parentage and raised in Germany, to classify and name the plant. His muse forsook him. He named the poppy for his Russian friend *Eschscoltz,* and gave it a botanical tongue-twister, *Eschscholtzie californica.*

David Douglas, the Scotchman, was next on the scene. He was ten years old when he began his seven-year apprenticeship as gardener's boy on a private estate before being employed at the Botanic Garden at Glasgow. There he sometimes accompanied Dr. William J. Hooker, then Professor of Botany at Glasgow University, on his botanical trips to the Western Highlands. Through Hooker's recommendation Douglas was employed by the London Horticultural Society as plant explorer to North America.

Douglas' first assignment was to make a six months' study of fruit-growing developments in the Eastern United States. In Philadelphia he met Thomas Nuttall, the English botanist, and familiarized himself with the collections of Lewis and Clark. Here he saw the herbarium specimen of the forgotten Clarkia, and in a New York nursery purchased another of their finds, *Mahonia aquifolium,* the tall Oregon grape.

In June 1824 Douglas sailed on *William and Ann,* a Hudson's Bay Company vessel, for the North Pacific Coast, to develop the vast flower field which Menzies had opened up. To Douglas' delight a school friend, John Scouler, naturalist and surgeon, had signed on as medical officer to the ship, and before sailing both studied Menzies' collections and were well briefed by Hooker.

It was nine months before they reached the Columbia, another six weeks before they could navigate the river and land at Fort Vancouver, the Hudson's Bay Trading post. Even before they landed Douglas noted the western hemlock, the balsam fir, and a "species which may prove to be *Pinus taxifolia.*" It proved to be the tree which Lambert, author of the work on the genus Pinus, named for him, the Douglas Fir.

All the excitement of his landing is in Douglas' own recording of the moment he picked his first Northwestern plant and held the salal, *Gaultheria Shallon,* in his hands: "so pleased was I that I could scarce see anything else." All around him were Menzies' plants. One of these, the red-flowering currant, *Ribes sanguinea,* Douglas considered "one of the finest and most interesting additions that has been made to our shrubberies for many years."

Scouler returned to England in late September, taking with him the first consignment of Douglas' seeds and specimens, and leaving his name for some of the plants he found during those companionable plant-hunting days: the willow, *Salix Scouleriana;* a pentstemon, a St. John's Wort, and the tall blue *Campanula Scouleri.*

From then on, except for Indian guides, Douglas explored for the most part alone. Fort Vancouver was his home base. The Governors and Company of Adventurers of England. Trading into Hudson's Bay, were his kindly hosts and friends.

They were hard and often fearful days. His rations were meager. Supper was often but a piece of sturgeon, a slice of bread and a basin of tea—tea, Douglas declared, was the "monarch of all foods" after fatiguing journeys. At the day's end he still had work to do, writing up his diary, often without the protection of a tent. At first he confessed he looked with "a sort of dread" on the prospect of a night under the stars, but in time all sheltering comfort was superfluous to him.

Douglas considered the Sugar Pine his greatest find; *Pinus Lambertiana* he named it after his friend Lambert. He found Indians eating its seeds, which they said grew farther south, and later an Astorian overlander brought to him at Fort Vancouver just one cone. His curiosity aroused, he set out to find the tree.

On a late October day, with the aid of an Indian guide, Douglas found the sugar pine in what is now Looking Glass Valley, about eighteen miles from modern Roseburg, Oregon. That night he wrote in his diary:

Being unable to climb or hew down any, I took my gun and was busy clipping them (the cones) from the branches with ball when eight Indians came at the report of my gun. They were all painted with red earth, armed with bows, arrows, spears of bone, and flint knives, and seemed to be anything but friendly. I endeavoured to explain to them what I wanted and they seemed satisfied and sat down to smoke, but had no sooner done so than I perceived one string his bow and another sharpen his flint knife with a pair of wooden pincers and hang it on the wrist of the right hand, which gave me ample testimony of their inclination. To save myself I could not do by flight, and without any hesitation I went backwards six paces

and cocked my gun, and then pulled from my belt one of my
pistols, which I held in my left hand. I was determined to fight
for life. As I as much as possible endeavoured to preserve my
coolness and perhaps did so, I stood eight or ten minutes looking at them and they at me without a word passing, till one at
last, who seemed to be the leader, made a sign for tobacco,
which I said they should get on condition of going and fetch-
ing me some cones. They went, and as soon as out of sight I
picked up my three cones and a few twigs, and made a quick
retreat to my camp, which I gained at dusk. The Indian who
undertook to be my guide I sent off, lest he should betray
me . . . How irksome a night is to such a one as me under my
circumstances! Cannot speak a word to my guide, not a book
to read, constantly in expectation of an attack, and the position I am now in is lying on the grass with my gun beside
me, writing by the light of my Columbian candle—namely, a
piece of wood containing rosin.

Douglas spent nearly two years in the Pacific Northwest
before going overland to sail from an eastern port for England. In May, 1830, he was back in his happy hunting
ground again among the iris-covered coastal slopes, the fields
of camass like "lakes of blue water," and the great forests of
the Northwest.

On this last expedition Douglas covered a much wider field.
In December he sailed down the coast, to land at Monterey,
California, in January, 1831. The first flower he picked was
Menzies' *Ribes speciosum,* the fuchsia-flowered gooseberry,
which he declared was not surpassed in beauty by the finest
Fuchsia. And on the same day he made the first discovery of
Baby Blue Eyes, *Nemophila insignis,* "A lovely but humble
plant . . . the harbiner of the California spring, which forms
. . . a carpet of tenderest azure blue . . . affording relief from
the effect of the sun's reflection on the micaceous sand where
it grows."

These were not yet the California gold-rush days, but Douglas knew that the small glittering particles in the soil where he collected were gold. He regarded it as incidental. He had already all the gold he wanted; he had gathered enough on the shore of Okanagan Lake in the Columbia region to make a seal charm for his watch. His plants, the blue-flowered silver sage, *Salvia carnosa,* most of all, were his treasure.

In 1852 Douglas was back on the Columbia, and continuing north to Puget Sound and the mouth of the Fraser River, penetrated the most inaccessible country he had so far attempted. But from then on the tide of fortune turned against him. Snow blindness in the summer of 1826 and the glare of the California sun had ruined his eyes; the sight of his right eye had gone entirely. On June 13, 1833, his frail canoe was dashed to pieces down the Fraser River; his collection of four hundred plants and his Journal of the expedition were lost, and for an hour and forty minutes he was swept about in the turbulent current before being washed ashore.

Once more he set sail from Fort Vancouver for California. In sixteen stormy October days he reached Drake's Bay. The ship anchored there three weeks, during which time Douglas climbed Mount Tamalpais above San Francisco Bay. Then in the late fall he sailed for the Sandwich Islands, and the following year, on July 13, 1834, met his strange and horrible death, falling into a bull trap and being gored by a captured bull.

David Douglas' reputation rests chiefly on the magnificent coniferous trees he discovered: pines such as the sugar, the Monterey, the Coulter, and the Digger; the white firs and the Douglas spruce; above all, the king of the northern forests, the famous and familiar Douglas fir. Yet even without

these his fame is assured. He not only re-discovered and introduced into cultivation many of the plants his predecessors
had found, but himself discovered countless Pacific Coast
plants. In California alone he collected eight hundred species. Many of the iris, brodiaea, calochortus, erythronium,
and camassia bulbs are his; and he was the first to take that
great bunch of California annuals—the clarkias, godetias,
mimulus, lupines, and the California poppy—back to England.

Curiously enough Douglas forfeited, as Menzies before
him, certain credit that was due to him. In his Journal he
gives the names of eastern American species to trees of the
West. He did not realize, nor did the men who edited his
Journal eighty-nine years later, that not a single conifer and
hardly one tree or shrub of any one genus is common to both
sides of the continent. Menzies' "great flowering dogwood"
and the Western Hemlock, which Douglas had first seen
from the decks of the *William and Ann,* still carried no
plant-hunter's name.

Before Douglas' death, other British plant hunters were
making horticultural history. Thomas Coulter visited California in 1831. His greatest find was the incomparable *Rom-
neya Coulteri,* which Harvey the botanist named for him
after his death, and for Romney Robinson, the Irish astron-
omer.

Dr. William Fraser Tolmie, another Scottish surgeon in
the service of the Hudson's Bay Company, was the first white
man to approach and collect flowers on "The Mountain that
is God" as the Indians called Mount Rainier. On September 1, 1833, he sat dressed in a green blanket without trou-
sers, eating a breakfast of dried meat boiled in a cedar bark
kettle. He was discouraged both by the weather and by the

reluctance of his five Indians to accompany him much further, fearing they might provoke the wrath of mountain spirits.

But on September third, at sunrise, and with one of the Indians, he stood on the snow "spangled summit" of the peak which was afterwards named for him, Tolmie's Peak. From that altitude of 5,939 feet he saw Mount Rainier, 14,408 feet, "surpassingly splendid and magnificent" above him. And there on the slopes of the Mountain he found the dwarf penstemon that Hooker named for him. There, too, he probably found his saxifrage, the mariposa lily, the deep-blue bell-shaped gentian *G. calycosa,* and the curious Youth-on-Age, *Tolmiea menziesii.*

Thomas Nuttall, the Yorkshireman, who had named the wistaria on the eastern seaboard, was already a famous botanist when he traveled overland with the Second Wyeth Expedition. He was forty-eight years old when he arrived at Vancouver, Washington, in September 1834, a Fellow of the Linnean Society, of the Philadelphia Academy of Sciences, and of the American Philosophical Society.

The journey overland was arduous. John K. Townsend, the ornithologist, whom the Academy of Sciences sent out with Nuttall, records the zest Nuttall brought to the whole undertaking. Along the North Platte River in what is now western Nebraska, the road was so narrow and difficult that the horses could hardly advance, and some of the men rode, a mile at a stretch, kneeling upon their saddles. But there were flowers everywhere. Even the men disinterested in botany exclaimed, "Beautiful, beautiful!"

Nuttall rode ahead of the company, clearing a passage with a trembling and eager hand, looking back at his companions as though he feared they would catch up with him

before he had finished his collecting, and tread his lovely
prizes underfoot.

He used the gun, given him for protection, as a tool to
dig up his plants, entirely stopping the barrel up with earth.
Once his plants were damaged by wetting. But no difficulty,
no fatigue ever daunted him. He sat on the ground, drying
his papers by an enormous fire, rearranging the whole collection plant by plant, while the drops of perspiration rolled
off his forehead unheeded.

Nuttall traveled back and forth on the Pacific Coast, to
California and the Sandwich Islands and the Pacific Northwest, before he returned to Philadelphia, sailing by way of
Cape Horn to Boston. Dana, in his *Two Years before the
Mast*, writes of Nuttall's passion for flowers. "Old Curious,"
the sailors called him for his interest in all things strange and
curious around, and the Captain refused to take his passage
money, because "you travel for the benefit of mankind."

"Old Curious" was the only botanist of this period who
traveled east *and* west in search of plants; he made more discoveries, Asa Gray said of him, than any other explorer of
the botany of the United States. He was also an ornithologist,
and an authority on conchology, mineralogy, and the American Indian; the author of two books, *Ornithology of the
United States and Canada* and *Genera of North American
Plants*. His collections are spread over the Philadelphia
Academy of Sciences, Harvard University, and the British
Museum in London. Scores of plants were named for him,
also the white-crowned sparrow.

How would Nuttall himself choose to be best remembered? Perhaps by the western dogwood, the Pacific dogwood which in California grows as a lovely understory tree
along Sierra streams, and in the Northwest towers to a sixty-

feet fountain of bloom. The same "great flowering dogwood" that Menzies first discovered, the same that Douglas
noted yet failed to distinguish as different from the eastern
tree.

But Nuttall, when he saw the tree in the fall—the Pacific
dogwood flowers again in autumn, the white "flowers" in
bloom beside the scarlet berries—noticed certain differences.
He counted six bracts instead of four, noted their larger size
and perfect outline, and detected the absence of the dark
scallop notch. The band-tailed pigeons were feasting on the
berries, and he sent a specimen of both birds and tree to Audubon. And there in the 1834 edition of Volume four of
Audubon's *Ornithological Biographies* you see the pigeons
on a flowering branch of the tree, and underneath Audubon's inscription of this "superb species of Dogwood, discovered by our learned friend Thomas Nuttall Esq.; when on
his march towards the shores of the Pacific Ocean, and which
I have graced with his name."

When Nuttall returned to England in 1842, he went hesi-
tatingly and most reluctantly to accept the condition of his
brother's legacy as heir to Nut-Grove Hall in Lancashire,
that he reside there at least nine months of every year. It
was the year that Archibald Menzies died, the year that Sir
William Hooker became the first Director of Kew Gardens.

The first half of the great exploring century was almost
ended. In 1844, forty years after the soldiers Lewis and Clark
came overland, Captain John Charles Fremont, The Path-
finder, came his military way. He was the first to see and
marvel at the flower tapestry of the Mojave desert in spring,
as Coulter had been the first to gaze upon the spring color
of the Colorado desert. The hills were purple, and orange
with bloom instead of green.

Fremont found the western redbud, the snow plant, and the alpine pussy paws. He also discovered the beautiful endemic *Carpenteria californica* in the foothills above Fresno, which Torrey named for his botanist friend Carpenter. Fremont is remembered by *Fremontia californica,* a thickset tree studded with golden flowers.

Lastly, there were three more plantsmen who have left their names for western flowers. Theodor Hartweg, a German gardener, whom the London Horticultural Society sent to California in 1845, found the Monterey cypress, *Cupressus macrocarpa,* the most widely planted of all cypresses today, which is native only to the coast at Monterey, a tree which oddly enough Douglas never mentioned. At Sonoma he discovered the Kellog oak; at Corte Madera he found the *Fritillaria lanceolata var gracilis,* which was for so long described as a species new to science. Hartweg was also the first to make known the flora of the Sierra Nevada foothills.

Dr. C. C. Parry, the American collector, made the first of his many trips West in 1849 and his name is coupled with scores of plants, including *Ceanothus Parryi* and *Delphinium Parryi*. And there is John Jeffery, another Scotchman, who stands outside the half century by just one year.

Little is known of Jeffery except that he was sent out by the London Horticultural Society to collect in the region explored by Douglas. He arrived at Fort Colville in May, 1851, and until the following year collected in Washington and British Columbia. The mystery of his silence and his disappearance is still unsolved. He never returned from an expedition in California in 1853. Because none of his specimens are left in any American herbarium, and because there is no trace of his Journal, he has been called The Forgotten Botanist. This is not wholly true. Jeffery's name still lives in the pine tree, *Pinus ponderosa Jeffreyi,* and in the lovely magenta-colored shooting star *Dodecatheon Jeffreyi.*

Thomas Nuttall, himself the discoverer of nearly one thousand new species of North American plants, had, in a sense, completed much of the work of pioneer plantsmen both in the Atlantic State and in the West. In voicing his own regret at leaving the New World to return to the Old World he spoke for them all:

> Hardship and privation are cheaply purchased if I can but roam over the wide domain of primeval nature and behold another Flora there of bolder hues and richer sweets beyond our garden's pride . . . I bid adieu to the New World, its sylvan scenes, its mountains, wild and plains . . . I return, almost as exile, to the land of my nativity.

17 Fool's Gold

SOUTHERN CALIFORNIA is so vast, so diverse, so rich in horticultural interest, that it would be absurd to attempt to write of it without spending a considerable time there. And I have never spent more than a week or two at a time in that huge territory which stretches from the Mexican border to two hundred miles south of Monterey. Not even a superficial reporting could ignore the Santa Ana Botanic Garden at Claremont, near Los Angeles, nor the Santa Barbara Garden with its great collection of California native plants; nor the Mojave desert bloom in spring.

If I had to choose one single southern California sight I should forgo all these, and the flower fields around Lompoc and Bakersfield, the Joshua Tree National Monument, and what remains of the once great private gardens of Santa Barbara. I should be content, instead, to search the Ojai valley behind Santa Barbara for the glorious Matilija poppy. This poppy, with its large white-petaled flowers growing on five-foot grey-silvered leaved stems, is to my mind not only the largest but one of the most beautiful of all California wildflowers.

As it is, southern California means to me orange and lemon, avocado and grapefruit groves and, above all, geraniums and eucalyptus trees. Geraniums grow like weeds and are used as ground-covers to plant steep dry banks with a brilliant profusion of color; as street decorations they often grow up the trunks of palm trees, as a nine- or ten-feet colonnade in pink and red.

As for the eucalyptus, which is perhaps Australia's greatest gift to North America, it has, more than any other import, adapted itself to the southern California landscape as box to Virginia. The eucalyptus belongs. It is the oasis tree and is grown widely as a windbreak; it marks much of California as a desert now made fertile.

I left Los Angeles, after my first Christmas there, early in January. After two nights in Santa Barbara, I then went on to Carmel, near Monterey.

Carmel . . . the word is like a bell, and as a bell it had been ringing in my head ever since someone told me that wherever I went, whatever I did, I must see it.

"Hurry, and we'll see the last of the sunset." So Mrs. Lester Rowntree greeted me when she came down from her Carmel Highlands home to meet me in the town of Carmel-by-the-Sea. The motor of her station-wagon was running. I had but a moment to throw my baggage in and fall into a seat. Almost before I had recovered myself we were standing beneath the Monterey cypress trees as the sun was setting in turbulent mood across the bay. It was a tremendous sight,

the vast vermilion sky above the wine-dark sea. In silence,
we watched as the color drained first from the sea, the purple fading to molten grey, until the sun went down a ball
of fire, and the angry vermilion faded to a carmine afterglow that spread upwards over the entire sky.

"That's a Turner picture for you," Mrs. Rowntree said.

"I'm glad we hurried."

Off we went, hurrying again, hurrying up the hillside, up
above the pines. It was almost dark when we arrived. I could
see nothing but the great shoulder of hill looming above the
house. At Mrs. Rowntree's bidding I picked up an armful of
grease wood for the evening fire from the pile beside the
door. As I bent down I could hear the long roll of the in-
coming tide below.

Lester, as people come quickly to call her, is an uncom-
monly hard person to persuade to talk about her achieve-
ments. "I write not as a botanist nor as a hybridist" she once
prefaced an article on lupins, "but as a wayfarer urged on by
conjectural curiosity." The dustcover of one of her books
gives a more accurate appraisal: "The name of Lester Rowntree commands respect everywhere current literature of gardening and horticulture is known. From her home at Carmel
Highlands the seeds of California plants go all over the
world."

There was so much I wanted to ask Lester that first evening. There was little chance. She was full of eager question-
ing herself, for she was going to England for the summer.
I think she had not been back since her family left the Lake
District house and big walled garden when she was a girl.

"I want to know about the birds . . . what is the mavis? Is
the thrush the same as the throstle?"

I knew, by such a question, that for Lester the childhood

memories of the English countryside had long since been overlaid by her intimate knowledge of the wide spaces of the West.

"Do you remember the lark—Shelley's skylark, singing as he soars into the downland sky?" I asked.

"Yes." She did remember then, and some of the other things she had forgotten. "But it's the nightingale I want to hear most of all. Where can I do that?" I told her where I felt sure she would not be disappointed: by such and such a belt of Suffolk woodland, and on such and such a hillside above the village where day as well as night the nightingales sing in the hawthorn trees.

After dinner we had spread a map of England and a map of California out on the floor.

"It's all so big," I said, my hand on California. "I'd have to live for years on the Coast before I could know it even passably well. And it's no use depending on others; every one sees things differently, each must see for oneself. Some," I said, "tell me that California is parched and dry and tree-less, others that it is wet for months on end and I'll never see the sun. What can I believe?"

"That's an old story," Lester replied. "Even Americans on the East Coast don't realize that California, if placed on the Atlantic side, would stretch from Connecticut to South Carolina. The state is almost eight hundred miles long. California has everything: mountains and desert, forests and bare rolling hills, rich valleys and treeless wastes, almost every type of terrain and climate. You may find here whatever it is you seek from sun-baked beaches to snow-caps."

She was silent a moment, then talked on. Her memory took her back to the big old walled garden in the Lake District. Always a rebel and a tomboy, she once saved her tea

biscuits in a tin box against the day she ran away to sea. She
remembered that one-third of that home garden was divided
into eight parts, one for each of eight children in the family; that her first heartbreak was at the age of two on being
told by the family coachman that if a cowslip were planted
upside down it would come up double.

It was late when we folded the maps. "You'd better take
a couple of books to bed with you," she said. "Unless you're
tired to death by my talking, you won't get to sleep right
away. There's a board under your mattress, no springs. I'm
so used to sleeping on the ground in my sleeping bag that
I don't like to sleep soft at home. I have to keep myself in
trim."

The books I took to bed with me were Lester's *Flowering Shrubs of California* and *Hardy Californians*. Perhaps
they would give me a clue to this firm-muscled, five-feet tall,
indomitable woman with the bright, sometimes puzzled,
brown eyes, whose face was burnt and wrinkled by the California sun. Although she chooses to forget her age, I know
Lester Rowntree was past the seventy-year mark when I met
her first.

Upon coming to America from England when she was of
early school age, her family had settled in the Middle West
first, later on the West Coast. She had been sent back East
to finish her schooling, and even then, I know, she had hated
the confines of walls and ceilings. After shuttling back and
forth between East and West in the years leading through
school to marriage, Lester had made her home high on this
chaparral-covered hillside, as she called it, above the pines
and within sight and sound of the sea. That much I knew.

The books told me more of what I had guessed. From a
youthful English tomboy, Lester had developed into a gypsy,

and although she does not like to appear as one, in public, she is essentially a gypsy at heart.

"What are you?" is a question she has often been asked by the police who, after a quick glance, have been unable to apply any of the conventional labels. Sometimes she has been hard put to give a convincing answer. Depending on whether her seedbags, her plant presses, or her notebooks are in evidence, she has declared herself a seed collector or a writer.

Once a passerby, noticing an apparently abandoned car in a dried river bed, reported the matter at the next town. Lester meanwhile was happily exploring a canyon. At mid-day two men, sent out in search for the "lost driver" of the car, climbed the steep hillside. "We've come to find you," they announced. "You can't because I'm not lost," Lester replied. In spite of their pleadings—they thought no doubt that Lester was slightly mad—she firmly refused to go along with them. "I'm not lost and I won't be found," she insisted, and remembered in time to call after them, to thank them for their thought and concern.

A gypsy's life is a wayfaring life. Seeds of wild flowers are not so easy to come by as an ordinary peddler's wares. It is arduous to go up to those high places, to that Arctic-alpine zone which stretches from timber line to mountain top, and which in California means from 9,000 feet to 14,500 feet. Nor is it appreciably less arduous to gather seeds in the parched heat of the desert sand. This is what Lester Rowntree had done for some thirty years. She has set out from her hillside in March and April for long shining days in the desert; for the foothills in May; for the northern counties in the new-mown hay and strawberry time of June; for the higher mountains in July, and with mule or burro in August and September for the high places of the alpine zone.

What did she get from it, this collecting of seeds and their distribution overseas? "Fool's gold." I hadn't a doubt that would be her answer—it was in her book. The small monetary rewards of seed collecting bear no relationship to the time and hardships involved. But to her, Fool's gold was enough to give her freedom of space and timeless days, freedom to follow her own chosen pattern of living, however costly the privations. She told me, over dinner, that she would rather eat bread and cheese, and be free.

The January sun was pouring into my room when I woke next morning and opened the door to the garden. I saw the bees swarming over the rosemary bushes thickset with lavender bloom. Jonquils were in flower. A blue jay streaked an azure line across the pines. I looked up at the shoulder of a hill rising abruptly on the north like a gigantic backdrop.

I asked Lester, at breakfast, what she meant by the term "chaparral-covered" hillside. Chaparral is a medley of shrubs, she told me, sometimes so jammed together that they lose all individuality in the service of general ground cover. It consists mostly of scrub oak, wild lilac, manzanita, sage, rhus, and toyon. The term chaparral comes from scrub oak or Chapano, and because chaparral contains so much formidable scrub oak those who used to penetrate it on horseback encased their legs in chapineros or chaparyos, commonly known as just plain "chaps."

"Fragrance is a marked characteristic of the chaparral," she said. "Especially after rain its scent is as typical of California as is the scent of orange blossoms. All the stands of it everywhere have the same basic aroma, something like that of chrysanthemums, overlaid here by one perfume, there by another, as the various shrubs come into flower."

"I'm going up the hill right after breakfast," I said.

"I guessed you would. You won't find the chaparral too dense. You can forget the clock. I'd come if I could, but my heart nowadays keeps me on low ground. Tell me what you see up there when you're back."

It was a stiff climb. I shrivelled a bit of sage in my hand and sniffed it as I went, looking back at the sea below as I paused now and then for breath.

High up on the hill I could see the foothills stretching away to the south, fold after fold of green. Below me the pines were evergreen shadows sweeping upwards from the hill-dividing canyons. Away in the distance I could see there was snow along the Coastal Range.

Beyond the pines and far below was the curve of Carmel Bay, and beyond that the Bay of Monterey. The sea was thundering in along the rugged coast, but no sound reached me on the hilltop, though I could see the spray, a surging eddy of driven foam, as the waves hurled themselves against the rocks.

What was this blue of Carmel Bay? For Mary Austin, who knew the contours of the West as well as any human can, it was a "blue lifting to chrysoprase and breaking white to foam." Years ago, homesick in New York, dreaming of the blue, Carmel Bay had called her back, back west across the continent. Gazing upon Carmel Bay I could understand that now.

The sun was hot. I took off my coat, and then my sweater, and lay flat on my back on the short turf, staring at the clear blue sky. I would never know what I absorbed from that green California hill. Only I know I did not leave it empty-handed.

The sun had traveled a long way by the time I started

down. A few blue lupine banners stood up among the big silver-leafed bushy mounds. Paintbrush and yellow violas flowered in the shelter of buckwheat twigs and grey-green sage. And then my day was made. I recognized Baby Blue Eyes, azulejita or little blue one as the Spanish call it, the humble plant that David Douglas called the harbinger of the California spring. I had found it on Lester's hillside, and near where Douglas found it first, at Monterey, on another January day.

After that I went down lickity-spit to find Lester weeding, crouched down over her plants, an alpine trowel in her hand.

"How was it, what did you see?" She sat back on her heels and looked up.

"I found Baby Blue Eyes . . . I wanted to ask you about lupines: they are legion here, aren't they, like the asters and goldenrods in the East?"

"What a question! I wouldn't know where to begin to tell you. There are three hundred to four hundred lupine species, not counting varieties and hybrids. In California alone there are more than sixty-five species and as many varieties. You'll find them everywhere. What else did you see?"

"I saw the blue of Carmel Bay . . . There's snow along the Coastal Range."

"What else," Lester persisted.

"I saw a hawk swoop down low over the chaparral," I said.

"Nothing else? I know," Lester continued, "you don't have to tell me. I wanted to live on this hillside, for the view and the aboveness, so that I could wave my arms and crow."

"I know."

She picked up my echo of her words. "How do you know?"

"You told me last night. I mean, I read it in your book. And you said that you had from your seed collecting what you wanted: Fool's gold. Now you ask me what I saw on the hill, and I tell you I saw a hawk and the blue of Carmel Bay. We've both got our wages, in different currency, that's all. I've even less to show. I haven't even a handful of seed."

Lester was poking away again in the soil.

"I've a tool just like that at home," I told her.

"It's the only thing among the old things I saved from the fire in my workshop which destroyed my notes and photographs," Lester said. "It's the tool my father used, he brought it with him from England . . . I wanted to grow things in gravel soil, that was another reason for my coming to the hill. I hadn't done that before, I'd never gardened in gravel."

"I used to hybridize those," she said, following my glance around her garden to the yellow and maroon-eyed gazaneas that were fully open to the sun. "But now I leave it to the bees and they do just as good a job, probably better. It's the soil I have to contend with still. I have had to start compositing. I couldn't grow the pinks and rock roses in this pure decomposed gravel if I didn't feed them . . . Discouraged?" She picked the word out of my question. "No, I'm never discouraged, it just doesn't do. There's always a way."

That is a cornerstone of Lester's philosophy. There is something indomitable about her for all her five-feet diminution. She herself might well be described by the title of one of her books, a *Handy Californian*. Yet the hard collecting years, working at high altitudes and on a too meager diet, have taken their toll physically.

In many ways there are striking similarities between Lester Rowntree and David Douglas. In fact, Lester could be called Douglas' plant-wise and spiritual descendant. No one since Douglas' day has developed so extensively the same California hunting ground; no one has distributed so far and wide the seeds and plants of California natives, many of which Douglas was the first to introduce. Lester's knowledge of California wild flowers in unrivaled; it is safe to say she knows more about them than Douglas ever knew.

Both of them grew to discount comfort, both shared an enthusiasm for their quest that carried them over almost impossible miles, both were content with Fool's gold. Both suffered blindness—Lester's sight fortunately has been partially restored.

She has not, so far, to my knowledge, had a plant named for her; she has not discovered a new genus nor any outstanding plant species. She has, however, introduced into gardens many plants and seeds that were not grown in cultivation before: *Ceanothus horizontalis, Ceanothus gloriosus, Lupinus peirsonii,* and two dwarf *dicentras* among them. She has, more than any other person, made gardeners aware of the use and beauty of California natives. And there is her writing.

Although Lester Rowntree belongs to the outdoors rather than the confines of four square walls, and although she prefers her wayfaring days, she can and does submit to the self-imposed discipline that writing demands. She is among the very few plant collectors with the ability and determination to set down for gardeners generally the knowledge she has so hardly acquired. In addition to her numerous contributions to magazines and botanical journals, her two books on the California plants and shrubs will long take their place in twentieth century horticultural literature.

For herself, the best by-product of all her plant collecting

days is the close and intimate relationship she has established
between herself and the natural world around her.

"It isn't only the plants," she once said to me, and the
puzzled look came into her eyes as she tried to put her
thought into words, "knowing what happens to them in the
night and in different weather, getting to know them; it's the
insects and animals, the whole living ecology. You feel part
of them, and they of you. You can feel the earth underneath
you—a oneness with the earth."

Lester's broad vision has allowed her to enjoy, without
hurtful nostalgia, the memories of the Old World and the
New. Likewise, though she infinitely prefers nature's plan-
less plantings, she gets a double thrill from the sight of wild
floods of flowers that she used to cultivate in her early English and eastern American gardens.

In a sense she has grown away from the busy everyday
life, and in doing so has become doubly perceptive of the
natural world around her. With an artist's eye for color and
form, she delights in the changing gradations of color in the
landscape, in the infinitesimal movements of a flower which
so many of us never see.

Sun and wind are, for her, the supreme engravers. No
lithographer, she declares, turns out anything more beautiful
than the twisted bole of a fallen lodgepole pine. She can hear
the wing swish of migratory birds, and her keenness for
scent, which equals that of a hunting dog, enables her to
detect the presence of a Sierra primrose before she sees it
with her eyes.

Few keep their childhood sense of wonder as Lester
Rowntree has done. By her awareness and her sense of oneness with the earth she has, especially in the mountains,
come very near to the heart of the world.

18 San Francisco

❧

SAN FRANCISCO stands at the tip of the San Francisco peninsula, on a promontory from which you may see the sun rise over the blue waters of San Francisco Bay and set on the deeper blue waters of the Pacific. Built on sand and granite, and on twice as many hills as Rome, it dominates one of the great, and one of the most beautiful land-locked harbors of the world.

There have been scores of books about San Francisco; there will be scores to come. People have written of the views over the city and the Bay from such high spots as the glass enclosed room at the "Top of the Mark" in the Mark Hopkins Hotel, and from Coit Tower on Telegraph Hill; of the stubby little cable cars which demand the right-of-way as they swing their loads of passengers precariously up the straight precipitous streets.

They have written of the elegance of San Francisco women, of San Franciscans' tolerance and hospitality, and their love to turn every possible event into a gala performance. They have written of the famous restaurants, the florists and the flower stalls; of the luxuries which flow in from the Orient, from the South Seas, and the Western World: of China Town with its silks and jade, and Fisherman's Wharf where the Neopolitans cook crab and lobster in their steaming brick coppers along the sidewalk.

For some the city may recall Marseilles and the blue Mediterranean; for others it has the flavor of New Orleans' Vieux Carré. But there is no other city that in any way resembles San Francisco. Almost everyone who knows it, loves it; yet no one has written *Everyman's* San Francisco.

How could they? For this is a city where East and West not only meet but live together. Russian and Oriental, Italian and Portuguese, Mexican, Negro, Spaniard and Filipino, and the English, the Irish, and the Scotch. All of them have added their ingredient to this most cosmopolitan of cities. The Irish nurse, the Chinese cook, the French gardener, the Italian fisherman were all, at one time or another, traditions of San Francisco living.

No artist of world acclaim has yet portrayed San Francisco on canvas. The Italians, busy with their fishing, have not yet provided a Caneletto to set down the clean lines of this water-washed city. The English have not provided a Turner to record the spectacular sunsets across the Golden Gate; the French have sent no Impressionist to record the constant variance in light and mood.

The surrounding waters which ebb and flow with the sea-going tides are calm and blue, and then are ruffled by the wind, green and grey. The sky is cloudless; or the channel fog drifts in across "the Gate," shrouding the city in opaque greyness, revealing and hiding hilltop by hilltop in turn so that you may look and see the city profile, a chiseled whiteness sharply drawn against the wide sweep of the Bay; and you may look again and see only faint shadowed outlines of what a moment before were straight, soaring lines of stone.

Geography and climate have done much to shape San Francisco's character and moods. General Fremont in a geographical memoir addressed to the Senate gave the name of Chrysophylae, or Golden Gate, to the narrow passage which links San Francisco Bay to the sea. He chose the name, he explained, for the same reasons that the harbor of Istanbul was called Chrysoceras, or Golden Horn, for the form of the harbor and its advantages for commerce, "Asiatic inclusive."

As for the weather, it is as perennial a subject of conversation in San Francisco as it is in England. Those who only know the city in summer, which is San Francisco's worst time of year, and who come expecting the fabled sun of California and find wind and fog instead, say it has the worst climate in the world. Those who live there any length of time think it has one of the best. With a mean annual temperature of 56.3 degrees, San Francisco is never too hot, and never too cold.

From the gardeners' point of view, the Bay area as a whole probably offers more diversity of climate and soil than any other comparable area. The temperate climate varies only within narrow limits, so that a gardener may choose his district by the flowers he wants to grow. Bouganvillea, for instance, will not thrive fifty miles further north, nor rhododendron fifty miles to the south, but both dwell within the city. Oddly enough, *daphne odorata,* by which the florists proclaim the arrival of spring flowers, will bloom but shyly in San Francisco, though abundantly in the surrounding districts.

It is not, however, such an easy gardening climate as it sounds. Spring is sunny, warm and mostly clear. Mid-May through to October are rainless months, when the westerly trade winds from the sea make people clutch their hats along the windy streets, and the high driving fogs form a sun-obscuring overcast. Although the fog gives a certain amount of moisture, it is not enough, and constant irrigation is needed to keep the plants alive. September is a difficult month when the hot, dry wind from the interior valleys sears the already parched gardens, but October brings a respite. From then until the winter rains begin, the city basks in a long and windless Indian summer.

There are always flowers in San Francisco, "the city with a flower in its buttonhole." By repute its citizens buy more flowers than the citizens of any other American city.

The Bay area nurserymen not only grow for the San Francisco market, but also export quantities of flowers; ten-car loads of chrysanthemums alone, at the height of their season, are shipped out daily to the cut-flower centers across the continent. And the florists not only buy from the local growers, and from southern California and the Pacific Northwest, but shop in the Hawaiian Islands for orchids and other exotics, such as ginger lilies.

You would think that San Franciscans, with their habit of buying so lavishly from the florists, and with the need for irrigation and high labor costs, would hardly take the trouble to garden and raise still more flowers. But they do.

Wherever there is a space between the houses and the

sidewalk, it is filled with flowers. They spill over the garden walls and the low curbings, so that it is true to say that
San Francisco's almost treeless streets are, at times, flower-
scented streets.

The real gardens of San Francisco, however, are behind
the houses, which mostly stand directly up to the sidewalk.
And since San Francisco is as restricted for space as New
York's Manhattan Island, the gardens are small. Unlike the
roof gardens of New York, the typical San Francisco garden
is generally a steep, terraced strip or square, although there
are some fine roof gardens too.

One garden I saw measured no more than twenty by forty
feet. Across the narrow strip of grass there was a narrow
border, a brilliant three by four feet wide ribbon of cinerarias, multi-colored in a Schaparelli range of blue to purple,
lilac to magenta, rose and white, all raised by the owner from
carefully selected seed.

Behind the cinerarias was a row of pin roses, and behind
these the off-white boundary fence of lattice-panelled square
where fuchsias, heliotrope, and blue plumbago were climbing up to join the Cecil Brunner rose. There was even a
bird's nest in a fork of the plumbago bush.

In another slightly larger garden, which opened from the
dining room, I walked into what seemed an indoor conservatory of massed flowers—only the small central square of
grass was open to the sky. The rhododendrons were over, so
was the wistaria trained against the house trellis, but a
superb double-flowering Japanese cherry was a cloud of shell-
pink bloom. This, according to its yearly habit, lasted a full
five weeks. Ferns and shade-loving perennials covered the
north border; camellias and fuchsias were blooming and
would continue to do so throughout the summer months.

On either side, low brick walls buttressed the raised
flagged paths, a patchwork of color with violas, primula,
and polyanthus, creeping thymes, yellow alyssum, and English daisies. The white dwarf azalea, Snowdrift, which flowers
from January through to May, was till a compact mass of
bloom, and was the highlight of the miniature flagstone
corner. What a crowd of flowers to find in a few square feet,
and around a trim green lawn.

San Francisco is a fuchsia kingdom; bushes become miniature trees, and flower in the city longer than any other flower.
Heliotrope climbs in heady profusion over the walls. These
two, and cinerarias, camellia, and jessamine are San Francisco gardeners' favorite flowers, and always somewhere there
are geraniums, pelagoniums, and the yellow genista bushes.

I wanted to see a garden across the Bay in Berkeley, and
wrote to ask if I might see it. The owner must have realized
I had no idea her husband was ill. The day after he died she
wrote: "We are always glad to have gardeners visit our garden. I have been ill with flu and do not know if I will have
reached the talking stage when you come. I hope so. Please
set your own time and bring any friend with you—no gardeners are strangers."

I quote her letter because it expressses not only that
spontaneous open hospitality of America generally, but also
the gallantry which is a part of the San Francisco character.
San Francisco has suffered hardship and loss among all the
bonanza extravagance. Fire has destroyed much, not once,
but many times. Always she has rebuilt, quickly and cou-
rageously, and after the 1906 earthquake and following fire,
rose from the ashes like the phoenix, which is the city's
seal.

It is also a trait of the city's character to do what public opinion says cannot be done. The Golden Gate Bridge, suspended by the great towers sunk deep below the racing tides, was a bridge which engineers said could not be built. And even San Franciscans themselves laughed derisively at the site which was chosen for Golden Gate Park.

Many a park superintendent can point a proud finger as he tells the story of land reclamation and the conversion of almost inaccessible marshes into spaces of sylvan beauty. But none can match the triumph of the men who, from a barren stretch of land, from shifting dunes and wind-blown sand, created the great green swathe, nine city blocks wide and four and a half miles long, which today leads from the city to the sea.

There were many builders of Golden Gate Park. There were the legislators who, in their search for a sufficiently large acreage, fought the long and bitter controversy over the "Outside Lands" to which squatters laid claim, as being outside the four-square leagued city limit contained within the original Pueblo of San Francisco. And there were the engineers who, in 1870, declared it possible to make a park on what was seemingly an impossible site.

In 1871 the first Park Superintendent, Hammond Hall, moved in. Wind and sand were against him, but he had the advantage of the Mediterranean-like climate, and an un-limited source of water from seaward-running subterranean streams.

Hammond Hall brought in tons of soil, tons more of grass cuttings and straw and city sweepings to mix with the sand. He hired small boys to collect wild lupine seed from the hills, and imported seed of the European sand-loving sand grass. With these and the native beach grass he started to harness the shifting dunes, and wherever an outcrop of rock or a sandhill valley afforded shelter, wherever a plant took root, he planted a seedling cypress, a pine or gum tree beside it.

In the first few years Hammond Hall planted twenty-one thousand trees, and acres and acres of grass. He laid down wide driveways and four miles of serpentine patterned roads to break the force of the winds. Here and there over the tawny hills spread a hint of green.

The Park had been in existence sixteen years under a succession of Superintendents; the treescape of the eastern end was well established, but elsewhere, in the park proper, there was everything to do. Then came John McLaren, a forty-one-year–old sandy-haired Scotchman.

"We want you to make Golden Gate Park one of the beauty spots of the world. Can you do it?" the Park Commissioners asked McLaren.

"With your aid, gentlemen, and God be willing, that I shall do," McLaren promised.

The Park, as we see it today, is the fulfillment of those hopes and of McLaren's word. Tirelessly, ceaselessly, he worked from dawn to dusk through fifty-six long years. He was a small, square-shouldered man with tremendous vitality and driving power: bluff and brusque but extraordinarily kindly, and fantastically loyal to the men who served him well.

He worked always with, never against, nature, striving to create the effect of natural beauty. "I'd go out into the country," he said, "and walk along a stream until I came to a bonnie brook. Then I'd come back to the park and I'd reproduce what nature had done."

Along the driveways and the margins of the lakes, from one long grassy meadow to another, he massed his shrubs and trees, setting out his flower gardens wherever the plants were happiest and most at home. His plant material came to him from all over the world, and he was the greatest introducer of non-native plants the West has known. In the Park Nursery he propagated every species of flower common to the Temperate Zone.

Rhododendrons were John McLaren's favorite flowers. Fortunately, for him, they flourish in the cool summers of San Francisco; some of the original plants which Joseph Hooker sent from Kew in 1880, before McLaren came to the Park, still thrive.

As early as January, when the acacia trees are showers of gold, the rhododendrons begin with a thin thread of color. They make the longest and also the greatest single flower display in the Park, growing in beauty and variety with the spring until, by long yearly custom, the street-car bannerings proclaim in early May that "The rhododendrons are in bloom."

The Park's year-round flower show is only part of McLaren's dream come true; color, though he used it lavishly, is always set against the predominant evergreen of shrubs and trees. Trees were his passion. He liked to tell the story of how his father once chided him for idleness. "Me boy," he said, "if ye've neething to do, go plant a tree an' it'll grow while ye sleep." When John McLaren came to California as a lad in the late 1860's he started straightway to plant trees. All up and down the Peninsula, during the several years he worked on private estates before coming to the Park, he planted trees, some two thousand trees, it is said.

He went back to Scotland once, to see his old mother. When he got out of the train at the little railway station, and saw one of the redwoods growing there, he asked the station master its name.

"That . . . oh, that's a Wellingtonia," the station master said, giving the tree the name by which it is known in Britain.

McLaren looked up at the tree again. "It's a Sequoia," he corrected, and then to himself: "It's a long way from home, and so am I."

McLaren hated and withstood any innovations that might mar the natural beauty of the Park. He abominated statues; "stookies" he called them, and screened those he had to accept with shrubs and trees. There was only one exception. When it was proposed to erect a statue of his countryman, Robert Burns, whose poems he loved to recite, McLaren himself raised the subscriptions in one whirlwind day. "Ah, the things I do for Skootland," he sighed when the statue was put in place and left open to public view.

He might as easily have sighed over some of the things he did for San Franciscans, except for the fact that he always remembered that the purpose of the Park was to serve the people. Back in the depression days of 1894 he opened the garden to a flood of unskilled hands, offering a dollar a day to any man willing to work there. At one time 2,600 men accepted that offer. Again, at the time of the earthquake and fire of 1906, when the people streamed out to the Park, bringing their few remaining belongings with them, shacks and shelters covered the grass lawns. It was a year after they withdrew before the work of replanting and restoration began.

There were, inevitably, attempts from time to time to oust McLaren, but no authority could face the storm of public protest that his forced retirement would raise. It was

his rightful boast that the Park belonged to the people, that
it was made by gardeners and not by politicians. City ad-
ministrations came and went, but John McLaren stayed.
He was still Superintendent six months before he died, at
the age of ninety-seven, on January 12, 1943.

Even in his lifetime John McLaren was a legendary figure.
Each spring the city's children came to pay him tribute;
each year his gardeners made him a birthday ceremony. But
first and last he thought of himself as a gardener. He was,
it is said, the only student of Edinburgh University to grad-
uate merely as "Gardener." And at the end, when honors
came to him from far and wide, he spoke of himself simply as
"the boss gardener who conquered the sand."

There have been many changes in the Park administra-
tion since McLaren's day. The boss gardener is no longer entirely boss; the Superintendents of the once separate Parks
and Recreation areas are now under the control of the General Manager of the Recreation and Park Department.
Otherwise, and outwardly, much is the same. The Superintendent, with a corps of one hundred and forty gardeners
and administrators, maintains the great pleasure ground in
the McLaren tradition.

Certainly Golden Gate Park is great; even by Californian
standards it is big: one thousand acres compared with the
New York Botanical Garden's two hundred and thirty acres,
with the three hundred acres of England's Kew Gardens. It
is so big that neither the civic buildings, the recreation areas,
nor the fifteen-mile network of paved roads rob it of a sense
of spaciousness.

In the trimmed and tamed evergreen wildness there is
room for all; meadow slopes where the buffalo and elk, the
deer, the antelope, and the sheep may graze; lakes for water-

fowl to feed and take refuge; shrubberies for the wild animals and tree tops for the birds.

Most visitors to the Park see the Oriental Tea Garden, which flanks the De Young Museum across the Music Concourse from the Academy of Sciences building. This garden was laid out by the Japanese gardener Hagiwara, whom McLaren called the greatest landscape architect he had ever known. For San Franciscans the zashiki, the traditional two-storied Japanese house, is a favorite rendezvous, where they come especially when the Japanese cherries are in bloom to sit on red lacquered benches, sipping tea from handleless cups and nibbling the three-cornered rice cakes.

Close by the Tea Garden is the Strybing Arboretum and Botanic Garden which was founded in 1937; it displays in a concentrated collection the wealth of plant material that over the years has become scattered in the wide plantings throughout the Park. The purpose of the Arboretum is two-fold: to serve the professional in botanical and horticultural work, and to show the home gardener and plant enthusiast the beauty of the innumerable ornamental plants that thrive in the Bay area.

The Arboretum is young, as arboretums go, but already some five thousand choice species and varieties of shrubs and plants are displayed in a variety of ways. There are unit collections devoted to garden varieties and species of ivy, of cotoneasters, pyracanthas, and barberries; ground covers, rock garden plants, and plants of merit which the Park has introduced to the horticultural trade. The geographical sections prove the most popular. There plants of various countries are grown together in a single garden; gardens of Australia and New Zealand, South Africa and South America, Mexico and the Mediterranean area; China, Japan and the Himalaya, while the Californian section features plants of the Redwood region and the wildflower meadows.

Many of these plants are chosen to be featured in turn as the "Flower of the Week." These are described in the press, and their history is told on the moveable placards placed beside the growing plant in the Arboretum.

The pink-flowered magnolia, *Magnolia Campbellii,* is undoubtedly the star among Arboretum celebrities. People come from all over the Coast to see the wide clear rose-pink blossoms open to the February sun; they are ten inches in diameter with twelve to fifteen petals of a faint, delicious fragrance. Discovered in the Himalaya around the middle of the last century, *Magnolia Campbellii* has remained scarce in cultivation because the trees do not flower until at least twenty years old. In 1924 Golden Gate Park acquired plants from England; in 1940 they flowered for the first time in the United States.

Since the Arboretum is not primarily intended either for recreation or for spectacular massed display, it is understandable that its botanist guards his treasures with a jealous care. He regards the genus *boy,* intent on mischief, as enemy number one, and he holds the adult who damages his preserves in high disfavor. And so he introduces certain discouragements. An innocent label hanging on a precious branch can sometimes make even an innocent inquirer blush with guilt when he reads HANDS OFF instead of the plant's name.

Golden Gate Park is forever growing—not in area but in completion. The Academy of Sciences plans as a centennial project the building of the Alice Eastwood Hall of Botany, which will give the Pacific Coast a plant center comparable to those of New York and Brooklyn. The Hall of Botany

will serve also as a memorial to another remarkable person-
ality and one of America's most distinguished women botanists. Alice Eastwood gave over fifty years' service as Curator
and Head of the Department of Botany at the California
Academy of Sciences, retiring on her ninetieth birthday but
retaining her interest as Curator Emeritus until her death
at the age of ninety-seven in January, 1954.

Each year the Park Nursery raises from thirty to thirty-
five thousand plants, and each year new generations of San
Franciscans and out-of-town sightseers come to the great garden. There are some who come but once or twice a year,
perhaps: the sailor on shore leave, the soldier from the
Presidio, the artist and the tourist, the visiting amateur and
professional botanist. But the everyday workaday San Franciscan, for whom the Park was made, comes year in and year
out.

Everybody comes. They come as families to picnic; children to play; the tired to lie on the grass and the old to sit
gossiping or dreaming in the sun; some simply come to
stand and look at the flowers. "The trees are in bloom,"
you hear people say in April when the cherry trees are out
in the Japanese Tea Garden. "The rhododendrons are in
bloom," you hear them say along the sidewalks in May.
They come then to see the massed tiers of azalea and
rhododendron bloom, and see the great scarlet-flowered
rhododendron that was raised in the park nursery. After
whom could it be named but John McLaren, for over fifty
years the Park's presiding genius!

19 **Poppies**

and

Snow-caps

$\mathcal{S}$AN FRANCISCO is one of the easiest cities to get away from. This may sound a doubtful compliment, but to the country lover who will always trade a grass trodden path for a city sidewalk, it is a rare asset.

Half an hour's driving, by the local direction of "Across the Bay," will take you across the eight-mile-long Bay bridge to the Bay cities of Berkeley and Oakland. Up in the Berkeley hills you are in country that is still the haunt of fox and deer, of quail and the horned owl, and on occasion of the mountain lion.

Half an hour's driving, by the local direction of "over in Marin," will take you by way of the mile-long span of the Golden Gate Bridge to Mount Tamalpais. This mountain, with its meadows and woods, its chaparral and wild flowers, also affords magnificent views. From the summit you

see the wide sweep of San Francisco Bay on the one hand,
the Pacific Ocean along the city's Ocean Highway on the
other, and to the north the rolling hills and rugged coastline
of Marin. In tourist jargon, San Francisco is the gateway to
an almost unrivaled variety of landscape and climate.

They say that spring comes, unofficially, to San Francisco
when the short sprays of *daphne odorata* come to the
florists, usually towards the end of January. The honey-
sweet sprays are unfailingly prompt, and are spread out according to custom, as boutonnieres in neat rows on the sidewalk flower stalls, and clustered in low wide bowls in the
florists' windows. But January is not spring in San Francisco,
even unofficially; it is still a month or two ahead, though in
distance it may be but two hours driving time away.

Early in February, in the wine-growing Napa Valley some
sixty miles north of San Francisco's windswept promontory,
the bees swarming up in the roofs of the old wineries know
that spring has come. The cross-stitched patterned vineyards
are still leafless, but the floor of the prune orchards is solid
with yellow mustard bloom, and the black boughs of the
trees carry a canopy of white.

On Easter day I had my first sight of the California poppy
in the Berkeley hills behind Strawberry Canyon. Not one but
hundreds of them, thousands, tens of thousands of poppies.

It needs no imagination to know why the Spaniards called
the California coastline *La Tierra del Fuego,* though a sailor
now sees from the sea but a faint streak of fire across the
hills instead of mile upon flaming mile of bloom. For, as
wildflower population goes, the California poppy is still
widespread. It is still a common sight though today only
torn fragments, such as I saw that Easter day, remain of the
once limitless poppy fields.

They say the poppy blooms most abundantly on land that has been seared by fire. But the poppies themselves are flowers of fire. They come like tongues of flame licking the hills and bluffs of the coastal ranges until, at the height of their flowering, they set whole hillsides afire with their molten bloom. Who can describe this fire poppy that is as beautiful individually as it is in its millions? It is neither gold nor yellow; rather it is a bright sun-spilled copper color with the sheen of lustre. I like to remember what John T. Howell, Curator of Botany in the California Academy of Sciences, said of this poppy in his *Marin Flora:* "Cherish it and be forever thankful that so rare a flower is common."

All spring you may follow the flowers across the hills, and find one hill all gold, another gold laced with lupin blue; sometimes lupins alone will turn a green hill blue. For poppies and lupins are frequent partners and are as widespread throughout the Pacific slope of California as the asters and goldenrod on the Atlantic seaboard.

Earlier in the year I had been shocked to find the nurserymen's forced daffodils dyed green. I have never understood why people tolerate dyed flowers, why English florists dye the white imperial Dutch lilac shrimp-pink, jade-green, and buttercup-yellow. It was a rude surprise to discover that in San Francisco a daffodil could be robbed of its gold and made a sickly green. The week after Easter, however, my faith was restored in the city's love of yellow daffodils. They used three hundred thousand of them to celebrate Maiden Lane's annual festival to mark spring's official entry into San Francisco. The narrow thoroughfare was a street of bloom. Daffodils festooned every building, covering the stone pillars of the doorways, replacing the usual display of goods in the store windows, and standing in great bunches wherever there was space to put them.

Spring had come to San Francisco. "Spring Superlatives," they hailed the yellow daffodils.

The florists' shops and the flower stalls were superlatively beautiful too, with their bouquets and extravagant arrangements of spring flowers. Union Square at the heart of downtown San Francisco was thickset with marigolds, pansies, and polyanthus. The streets of residential districts were flower-scented with jasmine and heliotrope. The Japanese cherries were at their height in Golden Gate Park.

Over the Bay, in Berkeley, the golden acacia trees had given way to flowering peach. In the Botanic Garden in Tilden Park, in a sheltered fold of the Berkeley hills, *Garrya elliptica,* the Silk Tassel bush hung out its pendant tassels; the yellow tree poppy, the western redbud, and scores of other native Californians were in bloom.

Over in Marin, the madrone and the buckeye were in flower. The hills of Tiberon were lilac-rose with the minute flowers of filaree, or Alfilerillo, as the Spaniards called the diminutive pin clover that the Franciscan padres brought to California from the Mediterranean for its value as a forage crop.

In Muir woods, pink sorrel carpeted the ground beneath the giant redwood trees. On Mount Tamalpais, ceanothus splashed wide blue patches on the dense green chaparral-covered slopes. The wide sheltering arms of the tanbark oak at Rock Springs put out its leaves.

In Sausalito, where you climb the stairways and winding roads to the houses perched on the steep hillside above the harbor, there were flowers everywhere. They escaped from the gardens, bursting through the fences, climbing down

over the walls in careless, disordered profusion. Julian Haw-
thorne called it The Stairway Town; he might as easily have
called it a stairway of flowers.

I spent a few weeks in Sausalito, in an old house that had
originally been prefabricated in Boston, brought round The
Horn, and paid for in California wool. Below me the terraced garden was brimming with spring flowers: anenomes
and ranunculus, the white and yellow marguerites which
had grown into shrub-like bushes. White calla lilies crowded
by the steps. Cecil Brunner roses climbed the roof with
prodigal carelessness, and the old blush-pink rose, Belle of
Portugal, a favorite throughout Marin, trailed down over
the windows. As I climbed the stairways in the evening the
warm lemon scent from the genista bushes mingled with
the wood smoke from Sausalito's friendly evening fines.

This Marin country has been a botanist's hunting ground
since Chamisso came with Eschoscholtz, and David Douglas
climbed Mount Tamalpais; since Menzies found the California laurel and Hartweg found his fritillaria at Corte
Madera. It was a hunting ground to me, too, in my amateur-
ish way, all the more attractive for its association with those
early plant explorers. I found almost all the flowers in the
bunch of annuals that Douglas sent back to England; I
found a clump of dusky purple bells above the mottled
leaves that I knew as Hartweg's fritillaria, and I picked the
pungent leaf of Menzies' California laurel.

One fog-bound day I went north up the coast to Drake's
Bay, a stretch of sand sheltered by the Point Reyes peninsula. Fog no doubt robbed Drake of the discovery of San
Francisco Bay, but he was the first white man to put foot on
the shore of Marin County.

It is a matter of controversy as to whether Drake spent

six weeks careening his ship *The Golden Hinde* in Drake's Bay or a mile or so further south. It is of no great consequence; the name Drake's Bay will stand whatever the archeologists and historians may finally determine, though the name Drake gave Marin has long since been erased. New Albion he marked it on his map, and it must have been the first name that came into his head when he looked up at the white shale cliffs and was reminded instantly of the white chalk headlands of southern England.

Along the sandy bay fishermen were trying for bass and salmon. They had made fires of driftwood to cook by, and to keep themselves warm; the acrid smell of wood smoke mingled with the salty tang of sea spray just as Drake must have smelt it too. The place can hardly have changed at all. His crew must have made fires there all through the six shivering summer weeks they had stayed—"During all which time," Fletcher the Chaplain recorded, "notwithstanding it was the height of summer, and so neare the sunne, yet were wee continually visited with like nipping colds as we had (never) felt before . . . thicke mists and most stinking fogs."

High up on the seaward side of Point Reyes, on a sheltered ledge between buttressing rocks, we had our lunch, huddled in thick mist and a "most stinking fogge." We sat holding mugs of hot sweetened tea in our hands, with the flowers about our feet. There was white wallflower and the brilliant magenta succulents, the grey-leaved mats of dwarf artemesias and tufts of rosy thrift. Sometimes a gull or cormorant swooped down and veered as suddenly away on seeing us, and sometimes the mist momentarily cleared and we could see seals swimming in the blue water or shambling up and down their private rock-guarded beach.

A short distance from the cliff edge were drifts of close

turf-loving plants. There were quantities of deep violet-blue dwarf iris, and the bright short-stemmed yellow flowers of *Sanicula arctopeidea,* Footsteps-of-Spring, among their mat of shining green leaves.

I have been to Point Reyes many times since then but the flowers have never seemed quite so bright as on that foggy day. The greyness seems to heighten, and the bright sunshine to diminish, the brilliant mosaic of those flower-carpeted cliffs.

Inland and north of the Point are barren rolling hills. On these and all across the slopes above the miles-long curve of Bodega Bay, the yellow bush lupin grows in dense profusion. This was one of Menzies' find, *Lupinus arboreus,* and a long-time favorite of English gardens.

The tree lupin in its native form comes in yellow, blue, pink, purple, and many shades ranging from pink to buff. The yellow is probably the best-loved form, and is familiar to all who travel the coast roads of central and northern California where it covers the foothills with huge domes of bloom and silvered leaves. This tree lupin, and another Californian, *Lupinus polyhyllus,* which haunts damp ditches, are parents of the famous rainbow-colored Russell lupins that so delight American garden visitors in England.

Through March you can find a score of Springs in central California within a day's drive of San Francisco: dramatic Springs that come so swiftly and so vividly that you see them more as an open flower in bright sunlight before you have seen the promise of the flowering year in the opening bud. By the end of April, Spring in the Bay area already seemed a long time ago. In the Sierra Nevada, however, which might be called the Switzerland of California, there was still another and a late Spring to see. Before going north I made my first trip to the Yosemite Valley. The words, "You must hurry if you want to see the dogwood," came back to me like an old refrain.

It was warm and sunny as we went over the Bay bridge. Across the wide open spaces of the San Joaquin or Central Valley we could see that the distant foothills had already lost their green and were turning from sepia-brown to their tawny summer gold.

Up in the mountains Fremont's lemon-yellow flowered Fremontia stood out, a bush of almost solid color, against the snow-capped ranges. Higher still we stopped to put on chains after a three-day snowfall on the road, and by the time we were past the old wooden hotel at Wawona and past Chinquapin, it was cold and snowing hard. At the entrance to the Yosemite Valley there was nothing to see but snow and the eddying mist.

Next morning we woke to intermittent sun and snow. Yosemite was going to reveal itself slowly, if at all. As we crossed the ice-choked Merced River and went up the trail to Vernal Falls we saw the incense cedars and the deep canyons below through a moving veil as the snowflakes whirled before our eyes. Waterfalls are part of Yosemite's glories, and for sheer beauty Vernal Falls in full spring flood has few rivals as it pours over the granite ledge, flanked by pines and cedars, to plunge in a sort of wild jubilancy to the rocks and boulders below.

Mid-morning the snow stopped, the mist cleared, and moment by moment as we watched, one part and then another of the surrounding walls of rock were revealed in sunlit winter beauty. A small pool mirrored the mountains, and the snow-mantled trees along the snow-clad peaks were as white lace etched across the surface of the water. The sheer two thousand-feet cliff of Half Dome's granite face was all but lost in lily leaves.

At last we could see the whole magnificence of the Yosemite Falls, which is probably the most spectacular waterfall in the world. In one prodigious leap the Upper Falls equals approximately nine Niagara Falls in the length of its plunge; the Lower, which continues with only a slight break, drops the span of more than two Niagara Falls. But the eye cannot take in the magnitude of such measurements. To tell the truth, the Yosemite Falls, for all its length, is less impressive than the mighty mass of Niagara Falls. The Yosemite Falls, by comparison, is a thread of water; moreover, the whole grandiose scale of the setting detracts from the incomprehensible height and fall of the down-thrusting white rockets of water as they shatter into clouds of white mist on the valley floor.

Along Tenaya Creek the western dogwood was in flower. The white saucer-like blooms gleamed against the heavy russet trunks of Ponderosa pines; the flowering sprays spread over granite rocks and bent over the swirling ice-green waters of the creek.

The waterfalls in full flood; the dogwood in bloom; the weekend was slipping away. If we made haste, and if we were in luck, we might see the Big Trees of the Mariposa Grove. At the valley head we looked back at the impressive view, and so saw last what ordinarily people see first. I think our way the better way.

Great thunderheads now sailed above the snow-capped peaks of the Cathedral Rocks, and Bridalveil Falls, another turbulence of sparkling water, split down the whole length of another granite cliff. El Capitan, a massive fortess-like bastion, guarded the valley head like some Crusader Castle.

Away in the distance the polished face of Half Dome glistened beneath its snow-clad summit, and far beyond we could see Sentinel Rock and Clouds Rest.

We turned to go. There was just time for me to do what most Californians feel they must do, at least once a year: feel granite under their feet. I clambered up a slab of grey rock where the manzanita spread its twisted mahogany-colored branches, red-limbed candelabra alight with pale pink bloom.

Along forested roads the long pointed cones of Douglas' sugar pines dangled against the sky. Lichen on the boughs of trees was a startling streak of chartreuse above the snow. The ashen bark of the white fir, which is the most perfect of all Christmas trees, was silvered in the sun; its symetrical branches spreading horizontally in layer upon layer of evergreen boughs were as the welcoming outstretched hands of the forest.

We went slowly over the snow-covered roads until the Big Trees of the Mariposa Grove were in sight, and I plunged knee-deep in snow to put my hand on the trunk of the Grizzly Giant. No one would dispute John Muir's phrase that the Big Tree is Nature's forest masterpiece. *Sequoia gigantea* may not be quite as tall as the coastal redwood, *Sequoia sempervirens,* but of what consequence are fifty feet or more in height above the 209-feet stature of the Grizzly Giant, which also measures ninety-six feet in girth!

I leaned against the huge trunk, buttressed at the base, surprisingly soft to the touch, and looked up the deep and widely furrowed living tower above me. For one fleeting moment I was reminded of ancient English oaks; there was something in the horizontal line and the vertical upward bend of a branch, something of the steadfastness and tolerance of the oak which crossed my mind. But that was all. I know of no one, single thing that I have seen, not the savage wild hostility of Utah nor the splendor of the Grand Canyon of the Colorado, nor the marvel of Yosemite Falls, that has affected me so strangely and so powerfully as this seemingly eternal tree.

They say the Grizzly Giant is 3,800 years old. It is alive, not dead; it still bears virile seed within its little cones. It is incomprehensible, by any known scale of reckoning, that a living thing should be so old.

Slowly I walked back through the snow. Odd to remember that Americans so often say they have nothing to compare in age with Europe, thinking always of the works of man. But what work of man has endured in use so long? Masterpieces of nature such as these trees are a part of the wilderness that America strives to preserve, while Europe tries to preserve the work of man.

How infinitesimal is man—how brief the rise and fall of empires in terms of the life span of the Grizzly Giant, which is taller than the Nelson Monument in London's Trafalgar Square, and was young 1,800 years before Christ was born!

The Grizzly Giant has seen more springs than any other living thing has seen; yet it is monarch only among a race of giants, among other Big Trees that are almost as old, almost as tall, almost as massive. What will the world be like when the young sequoias at their feet, now but shoulder-high, shall be full grown?

20 Portland Means Roses

THE 670-mile journey between San Francisco and Portland in the Northwest is a magnificent journey whichever way or however you go; I have made it along the two connecting highways many times, at every season of the year, both by auto and bus, and have traveled the route by train and plane. The coastal road—the Redwood Highway, part of it is called —is one of the most spectacular and varied highways of North America.

Perhaps it is because the Pacific Coast's flowers and trees are now my familiars, or that traveling by bus I could look my fill without having to keep my eyes on the narrow, winding portions of the road, but the flowers along the Coastal Highway have never seemed quite so bright as on the mid-May day I first fared north. Contrariwise, by whatever method of travel, the giant trees remain as impressive as, ever, though they have long since become less austere and remote and seem now welcoming and friendly.

Mid-May is the best time of year to make your first journey; it is the time before the high fog hides the summer sun from San Francisco, when the wild rhododendrons and azaleas start to flower northward up the Coast.

It was late afternoon when, on that first journey, we were in the Redwood Empire. There had been flowers all the way. Around Cloverdale there were orchards and vineyards, and rolling wooded hills; around Hopland were hopfields. Everywhere the elderberry was in bloom, and the live oaks on the brown hillsides made a green oasis of shade beneath their densely spread leafy heads. But as we entered the redwoods' domain the light went out of the day, and the warmth out of the sun.

I spent a night in a cabin under one of the great trees. There was almost no one about, for it was still early for tourists. When I walked through the forest to a bluff above the Eel River, with its wide mid-stream stretches of white gravel, the long pointed shadows of the trees were already far across the water. Clusters of coral-pink bells threaded the huckleberry's glossy leaves, and a ceanothus trailed its blue sprays across the cinnamon bark of a madrone. A startled deer bounded away, the stones clattering down the rocky slope long after it had disappeared; then the silence edged back again.

The deep-shadowed groves seemed chill and solemn, even oppressive. I looked up at the enormous columns, but their canopy of green high above shut out the sun, and there was little sky to see. It was a perpetual semi-twilight of the gods, where only an occasional shaft of sunlight reached the ground. What brightness there was in that hushed place came from the frail and humble Sugar Scoop with its thread-like stems, which covered the forest floor with its leaves and tiny pure white flowers.

Next day the road northward ran for some fifty miles through the tremendous forest on either side. Redwood Empire is no idle tourist phrase. It is unquestionably the kingdom of the giants. Where the trees were less densely grouped they were even more impressive. There were glades where the sunlight revealed a ground cover of ferns and iris, an ideal stage setting for a sleeping beauty.

Gradually the forest thinned, to reveal the full beauty of individual trees. The sun lit up the now open glades. The ground was thick with forest flowers.

The redwoods were then behind me, the flowers now widespread along the roadsides and across the hills. The bus window was like a projector screen, the color slides changing constantly and all too rapidly. A madrone in bloom. A pure stand of western azalea smothered in creamy-white flowers. A logged-over hillside blue with ceanothus, and, beyond, the snow-capped Siskiyou Mountains. A patch of pale pink Dutchman's breeches, then a hillside where azalea and ceanothus flowered together, and, beyond, bright blue pools of tall larkspur in a meadow white with ox-eye daisies. I saw wide patches of camas, as David Douglas once saw them —lakes of blue flooding the green valleys.

As we drove on north from Crescent City, the ceanothus gave way to mile after mile of the native rhododendron and the western azalea; their laden sprays were outlined against the Pacific Ocean far below. Deep blue and white iris covered whole hillsides as thickly as primroses cover sunny slopes in the English spring.

The two-day journey along that coastal road was a fitting

approach to Portland and Fort Vancouver close by, over the river, which was the home-base of the early Pacific Coast plant explorers when this was Indian country. It was territory they must often have looked across with some affection, as the familiar oasis in the unmapped wilderness around. For my part I hold Portland in affection too. The city's welcome to all travelers in the words "For you a Rose in Portland Grows" was to prove especially true for me, and the views from the surrounding hills gave me my first sight of the mighty snow-caps of the Northwest.

Looking down over the roofs of the city, your gaze will travel across the Willamette River and the forested foothills to the snow-capped peaks of Mount Hood and Mount St. Helen's beyond. It is too wide and too diverse a view to comprehend in one glance, and the mountains rising above the summer mist add a breathless unreality to the humanized landscape below. It is hard to believe that a traveler, standing at such a viewpoint a hundred years ago, would see only a forest clearing instead of the settled city that celebrated its first centennial in 1952.

Though it is but a young city, Portland feels old-established, perhaps because the first settlers, the British and later the New Englanders, brought a sense of continuity and love of gardens with them, or perhaps because the mountains impart a sense of unhurried timelessness.

It is in character with this unassertive home-loving city that both its name and renown came haphazard and unsought. The name of Portland was determined by the mere toss of a coin. The proud title "City of Roses" was given by early travelers who were impressed by Portlanders' habit of growing roses along the streets, between the sidewalk and the highway. At the turn of the century there were miles of roses, mostly the old pink Caroline Testout rose, but today the automobile has pushed the rose bush from the downtown sections, so that you are not immediately aware that Portland is either rose-loving or rose-growing. But you have only to go north, south, east, and west into the slower moving residential areas to know that Portland is still fundamentally a city of roses.

Roses are part of Portland's life. The Portland Rose Society first staged its annual show in June, 1889, the city its first annual rose carnival in 1907. Five years later, one hundred business and professional men, The Royal Rosarians, pledged themselves to love and cultivate the rose, and it is they who represent Portland during the rose festival week.

"Caroline Testout" is Portland's official rose. The French hybridizer Joseph Pernet-Ducher of Venessleux, France, introduced Caroline Testout around 1890 and regarded her somewhat as a Cinderella. But a London dressmaker, liking Caroline, paid Pernet-Ducher a better price than he thought his Cinderella would bring him, and used the rose for a publicity show. Pernet-Ducher lived long enough to know that the dressmaker had a better eye than he for a winner; he died in 1928 knowing that his Caroline had long since been Portland's favorite rose, that through her, more than any other rose, Portland was dubbed the City of Roses.

It was June and the week before Rose Festival Week when I arrived. And because I was there without "former friends in the Portland area" as Robert Pyle put it, he had issued one of his occasional visas. He wrote to Mr. Fred Edmunds, who had just retired as Curator of the City Park Rose Garden, asking him to help me get any information I might want. And Mr. Edmunds forwarded the letter to

that year's President of the Portland Rose Society, Dr. Mar-
lowe Dittebrandt, a young woman doctor. The incredible
happened. The Rose Society asked me to be their guest
during my two weeks' stay, the Rosarians and their wives or-
ganized all my sightseeing days, and Mr. Ferd Edmunds
undertook to put me rose-wise in the Portland area.

The name Fred Edmunds was legend among rosarians
long before he relinquished the curatorship of the City Park
Rose Gardens and the International Rose Test Gardens.
His long life has been spent, for the most part, with roses,
and he has stored up in his head more history and anecdotes
about roses and hybridizers than probably any other man.

A long way back he worked as an apprentice for the
famous old English firm, Cant of Colchester. The highlight
of that apprenticeship was the day he worked from three
o'clock one afternoon until one o'clock in the morning, with
only a cup of coffee to keep him going, staging seventy-five
different varieties of roses for the Crystal Palace flower show
in 1887, the year of Queen Victoria's Diamond Jubilee.

Three years later he came to America. He fought in the
Spanish war in the Philippines; once he was in the jungle
eighty days and the clothes rotted off his back. Then, as
contrast, he went to Alaska where he built greenhouses and
raised vegetables, and was doing very nicely there until he
went to look for gold.

Fred had taken on an apprentice, but the lad's heart was
not in vegetables. He wanted adventure, gold-seeking adventure, and he left his pack with Fred and went north. In
six weeks he was back.

"What, back already?" Fred asked him. "Tired of gold?
Is it vegetables after all?"

"No," the boy threw back his shoulders, tipped the cap

back off his head. "I promised Mom that when I'd made
$10,000 I'd go straight back home, and that's where I'm go-
ing now, straight back to Mom." He had chalked his name
on a stake, and driven it firmly into the ground. A few
weeks later a syndicate had bought out all the stake holders
at $10,000 a piece.

It was too much for Fred. He abandoned his glasshouses
and went to look for gold too. He lived in the Arctic for
years, snowed in sometimes for all but two months of the
year. He lost what he had made. Worse still, he lost his
health and came back to the United States a very sick man.

"Mother," he nodded at Mrs. Edmunds, "she refused to
give me up when the doctors said I'd only a few months to
live. She kept me going, and she's kept me going ever since."

Finally Fred realized he must settle down, and he made
Portland his home, working first as a private gardener. When
his employer offered him a permanent position, Fred explained that he wanted to work for the City and had already
taken the civil-service examination. "Portland," he has said
to his employer, "will be here long after you and I are gone,
and I'd like to do something for the place."

Fred's work has become one of the crowning glories of
a rose-loving people. About 1925 he started to create an
immense terraced rose garden high above the city in Washington Park. When he retired as Curator in 1951 it was with
the knowledge that the Portland Rose Garden, which is
also one of the International Rose Test gardens, is now considered one of the world's finest civic rose gardens.

Looking back over his long years, Fred recalled for me
that Cant of Colchester had said in 1890 that Fred had
come into the rose business fifty years too late, that the new
roses being introduced at that time were nothing in com-

parison with the old ones; that the rose would go right out of fashion for a period unless the hybrid tea caught the public's fancy.

The hybrid tea won out and roses remained in fashion up to World War I when their popularity flagged. After that war the Pernetia strain, on account of its novelty, revived the rose fashion again. "Now we're back in the rut again. I don't think there is anything new enough today to be sufficiently worthwhile," said Fred, echoing, perhaps without realizing it, what Cant of Colchester had told him more than fifty years ago.

"It's just possible," he said after a few minutes reflection, "that Masquerade will do what the hybrid tea and the Pernetias did for roses. It's a new break, it's a novelty . . . it's just possible. Its chief virtue is that it improves and enriches with age. In youth it is pink turning to gold, finally to wine-red. It was found originally in an old Italian cemetery. I was asked to think of a good name. I thought of Pinoccio, the clown, Harlequin dress you know, and then it came to me—Masquerade."

Later, in his own garden, Fred showed me "Garten Direktor." Otto Ninnie was its original name, a small double pink bush rose smothered in long sprays of bloom. Niedermeyer had once said to him: "Give me a rose that blooms throughout the summer, that is completely disease free, that will grow from a slip put in the ground by a woman—then name it for me." It held its place in Fred's garden in company with two other favorites, the white climbing City of York, and the rich red, deeply fragrant rose, Mrs. Miniver.

Fred's son, Freddie, was with us. He, too, had grown up with roses, and today has his own nursery. "Tell me," I asked him, "when you look at roses, can you ever look with the amateur eye now, instead of with the professional's criticism?"

"Yes," he gave his big wide smile, "but it's not always easy. When you cease to look as an amateur, you know, you are lost. It isn't fun any more."

Rose Festival Week opened the day before the Parade. It was a simple opening ceremony. The Rosarians in their white suits, white boaters, and white gloves accompanied the Rose Queen and her Maids of Honor. Visiting rose celebrities were "knighted" according to custom. The President, Dr. Dittebrandt, made a short speech:

"Do not forget the rose itself among all our festivities, for it is the flower which is the symbol of this city and the center of our carnival. Grow roses. Cherish them."

From the steps leading into the auditorium a baritone's voice carried over the crowd, and trailed away between the avenues of trees:

> Only a rose I give you
> Only a song dying away
> Only a smile to keep in your memory
> Until we meet—another day

To put that down now, in cold print, sounds absurdly sentimental. At the time it was moving. The crowd stood motionless, hushed into silence. Then another Rose Festival Week had begun and everyone streamed into the auditorium to see the roses on show.

There were many old friends among the present-day rose socialities: Crimson Glory and Ami Quinard; Paul's Scarlet and Geranium Red; Mrs. Sam McGreedy, and Mc-Greedy's Ivory; President Hoover, the Duquesa de Pena-randa, and the Doctor. The rose Fred Edmunds, of a wonderful golden orange flame, was among the finest exhibits.

And there was dear old Caroline Testout, represented by but two single and rather poor entries. If she were not Portland's official rose, Caroline would probably not have been there at all. As rose fashions go, Caroline Testout is an old lady, about sixty years old. Yet among all the varieties I saw that day I could think of no other rose as suitable or as lovely for officialdom as Caroline. She is staunch and faithful, blooming profusely year after year even when utterly neglected, and possesses a stamina that is lacking in many a more modern-day rose.

An elderly man, who paused to look at the two roses, touched his wife on the arm. "My mother grew those fifty years ago," he said musingly. Another couple were at variance as they, too, stood there.

"You pride yourself on this old rose," the woman said peevishly, comparing the roses of Portland disadvantageously with those of her native California. Her husband, no doubt used to the comparisons, let the argument rest.

"I can't think," his wife went on, "why no one ever grows La France. There's a rose for you now, La France." He could so easily have retaliated, though probably he would not have thought it worthwhile. There is no wide difference between La France and Caroline. La France is more pointed, more silvery-pink in bloom; Caroline has deeper color and is more cabbage-minded; that is all.

That evening the Portland Rose Society gave their annual banquet. The "guests of honor" lined up as members of the Society came in, and as there was nowhere else to stand, I stood with them. A woman carrying what was obviously a great paper-wrapped bouquet over her arm, murmured something about a guest of honor. I tried to explain as she passed up the line that I just happened to be there. Then, when everyone had found their places I slipped into the seat Mr. and Mrs. Edmunds had kept for me.

There was a momentary sense of waiting. I looked up. Reluctantly and as quickly as possible, I slipped into the empty seat at the high table to which I was beckoned. I caught a comment on my way up: "That's she, I might have guessed from her accent." My heart sank for the second time. Were the Rose Society going to spring another surprise? By the time we had reached the ice-cream stage my fears had disappeared. It was nice of them, I thought, to have me seated there among the rose celebrities from all over the continent. But I did not belong, and it would have been so much easier to sit with the Edmunds.

The speeches began. I heard the President imitate the English accent. The rest of the speech was lost to me; I knew then I was doomed.

Mrs. Zimmerman of the Women's Advertising Club of Portland rose in purposeful manner, carrying an enormous bouquet of roses—she had taken the wrapping off. More reluctantly than ever I obeyed her beckoning, and followed her to the center of the table.

"R.P." I thought—that was how I now spoke of Robert Pyle—"what am I going to do? You let me in for all this, and now I've got to say something that won't let you down. I would not be here as guest if you hadn't issued that visa."

I pulled my mind together. None of this, I reasoned, had anything to do with me personally. If they asked me to speak it was because they wanted to hear what I would say. I couldn't let them down any more than Robert Pyle. What could I, an amateur, say among the professionals? I wasn't smart enough to say a thing I did not mean.

Mrs. Zimmerman made a long speech; most of it was lost

to me. My mind swam. I looked at the roses. I tried to smile but the smile seemed to freeze on me. Everyone appeared to be listening intently. I could pick out the faces I knew, of rosarians I had known in the East. Then Mrs. Zimmerman was speaking to me and not to them.

"We have the great honor of making you a life member of the Mystic Order of the Rose on one condition. Will you raise your right hand? Will you, when you speak of Portland, always say: 'Portland, the City of Roses?' "

"Yes," I said firmly. "Yes, most certainly I will." And the guests relaxed; there was a smiling stir and they did not appear quite so serious any more. Suddenly I knew that I was among friends, and I was speaking to them:

"My American adventure is a series of surprises, and each surprise is more surprising than the last. How could I guess, when I first came to America through the rose man in the East, that a year apart in time, and three thousand miles in distance, east to west, I should come into this rose world of such kindness and hospitality . . .

"Dean Collins the other day wrote in his column that other American cities vied for the title City of Roses. Portland has never asked, she has never tried to compete for the title, which was given to her freely, long ago. The world over she was known as the City of Roses, and she gave a simple and characteristically generous reply: 'For you a Rose in Portland Grows.'

"Months ago when I sketched the outline of my journey on the map I wrote that phrase down on my itinerary instead of the word Portland. I could not possibly imagine a slogan would ring so true. You have given me not one, but many roses, and for this beautiful bouquet you have given me tonight I thank you with all my heart."

I sat down. Was it all right, R.P.? I remembered the rose Mrs. Miniver that I was wearing as Fred Edmunds' gift. Mrs. Miniver would have known exactly what to say.

The theme of that year's Rose Parade was "Do you Remember?" I walked among the floats during the judging, and almost all of them were strikingly beautiful. The designs were less ambitious, and for that reason more pleasing, than those at the Pasadena Parade in California, but the effect was just as successful. There was exquisite workmanship and close attention to detail.

The Firemens' float, apart from a few white pinks, was made entirely of dark red roses. Another signed its signature "The Story Book Hour" in white marguerites and shell-pink peonies. My choice was a float depicting the horse-and-buggy days. The coach itself was of red roses lined with white peonies, the roof and side supports of sweet williams to match. There were red roses for wheels, and white sweet williams for the supporting spokes. The entire base of the float was also red roses, thousands and thousands of them, and the horse of white sweet williams was driven with a bright red-rose harness.

It was all over by mid-day, hours and hours of work that must have rivaled Fred Edmunds' staging at Queen Victoria's Jubilee.

"You will remember?" someone asked me next day as I left to go farther north. "Yes, I'll remember. One day I'm sure I'll be back."

The Story Book Hour was over.

21 ❧❧ Forestland's Gardens

THE most outstanding gardens of the Northwest are those of Portland, Oregon, and of Olympia and Seattle, Washington. They share common characteristics in design and plant material, yet have distinct differences. Their climates vary to a surprising degree, though the distance between Portland and Seattle, with Olympia about midway between, is only 184 miles.

"In a sense you have come home," a Seattle gardener said to me, leaning on his spade as he stopped to talk. "I mean," he continued, "you must have the same climate and plants in England as we have here."

In many respects that is true. Broadly speaking, the climate is similar to that of southern England. Over the last thirty years the average rainfall in Seattle has been 31.8 inches; at Kew, England, over a corresponding period, 23.8

223

inches. But England has a relatively high rainfall through-out the summer, which allows the gardener to keep an al-most permanently green lawn without the aid of sprinklers. Seattle's heaviest rainfall occurs in the winter months, and, after July fourth, the summer as a rule is reliably warm and dry.

There is also an important climatic difference in frost dates. England's first killing frost usually falls in October, not infrequently in September; in Seattle it falls usually the last week in November. And the last killing spring frost in England is usually late April, not infrequently late May; in Seattle frost is rare after April.

Olympia, sixty-two miles south-west of Seattle by road and considerably less as the crow flies, is one of the wettest cities of the Northwest, with an annual rainfall of 51 inches. July and August are counted as the "dry" months with an average of less than an inch rainfall per month.

Portland's climate is less favorable than Seattle's, even for roses. The winters are more severe, the summers are hotter. The east wind strikes down the Columbia gorge, and there is no surrounding water to keep the summer nights cool, though the days generally are temperate.

Weather, however, is always unpredictable. The North-west will long remember, as the great freeze, the early November night, 1955, when there was a frost of 20 degrees. Olympia came off lightest. Seattle gardens were harder hit than those of Portland. In Seattle's Washington Arboretum, twelve hundred rhododendrons alone were killed, and hardly a flowering cherry escaped death or serious injury.

Portland was settled by the British and New Englanders. This basic ingredient, added to a favorable garden climate and a superb native flora, have, I believe, made Portland the most garden-minded city in North America. In almost every American community you see some people, trowel in hand, working away at their gardens, but in Portland they are more the rule than the exception. I saw more home gardeners in Portland than anywhere else. The City of Roses is also a rhododendron, iris, and a primula stronghold—as Fred Edmunds said, there were indications that roses were losing some of their overwhelming popularity.

In any community of plantsmen there are inevitably some amateurs and professionals who, in one direction or another, make their influence felt. John Grant, when he lived in Portland, appreciably influenced the design and planting of northwestern gardens in recent years. His *Trees and Shrubs for Pacific Northwest Gardens* is a well-thumbed guide book and has a place on many a gardener's shelf.

Portland's gardeners wanted something new and easy of maintenance. They had a liking for a touch of Japanese- and California-type gardens, but wished to keep the soft informality of the English garden without the romanticism of the Orient. John Grant's ideas fitted their need. His aim was two-fold. He sought to develop an American garden of independent design, one that broke from the European tradition. Too, he wanted people to become aware of the texture, height, and color of their native evergreens, and of those from other countries with similar climatic conditions. The Asiatics proved acceptable to this trend, and were remarkably adaptable to the northwestern climate. With such material John Grant created a garden room that was a pleasant place for relaxation in summer, and an attractively furnished room in winter. He avoided the cover-up, disused drawing-room effect that herbaceous borders, formal beds, and rose plantings so often leave behind them after their summer bloom.

Further, Grant made Northwest gardeners more aware of
the horticultural value of their native plant material. Three
plants which delighted pioneer plant collectors are today
used widely as the basic semi-permanent garden structure:
salal, *Gaultheria shallon,* the first plant which David Douglas
gathered when he landed at Fort Vancouver; the Oregon
grape, *Mahonia aquifolium,* which Lewis and Clark discovered, and the evergreen huckleberry *Vaccinium ovatum,*
first found by Archibald Menzies growing in abundance
along Hood's Canal.

Around this trinity of evergreens, all inhabitants of the
lower forested regions, gardeners now build upwards to
the native azaleas and rhododendrons, to the hawthorns and
crab apples, the dogwoods and the madrones, and down-
wards to ground covers of kinnikinnick and pasthendra.
These are predominant Northwest garden fundamentals.

The Asiatic bamboo and the mountain laurel of the eastern states blend with the rhododendrons and azaleas. Yellow
wood from the Carolinas, magnolias from the American
South and Asia, the Eastern and the Kornusa dogwood,
merge with the Western dogwood and the madrones.
Primulas, auriculas, and polyanthus enjoy the same shade
and filtered sunlight as the ferns, the Western trillium, and
the starry Solomon's plume of the far western forest. The
amateur would find it hard to know which of the beardless
iris are native, and which are hybrid or alien. The list is
endless.

Both in Portland and Seattle long-established gardens are
generally still markedly English in design and planting. But
in the more recent plannings, the American garden of independent design is strikingly apparent.

Mr. Peter Kerr's magnificent garden in Portland was

easily among the most outstanding of the older gardens that I saw in the Northwest. As I looked at the grey stone house across the lawn with the trees and the Willamette River beyond, a cock pheasant crowed from the woods above. For a moment the scene took me back to a garden in Scotland's Invernesshire. Aubretia and thrift, dwarf blue campanulas, and creeping thymes shared the rockery with the rarities. Along the stream were lily of the valley, auriculas and polyanthus, and the native English primrose beneath the Solomon's seal.

Mr. Kerr, a green-fingered Scotsman, proved to be also a plant connoisseur. Rare plants and shrubs were blended among the old favorites. A magnolia enthusiast, Mr. Kerr could say like Thomas Jefferson that though he was an old man, he was still a young gardener. He was then ninety-five, and still planting magnolias, which he expected to live to see in flower.

Mrs. A. C. U. Berry is another Portland plant connoisseur. Well-known as a grower of American alpines and rare plants from all over the world, her collection of primulas and rare rock plants was probably unmatched throughout the United States. In addition, she had something like ten thousand rhododendrons in her ten-acre woodland garden.

Rhododendrons are fast becoming as widely used by Portlanders as roses. The new Experimental Garden of the Rhododendron Society of America is another example of the city's garden-mindedness. The Society plans and organizes the garden, and supplies the plants; the City of Portland furnishes the labor.

John Grant's influence was plainly evident in Mrs. Hoffman's garden, eleven hundred feet above the city on a bluff of land with tremendous views. It was as fine a setting,

among many superb sites, as any landscape gardener could
hope to find. The plateau-like expanse gave me the impression of standing on the deck of an aircraft carrier from which
I looked down through the fir trees to the Willamette River
and the mighty Columbia beyond, and across the city and
the foothills with the snowcaps of Mount Hood and Mount
St. Helen's floating like icebergs above the summer haze.
Native plants were widely used in Mrs. Hoffman's planting,
the fragrant western azalea predominating; they grew as
big bushes along the crest of the bluff, and massed along
both sides of the winding driveway leading up to the house.

John Grant loved the azalea. It was, he said, breathtak-
ingly beautiful to see the western azalea flowering among the
ceanothus and huckleberry along the Oregon coast, "a sight
never to be forgotten." That is without question. But it
struck me as characteristic for an Englishman to write the
words "never" and "forgotten," which are slightly negative,
reticent words, and convey a backward-looking implication.
Never and forgotten are leave-taking words, as are forever
and farewell. I would rather superimpose the words "ever"
and "remember" for a sight that is perennially beautiful and
constantly renewed. Certainly I shall remember the azalea
along the coastal road as John Grant saw it, and in this
garden in the sky which he once helped to make.

It would serve no purpose here to list garden after garden in Portland. Like the variety of plant material available to Northwesterners, the list would be endless. So many
gardens were woodland gardens; so many others reminded
me of English gardens by their grass-mown apple orchards
and patches of tall grass where bulbs had flowered and now
might wither to harvest well later. Sometimes I saw the old
Scotch rose Max Graf, trailing along a garden fence, and

grown for association's sake as well as for its single pink
blooms and virtue of immunity from disease and blight.
Clematis, in many varieties, were among other Portland
preferences; pear and apple trees cordoned along grass-
pathed borders, and that old favorite of English gardens,
the Mrs. Sinkins' pink.

It may be mere chance that I saw more woodland gardens
in Portland than in Seattle, that I saw more stretches of
green lawns and massed borders of bloom in Seattle than in
Portland. But I have kept the impression that Portland was
more influenced by the forests, Seattle by the mountains.

In Seattle outcroppings of rock are a central feature of
many gardens; rock slopes as sidewalk boundaries are the
rule along many streets, planted for the most part with prostrate juniper, and yews, and other low-growing plants and
shrubs. Almost unfailingly there is heather. Perhaps this
wide use of heather was first inspired by some gardener
who discovered it does so well in the Northwest, or it may
be that the red and white so-called native heathers of the
mountain slopes inspired its wide use.

Apart from the climate, there was another reason for the
Seattle gardener to say that in a sense I had come home. In
the larger gardens of the two wealthy residential districts
—The Highlands, north of the city and among wooded hills
overlooking Puget Sound, and along Lake Washington Boulevard overlooking Washington Lake—the gardens are unmistakably English in character. This at first seems curious,
since, unlike Portland, there is little else about the city of
Seattle that is English. No doubt the Olmsted Brothers,
landscape architects of Boston, are responsible for this
anomaly. Almost before Seattle was an important city, the
Olmsteds urged that these two residential districts should

be reserved, and then set to work designing the English-type garden that dominates them.

The chief glories of these gardens are their magnificent herbaceous borders. In one I saw delphiniums nine feet tall growing beside the beautiful *Thalictrum dipterocarpum* with its four-to-five feet branching stems of rosy-lilac flowers and golden stamens. A long alley with lilac bushes on either side, and below them a broad planting of perennial mixed colored phlox, was another popular feature.

Each of the three cities I have named has, at least, one outstanding public garden—Portland, its Rose Garden; Seattle, the University of Washington's Arboretum, and Olympia its fifty-five-acre Capitol Gardens.

The Arboretum in Seattle is nearly a quarter of a century old. Brian Mulligan, formerly Assistant Director of the Royal Horticultural Society's garden at Wisley, England, has been its Director for ten years. He and his wife Margaret are both plantsmen at heart, spending their spare time in the mountains, plant hunting and collecting seeds for the International Exchange. Seattle gardeners regard this Arboretum as their own, and there is little doubt that John Grant's prediction for its future will come true. As it develops, he said, it will "inevitably become the backbone of horticultural achievement in the Pacific Northwest."

Little Olympia has just one great garden. Like so many American capitol cities, it is a modest, unassuming place, more a town than a city. Although transversed by the ever-crowded northern route, Highway 99, it is an otherwise unspoiled old-time town, and has as neat a collection of simple white-boarded houses, trim lawns and little gardens, and tree-lined streets as any town in the Northwest. But the fifty-five-acre garden around the State Capitol buildings,

high on the bluff of Budd Inlet at the southern extremity of
Puget Sound, is, in the opinion of many, the most beautiful
Capitol garden, if not the finest of all public gardens, in the
United States. With this I entirely agree.

Oddly enough, however, this Capitol garden has had no
publicized acclaim, partly because Olympia, as a tourist
center, cannot compete with Seattle, and partly because Mr.
Albert E. Hart, the garden superintendent, is a very modest
man. English-born, he served his apprenticeship like his
father before him, as gardener's boy and then as working gardener on several large estates. In 1911, he left England for
Canada. Eventually, at the famous Butchart Gardens near
Victoria, Vancouver Island, he absorbed, or rather added,
an extraordinary sense of flower color-blending. In this
few men can count themselves his equal.

In 1930 Albert Hart had a real break; he seized the golden
chance with both hands, using his stored-up experience to
create, as a painter with his palette, the master flower-piece
of his dreams. He had by then left Canada to try his hand in
the United States, and was working as gardener to Mrs.
Chester Thorne, the owner of a twenty-five-acre garden
within one hundred-acre estate at American Lake, Tacoma,
Washington. It was the year of the Garden Club of America's Convention in Seattle and a visit to Mrs. Thorne's garden was on their program. She gave her gardener the responsibility of doing his best to make the garden a show-piece
in honor of the event, and trusted him with a blank check.

With his English training to do every detail of his work
"right," and not simply strive to make just one momentarily
stunning effect; with the memory of the massed herbaceous
borders of his youth; with the sight of pastel-colored flowers
which are used so lavishly at the Butchart Gardens and

which thrive so abundantly in Canada and the Northwest, fresh in his mind, he brought Mrs. Thorne's garden to its all-time perfection in mid-July.

He has kept no clippings of the acclaim that garden won. It was enough for him that he not only met but exceeded Mrs. Thorne's shrewd value of her blank check. But in the yellowed pages of the old *Tacoma News Tribune* there is a record of The Garden Club of America's appraisal. The members judged the garden as "the most beautiful garden of any they have visited during their tour of America and England," and added "this is the only garden for which the group expressed any special preference." That, in itself, was an unusual and extraordinary tribute.

The garden at American Lake is no more. But the Capitol Gardens at Olympia are a reproduction and a further development of Albert Hart's garden art. For the last sixteen years he has been Olympia's master gardener.

Since my first visit to Olympia, I have spent the months of April through to September close by his garden. People have told me that whatever the frost, whatever the wind, and whatever the rain, the garden is always as I saw it—a perennial sight of spring to summer-long bloom.

Even a casual garden sightseer will notice some features of Albert Hart's skill: the succession and continuity of bloom; the range and harmony of his color effects; the fragrance that pervades the walks, and the overall careful upkeep which gives the impression of a well-tended private garden; a natural formality without any deliberate overgrooming.

Towards the end of April the double pink Japanese cherry trees are in full bloom, and avenue of some thirty trees which rival in beauty the cherry trees along the Potomac in

Washington. No sooner have they faded than the massed plantings of rhododendrons and azaleas come into bloom and the garden is filled with pungent azalea fragrance, and the sweet daphne Somerset.

Some fifty thousand annuals are raised to fill scores of flower beds. The second and third weeks of May is the great annual planting-out time. This follows no fixed drawn-up plan. As Albert Hart draws out a circle here and there on the bare, well-dug earth for his men to plant a clump of this or that, he already sees with his mind's eye the color that the public will see in two to three months' time.

Highlight plantings include two large herbaceous borders and the Sunken Garden. At least a third of his great perennial borders are given to the gap-filling annuals. One border, about two hundred feet long, faces east and marks the tree-backed boundary from the Governor's Mansion to the bluff above the Sound; it is known as the yellow border. As its name implies, the effect is predominately yellow and is attained by using simple flowers—sunflowers, marigolds of all kinds with wide patches of white, chiefly white phlox. There is a contrasting touch of zinnia red and a mist of blue sage, which serves to underscore the predominating white and yellow and the green of lawn and evergreen trees. Such restraint and narrow choice of color is both highly effective and restful.

The west border, in quite another part of the grounds, runs through the gamut of pastel colors for its entire 220 feet, and is the finest herbaceous border I have seen anywhere across the American continent. But it is the Sunken Garden that is the center of attraction throughout the summer; people crowd to it as the bees crowd to the flowers.

This garden, which measures some one hundred and fifty

by one hundred feet, contains a dozen flower beds around a central oblong bed of roses and is surrounded by narrow rose borders, raised to a gentle slope. Already by the end of May, and through June, it is a rose and delphinium garden. The two- to three-year–old delphinium plants bloom early and last until the other perennials take over at the beginning of July.

The Sunken Garden comes to its full height of bloom towards the end of July and the flowers, a vibrant pool of color in the surrounding green lawns, last until the summer draws to a close. There are four large beds, the larger two sixty feet long and fifteen feet wide, planted with perennials and annuals; eight smaller beds are planted with annuals only.

A close examination of one of the larger semi-permanent beds shows that roughly two-thirds is planted with perennials, about a third with annuals. The delicate lavender-flowered *Thalictrum dipterocarpum,* purple lythreum, *Campanula lactaflora* and a variety of widely planted phlox are the perennial backgrounds; the foreground is built up from the grass edge with such annuals as pink verbena, schianthus, cherry pie or heliotrope, pink and salmon-colored snapdragons, blue statice, and Dianthus var. Gaiety. Taller annuals blend in height with the low-growing annuals and the tall background perennials: salphiglossis, rose mallow, spider flower, and annual phlox in great variety of color. Deep salmon-pink to cerise, mauve, blue and white phlox, both perennial and annual forms, form the body of these beds. The smaller annual beds, low and medium in height, carry out the same color schemes and are planted with the same kinds of annual plants.

Elsewhere there are many other details to delight the eye

in this fifty-five-acre garden, which Albert Hart, with nine-teen men to help him, maintains. The lawns, which get ten tons of fertilizer each spring and a generous all-year long supply of water—they are irrigated daily during summer—are magnificent. Occasionally you see people stroll across them, for there are no notices saying "Keep Off the Grass," but the paths are so practically laid out that people, for the most part, let the grass stay untrodden.

Here and there the old influence of the great era of bed-ding plants shows itself, and happily, as it does in the gar-dens of Vancouver Island and some European city parks. There is a walk lined with the annual multi-colored dahlias, bordered with the misty blue ageratum, a large circular bed of red and white geraniums, planted in pin-wheel strips with a surrounding band of the light-spraying anagalis, the bright blue version of the scarlet pimpernel. The long flight of narrow steps leading up to the Governor's Mansion is gay in spring with pink tulips and forget-me-nots, and later with bright pink geraniums. There is a separate rose garden, a fine collection of the great and fragrant tree-peonies.

And lastly, only because it is the last border to come into its full glory, there is a narrow roadside border ninety by eighteen feet that is planted entirely with the pink verbena Helen Wilmott with white, blue, and mauve delphiniums. There are delphinium seedlings, sturdy plants, bearing five- to six-feet spikes of bloom above the broad band of pink verbenas at their feet. This border illustrates another flair of this master gardener, Albert Hart, his flair for matching his garden plantings to their background. The border is situated at the edge of the bluff, where the land drops abruptly away to the wide view of Budd Inlet, with its sawmills, floating timber logs, the freighters and the wharves, and in the dis-

tance the forested foothills and the cloud-capped Olympic
Mountains. Towards the end of July and into August you
see the tall spires of delphinium in outline against this view.

As I write with enthusiasm of gardens such as these, I
must admit to an unreserved preference for the gardens of
the Pacific Northwest. It may be that my eyes, long-accus-
tomed to the soft light and mists that England shares with
this part of the United States, find the paler colors and the
greenness the most pleasing; or it may be that I share my
national preference for an unobtrusive and natural beauty
rather than an artificial and spectacular display.

However individual preferences may run, there is no
denying that the gardeners of the Pacific Northwest are fully
aware of their natural advantages. Their climate is the best
gardening climate in America. They have at hand plant
material of exceptional horticultural value which they not
only appreciate but know how to use. They have everywhere
around them some of the most beautiful scenery in all of
North America: mighty rivers, lakes and land-locked harbors,
forested foothills, and a string of snow-capped extinct vol-
canoes which can be seen, on clear days, from hundreds of
miles away, rising in splendid isolation to dominate the
surrounding land. They are gardeners who have matched
their gardens to their setting, and are the most naturally
minded gardeners in the United States.

22 Bulbs by Beaver Dams

THE Northwest, as may be expected in such garden strongholds as Portland and Seattle, can boast of many outstanding plantsmen. The area has maintained its tradition of the early pioneering collectors, and is also the stage of revolutionary hybridizing.

Sleepy Hollow, the home of Mr. and Mrs. John Leach, a mile or so outside Portland, is a contemporary botanists' landmark. It contains Mrs. Leach's collection of six thousand plant specimens that she and her husband have collected. In the five-acre woodland garden which they made together, the water from the foothills of Mt. Hood flows down between steep banks along Johnson Creek to join the Willamette and Columbia rivers. Where the beaver still has his dam, they have planted about three thousand plant varieties which include rare native plants and other unusual ornamentals.

239

Many botanists in recent years have found new species, but few find a new genus. Lilla Leach has to her credit the discovery of fifteen species and varieties formerly unknown to science, and two new genera: *Bensonia oregona* and the now famous *Kalmiopsis leachiana,* which is named for her. Among the new species she collected, gardeners will probably name the golden iris *Iris innominata* as her choicest find —the "unknown iris" as it is commonly called, because it is the first new iris to be found on the Pacific coast since David Douglas' picked the lovely, widespread *Iris tenax.*

Raised on a stock farm in western Oregon, Lilla Leach rode horses from childhood, was a successful student and, later, teacher, of botany. John Leach, the pharmacist, is not a botanist, but a country man. He, too, was raised on a stock farm, in eastern Oregon, and at an early age learned to throw the diamond hitch and become mountainwise. Since their early married years John and Lilla Leach have shared a partnership of interests, making their garden and exploring the comparatively unknown regions of Oregon together.

Year after year in the long spring and summer vacations they set out in search of plants. During those first years they collected in places within auto-reach. Such territories yielded few new plants, having been too well worked by earlier collectors. So the Leaches decided to change their course, and penetrated into the interior of Curry, Josephine, and Douglas counties, along trails where only a few trappers, forest rangers, and prospectors had made their way.

For nine summers they "wandered," as they describe their plant-hunting holidays, across the lonely, unnamed, and unmapped territory of southwest Oregon. Two faithful companions, Pansy and Violet, their Mexican burros, accompanied them. From Sleepy Hollow, their first base, they

would set out with one burro in the trailer, to join the other
burro waiting for them at their second base. Pansy carried
the botany presses, Violet the axe, the food, cooking utensils,
and sleeping kit. Then all together they set out to explore.

All four have shared the discomforts and adventures common to all pioneering plantsmen. Mountain lions, or cougars
as they are commonly called in Oregon, would on occasion
lie in wait to attack the burros if they thought them unpro-
tected. Once Lilla shot a waiting cougar they surprised as it
bounded up a Douglas fir. John and Lilla Leach always felt
a responsibility in taking the burros from safe pastures,
especially because they could not share in the excitement of
plant discovery. But the burros could provide their own
entertainment, and once ate up John and Lilla's under-
clothes while they were swimming in a river.

The crossing of creeks and rivers was often hazardous.
Burros, being desert animals, are unused to water; even a
few inches will scare them, and ordinarily when forced into
deep water they will go into a spasm and drown. Pansy and
Violet were different. Although they always needed a push-
ing-pulling persuasion and sometimes argument, they tried,
terrified as they were, to swim.

Deft negotiation was needed to cross the larger rivers,
with John paddling an Indian canoe and Lilla holding the
burros' heads out of water with a tow rope. When no canoe
was available, they used their air mattresses to buoy the
burros up. Once Pansy slipped on a boulder and went down
a swift stream, rolling over and over until John lassoed her
and pulled her to the shore. Drying her soaked load was but
a small matter compared with what might have been a total
loss of both beast and burden.

On a hot day in the middle of June, 1930, fatigued towards the end of a long plant-hunting day, they came out of the forest on to an arid and seemingly flowerless ridge. "And there," Lilla Leach recounts, "before us, beside the trail, lay a patch of low bushlets, evergreen, profusely covered with deep rose flowers, vivid beyond description in the sunshine. Were we thrilled? We forgot how tired we had been. It looked a good deal like *Kalmia polifolia,* but it wasn't. I thought it might be a new kalmia."

It needs an expert among even expert botanists to classify correctly. Kalmiopsis, though neither a rhododendron nor a kalmia, but resembling both, was first considered to be a member of the rhododendron genus. Dr. Alfred Rehder, writing in the Journal of the Arnold Arboretum, gave the shrub its formal botanical christening, naming it *Kalmiopsis leachiana,* with the following explanation:

> The discovery in Oregon by Mr. and Mrs. Leach of a new ericaceous shrub, subsequently described . . . as *Rhododendron leachianum* is highly interesting, particularly as this shrub turns out to be a new genus related to *Loiseleuria* and *Kalmia* and also to *Kalmia polifolia Waugenh.*

It was also Dr. Rehder who suggested that steps be taken to reserve the forest section, the only place in the world where the scarce and rare plant lives. Today there is a Kalmiopsis Wild Area which no road will ever cross, 320 acres of private land and 78,530 acres of national forest land which the United States Forest Service has set aside to preserve the shrub in its native wildness.

This is all the more important since kalmiopsis is not easy to propagate. Even Mrs. Leach with her green thumb had difficulty in finding the shrub's exact requirements in her garden—slight shade with perfect drainage. Ironically, it first flowered in cultivation at Kew in England, winning the

Award of Merit of the Royal Horticultural Society a year
or more before Mrs. Leach herself succeeded in flowering it
in her garden at Sleepy Hollow.

Of all the rewards that have come her way, Lilla Leach
undoubtedly counts as greatest among them her discovery
of the Unknown Iris and Leach's kalmia—the one scattering
its typical golden blooms, the other making low single
masses of brilliant carmine deep in the fastness of southwest
Oregon's wild mountainous forest country.

In the extraordinary story of American lily hybridization,
Jan de Graaff is the star lily builder. He comes of ten generations of De Graaffs in Holland, a family that has been foremost among Holland's famous bulb growers for two and a
half centuries. Gardeners instantly recognize the name, for
daffodils and De Graaff are practically synonymous; it was
Jan de Graaff's grandfather who raised the famous daffodil
that bears the family name. As his grandfather once pioneered in daffodils, Jan de Graaff has pioneered in lilies.

He was trained for diplomatic work, since his elders
thought it time to introduce a new interest into the family.
But Jan thought otherwise. He returned home, worked in
the bulb industry, then packed his bag and sailed for the
United States.

The story of the Oregon Bulb Farms is the story of this
tenth generation De Graaff in the New World. In New York
he met a group of agricultural college professors who wanted
to go into the bulb-growing business in Oregon. He persuaded his family in Holland to invest in the venture and to
give the new growers a start with their breeding stock. But
the professors, experts in horticulture, were not business
men, and Jan took over the Oregon farm to get the family's
money out.

With the use of labor-saving machinery which he adapted and sometimes invented, by breaking away from the old by-hand methods of planting and harvesting, Jan de Graaff soon had the farm a going concern. From time to time the Old World De Graaffs came to see how he was getting on, and they were shocked by his new-fangled methods to speed up bulb production. In 1934, the family agreed to sell out its entire interest to Jan, who then took out American citizenship, married an American and started out on his own. Today, the Oregon Bulb Farms is one of the nation's largest bulb-producing farms and famous for its lilies, daffodils, and other ·bulbs.

As a hybridizer, Jan de Graaff has blended the qualities of European and American plantsmen. He still has a great respect for what he calls the Old World viewpoint, and maintains that the Europeans are still masters in originating new varieties, which takes time as well as skill and patience. Americans, he says, don't have time.

Even by European standards it takes an extraordinarily long time to produce new and outstanding daffodils, tulips, and Dutch iris. What, wondered Jan de Graaff, the American rhythm now running in his blood, what flower could he renew and remodel in a lifetime?

Lilies were his choice. Lilies increase more rapidly than other bulbs. They not only bear pods of seeds that will grow into small bulbs in from two to four years, but often have bulblets at the bases of the main bulbs. Even a few scales from the main bulb itself will soon grow into small individual bulbs. Lilies, unlike most other bulbs never go wholly dormant, as Jan de Graaff often repeats: "Lilies never sleep."

Here then was his natural resource: as a stock market

phrase goes, lilies possess a tremendous potential for reproduction. For Jan de Graaff it was comparatively easy to find ways and means to develop this potential—his labor-saving machinery and his willingness to experiment in new growing methods enabled him to apply the methods of American mass-production. But this was not enough. He wanted new lilies, and also to do what had not been done before: combine mass-hybridization with mass-production. To accomplish the dual fact he had first to do what other lily hybridists had long been trying to do, break through the so-called sterility barrier in certain lily species.

Jan de Graaff told me the story of the development of his rejuvenated Madonna lilies when I went to the bulb farms high up above the great horseshoe bend where the Sandy and the Bullrun rivers meet, encircling the dense coniferous surrounding forests. It is one of the strangest stories of twentieth century plant hybridization. As we sat sipping mint juleps I wondered whether I could be hearing the story aright, but it can be verified in detail in his *The New Book of Lilies.*

The Madonna lily, as many people know, is one of the oldest lilies in cultivation. It was the lily of the Crusaders, and of the Roman legionnaires who carried the bulbs to cleanse their wounds. But over the centuries it had grown soft and had lost some virtues, becoming weakened and disease-ridden. It had, moreover, been propagated so constantly by scales that it now resisted propagation by seed, which prevented hybridization.

Madonna lilies were Jan de Graaff's favorites. They were also the beloved flowers of Father Souillet, noted botanist and priest in a small French town near Paris. He, too, wanted to invigorate the lilies in his garden. So he brought

in fresh stock from old French gardens and some still growing wild in the mountains of Syria. But even these did not
give Father Souillet the hoped-for results, and he resorted
to the technique of mutilating the finest bulbs until they had
to seek other means of preserving themselves. They turned
into annuals and reverted to their old practice of setting
fertile seed.

In the fall of 1938 Jan obtained from Father Souillet his
secret and a generous packet of fertile Madonna lily seed.
By 1946–47, thanks to what he called Father Souillet's skill
and patience, Jan de Graaff had his first ten acres of seed-
producing, disease-resistant Madonna lilies in bloom. This
reborn, rejuvenated strain raised "in the shade of our beautiful Cascade Mountains," he called his *Cascade Hybrids*.

Since then Jan de Graaff has taken his Madonna lilies a
step further. He crossed them with other lilies, and thereby
raised a number of Madonna lilies in beautiful and various
colors. One result he had not bargained for was the public's
reluctance to accept readily the colored hybrids. People
had so long been accustomed to the pure white Madonna
lily that they were slow to associate or accept the colored
with the old white form.

The Madonna lily development was but one of De Graaff's
experiments. Far and wide he sought for fresh "lily blood"
that he might create new hybrids by intermingling the
members of the lily race in his mass-hybridization program:
scarlet martagons from Constantinople, candlesticks and
tigers from Japan, princess lilies from Tibet, regals from
China, and from nearer home the red-bell shaped Preston
Hybrids from Ontario, Canada, and the Bellinghams from
Puget Sound.

His book and the Oregon Bulb Farms' catalogues show
impressively how far Jan de Graff has succeeded in produc-

ing new and outstandingly beautiful lilies. They show also
that he believes in sharing his success; he keeps no secrets
and urges other lily enthusiasts to get into the game. Nor
does he fail to give full credit to other successful hybridists,
listing his own hybrids with a note on their history and
pedigree attached.

As we went out to walk over part of his land, Jan de
Graaff told me how he had come West as a young man, and
had stayed because he liked western living, the climate, and
the West's spaciousness and freedom. Fields of lilies were
coming into bloom. In the sheltered valley where he showed
me how the beavers had felled his trees along the stream,
the smoke burners were already at work in the afternoon
sunshine. It was a surprise to know that there was the pos-
sibility of frost damage so late as June.

We talked about gardens in America in a general sense.
On the whole, he considered the climate unfavorable; he
thought too that Americans are not so intuitively garden-
minded or flower-minded as the English or the Dutch. He
shrugged: "A garden is in a man's mind," he said.

He might have added that bulb raising and hybridizing
are in Jan de Graaffs' blood. The dividend that he makes
is far bigger than a mere dollar dividend. Raising new and
beautiful hybrids is not his only ambition. He is strictly a
wholesaler. Oregon Bulb Farms supply bulbs by the thousands to big mid-western firms and others who sell them to
home garden owners—bulbs at ten cents apiece, a price
within range of the humblest pocket. That is what he likes.
One of his aims is to produce plants, especially lilies, that
are as easy and reliable to grow prodigously as are tulips
and daffodils, plants that display their gay blooms afar.
And that, perhaps more than anything else, as he sees it, will
contribute to the making of a garden in many a man's mind.

23 *Mountains*

in

Flower

I CAME to Seattle desperately tired after my festive round in Portland. Now I had to earn quickly to buy my ticket east and buy time of my own so that I might see the mountains in flower between July and August.

My luck held. I had free hospitality in a house on Queen Anne Hill whose owner was away for the summer, and my room looked out over Eliot Bay to the city and the Cascades, and over Puget Sound to Mount Rainier. And I took the first job that offered, secretarial work in a city office. It wasn't very amusing.

"Kwitcherbellyaken." I had not used a dictaphone before, but fortunately the man who used it to dictate his letters had spelt out certain words which he thought I might not understand. Even so I ran the recorder back several times before I had the word "kwitcherbellyaken" right on paper,

and it took some more time to translate its meaning. Then
I had it. Although the word was not used in reference to me
but to one of the traveling salesmen who complained his
takings were only peanuts, it fitted my mood exactly. "Quit
your belly-aching." As the outdoors called every hour of my
office day, I would repeat the word to myself, again and
again, knowing that in due course the mountains would be
my reward.

The end of June gave me my first foretaste of the Cascades,
a Sunday with the Seattle Mountaineers on Sun Top. Spring
had fled the valleys weeks ago, but as we went up through
the forest the western trillium and the miniature dogwood,
Cornus canadensis, were in flower, and above the forest the
hillside was alight with the incadescent torch-like beargrass
blooms.

From Sun Top, a few of us made a dash to reach the
summit of the Chinook Pass before returning to Seattle. We
raced down the long hillside up which we had toiled so
slowly an hour before, leaping over the fallen logs where
the lumberjacks were at work, and soon were driving swiftly
up to the Pass.

We found the first Avalanche lilies, the yellow fawn lily
and the western anenome breaking into bloom at the edge
of the retreating snowbanks. In our excitement, we ran over
the soft snow to bend down and see them closely, and then
looked at the tremendous panorama of Cascade mountain
country all around us. We did not stay long. Thunder
rolled, lightning jagged the sky, and a hail storm broke
over our heads. The mountain gods had decided, so we
thought, that we had seen enough for one day. We obeyed,
leaving the high places for the lower slopes, winding down
and down, past foxgloves and columbine, tiger lilies and

ocean spray, and white fragrant mock-orange bushes that grew side by side with the brilliant scarlet-berried elder.

My Sunday on Sun Top was the prelude to my first Northwest camping weekend. In company with a few Alpine Society enthusiasts, Brian and Margaret Mulligan took me with them to Miller Creek. Sunday morning I woke early and stared up through the tall mountain firs above me. Then I turned over cautiously, relieved to find no sign of stiffness after the twelve-mile walk the previous afternoon, a brief training for Sunday's big climb.

The others stirred, too, and from the moment we emerged from our sleeping bags all was abustle. You do not linger in the crisp mountain air of early morning even in full summer. After a breakfast of freshly caught mountain trout, we set off.

The pace was brisk enough, but the flowers everywhere about us in the forest gave us legitimate excuses to pause for breath. We stopped to see the short standards of the bell-like pyrola blooms above their marbled leaves, and to smell the sweet-scented valerian and the minute shade-loving wood rose, *R. gymocarpa.* Once, we rested by a small mountain stream splashing its way down between the white thimbleberry, white *dodecatheon,* the holly fern, and the mountain rhododendron, *R. albiflorum.* We lay down, propping ourselves on the rocks to drink the white-green water as it tumbled down through the natural woodland garden.

Then on we went again, up and northwards. For upward travel here is ever northward travel, every hundred feet in altitude being equivalent to about sixty miles farther north in latitude. And by the same measurement, wild flowers bloom ten days later as every thousand feet in elevation is gained.

The forest began to thin. The lower alpine meadows filled the spaces in between, rank with grass, white orchids, and the magenta shooting star, *Dodecatheon Jeffreyi.* Maidenhair fern and elkslip marigold grew along the streams; ledum, the Labrador tea, was in full bushy cream-white bloom.

We had our lunch alongside a stream, sitting among bosses of the so-called white and red heathers. Far in the distance, Mount Rainier was a turbulent mass of snow and cloud; behind us the peaks of the Three Brothers thrust their jagged outlines above the surrounding snow-covered crests.

I forgot what George Kelly once had told me in Colorado. "Reach your objective first," he had counseled, "then eat lightly, and you'll make the trail down refreshed." I never gave a thought to that advice, sitting there by the stream among the flowers, and after my sandwiches I bent down and drank deeply from the mountain stream.

We were off again, crossing the valley to the lake that lay at the valley head and surrounded on three sides by the precipitous mountains. On a small peninsula, and close to a wide stretch of shooting stars, we found a mat of Alpine Laurel, the two-inch high miniature of Peter Kalm's Mountain Laurel of the eastern woods.

Would I ever remember all the names? Red heather, *Phyllodoce empetriformis;* white heather, *Cassiope Mertensiana;* Alpine Laurel, *Kalmia polifolia; var. microphylla?* They were what Lester Rowntree once called them, a lovely trio, and I tried to remember their names as she had told me, and not have to ask my companions so constantly what this flower, or that, was called.

Margaret, intent on her color slide, asked me:

"Would you mind holding my measure so that I can focus?"

"Phyllodoce, Cassiope, and Kalmia." I said aloud. She looked up, surprised, and then realized the effort I was making to memorize what she had told me at least twice before.

Brian was away ahead of us up at the mountain slope. We started up, passing clumps of false hellebore and a small pool like an English dewpond, which was entirely ringed with elk-slip marigold. We sat down a moment to watch him climb a white-barked pine to get the mahogany-red cones.

As we got up, I was stricken with an appalling stitch. I slowed up, dragging myself slowly and painfully inch by inch across a patch of snow and up the steep shale slope beyond. I remembered George Kelly's words then, too late. Even "Kwitcherbellyaken" lost its magic. Humiliated, I had to confess. I could not keep pace.

"You needn't worry," Margaret assured me, "we'd both much rather let the others get to the top while we stay longer here, photographing and collecting." But I wasn't comforted; it was the first time I failed to reach a given summit. However, there was compensation. Had we pressed on and upward we never could have stopped to enjoy the flowers as we did, nor let the sight of that mountain country absorb us.

We were no more than six thousand feet up, but it was high enough to level our eyes with the vast wilderness of the Cascades; mountain peaks and crags stretching into the distance as far as we could see. There were the natural rock gardens of the high places, where the yellow cinquefoil grew with the blue delphinium, where the penstemons and columbine reveled in the bare rocks and volcanic shale, and the diminutive mountain phlox poured out its heliotrope-like fragrance.

By the time we reached our camp again we had done about fifteen miles. The Mulligans still had go in them.

Brian made notes for later seed collecting; Margaret, of the photographs she had taken. I lay flat out on the ground, like a dog resting its head on its front paws after a long day's hunting. Some of those who had been with us had gone much farther. I raised my head to watch them as they came in, laggard; one, two, or three at a time, walking automatons, too tired to speak.

It was the end of my first camping weekend. When I was a child, people had smeared me with the otter's blood at the end of a hunt, and I had been given the otter's rudder to take home. Now I felt I had been initiated into the plantsmen's brief open season, when from mid-June to the end of August he hunts among the spring and summer flowers that crowd along the skyline. Instead of an otter's rudder, I took back with me from that weekend a mahogany-red cone from a white-barked pine.

A week later, I made my first trip to the Olympic Peninsula. In fact as well as in name it is The Last Frontier. To say that almost everything about the great area is unusual is sheer understatement. Climatically, geographically, and in many ways botanically, the peninsula is exceptional. It is almost an island, surrounded by the open sea, by the Strait of Juan de Fuca and the winding waterways of Puget Sound. One of the largest—as the crow flies, the peninsula is about 88 miles wide at its northern-most portion, and from 58 to 78 miles deep—for a little while longer it will also remain one of the least known of the primitive areas existing in the continental United States.

The west side of the peninsula is the wettest area in America. Moisture-laden winds of the Japanese current, pouring in from the Pacific, are deflected by the Olympic Mountains; the resulting rainfall reaches up to 140 inches a year in some places, and to much more in the high country, though mostly in the form of snow. The peninsula's east side lies in the so-called Olympic "rain-shadow," and by contrast, is the driest area on the West Coast outside southern California, and irrigation is necessary for farm crops.

This great land mass, with its crown of snow-capped mountain range, is girded with an almost unbelievable density of evergreen forests, and contains on the western slopes the greatest stand of coniferous timber in the world. In the lowlands of the western slope, the luxuriant Rain Forest, a phenomenon of the Temperate Zone, has produced the largest known individual specimens of Sitka spruce, Western hemlock, Douglas fir, and Western red cedar. Among the cedars a giant of sixty-six feet in girth, found in a wild and hitherto unchartered area, stood unmeasured until as late as 1954. These trees—except the Sitka spruce which prefers valleys—spread upward in company with Western white pine and Pacific silver fir. Near timber line the Alaska yellow cedar, the mountain hemlock, and the alpine fir predominate.

Timber line on the Olympic Peninsula has a measurement peculiarly its own. The Hudsonian Zone (as botanists call the higher forest levels where, in the upper reaches, the forest thins) becomes stunted and windswept; it is interspaced with open meadows and at timber line merges into the treeless, rugged, mountain Artic-Alphine Zone. The Hudsonian Zone in the Olympics has altitudinal limits only of about 3,500 to 5,000 feet, whereas in Colorado, this zone occurs at 10,000 to 11,000 feet, and in the Sierra Nevada of California at 7,000 to 9,000 feet. Thus the Olympics have at comparatively low levels a climate, a vegetation, and animal life that is characteristic of mountains at much higher altitudes. To reach the Arctic-Alpine Zone in the Sierra Nevada you must climb to an elevation of from 9,000 to 14,500 feet; in the Olympics you must climb only to 5,500 to 8,000 feet.

It sounds so easy. But no one who has traveled the road to Hurricane Ridge will call it anything but a harrowing route to a plantsmen's paradise. A thirteen-mile drive up the mountainside, from the valley floor at less than five hundred feet to the ridge at more than five thousand feet, is a dizzying experience of curling hairpin bends and sheer drop-offs. And from the Hurricane Ridge objective there is still a further nine miles, along the ridge, to Obstruction Point, the end of the road.

On my first journey to that alpine garden-land, the avalanche lilies were still in bloom along the Ridge; acres of mountain meadows were washed by a tide of white bloom drifting between the wide-skirted alpine firs. Across the valley, the steep ravines and lower slopes were a mass of seemingly impenetrable dark green forest; above them rose the magnificent arc of snow-capped peaks of the Olympic range.

Every turn of that spectacular ridge showed us something different, but the predominating colors were always the same: white and green; white and blue, with the vivid interspersing of brilliant scarlet and magenta paintbrush, yellow-red columbine and spotted gold of the Columbia or wild tiger lily.

One alpine meadow was crowded with these tiger lilies and flecked with countless white spiked mountain dock, *Polygonum bistortoides,* another was blue with the subalpine lupin. Along the roadway the Olympic harebell, *Campanula rotundifolia,* made vivid blue borderings; in places the harebell nodded among clumps of white pearly ever-lasting.

We camped at Obstruction Point. High up, beneath a sheltering ridge, I put my sleeping bag down by the skirts of a mountain fir. I went down to fill the buckets with water from a pool by a shelving snowbank, while my companions made a fire to cook our supper. The snow which was about eight feet deep along the ridge in April had partly melted, and had been partly wind-blown off the summit ridges into wide piebald patches in the depressions—called "wind-shadows" of snow—which remain unmelted throughout the summer. It was dark by the time we cooked our supper, and we turned in early to be ready for the long tomorrow.

Snug in my sleeping bag, I tried to memorize something about the plants I wanted to find. I knew that if I found but one rarity I could count myself lucky. Of nearly one thousand varieties of flowering plants in the Olympics, many of those above tree line are identical with plants of Alaska, Northern Canada, and Greenland. About ten that grow mainly on the slopes and ridgetops above four thousand feet are to be found nowhere else in the world.

When the sun touched the peaks of the mountains across the valley I scrambled out of my sleeping bag, and while the others were still sleeping went up the steep slope to the ridge above Obstruction Point. It was a dizzy enough place from which to take in that immense view. The Olympics glistened white in the sun, and from that narrow strip of volcanic soil some six thousand feet up, with the rocks falling sheer away, I looked out over the Straits of Juan de Fuca, the twenty-six-mile-wide stretch of water which divides the Olympic Peninsula from Canada's Vancouver Island.

Around me *Heuchera racemosa* marched along the summit with its six-inch-high creamy white bells in regimented battalions. The diminutive flower spikes of the Lyall lupin made a ring of white and blue above the hand-spread mat of gray-green leaves. Dwarf purple-blue penstemon, *P. Procerus,* grew among the prostrate juniper, and the thrift-like heads of *Erigeron ovalifolium* were opening their cream-white flowers above silvery rosettes.

I searched but I did not find what I was looking for, one of the rarest of rare plants. Brian Mulligan had given me alternative places where I might find this treasure, and landmarks to guide me. Now I could smell the bacon and eggs cooking, and the coffee brewing, so breakfast interrupted my hunt. Over breakfast I surveyed the ground more closely, and decided to cross the valley to the rock saddle above the snowbank where I had filled the buckets with water the night before.

Slowly I worked along that rock face, searching. There was Tolmie's saxifrage, mats of the white fragrant mountain phlox, and clumps of the pink *Douglasia laevigata* on the rocky outcrops. Silky phacelia, *P. sericea,* bore its lavender-colored silken-haired flower bosses a foot above its silken-haired leaves. A pinacled buttress of rock blocked my way until I found a foothold on a narrow ledge, and pulled myself round.

As I looked back, past the pointed jag of rock to the snow-patch wind-shadows and the clumps of alpine firs which had sheltered us at night, my eye caught a thread of blue in the bare rockface above my head. I did not need to ask anyone what I saw. I knew that my eyes would answer the identifying questions for me. Is it "vine-like in habit?" Does it grow "in the tiny crevices of rock faces?" Is the "flat star flower an inch across?" I reached up to measure by my thumbnail. It was all these, and something more. It was "of the most exquisite blue." Here was the star of all the alpine bellflower group; here was Piper's Bluebell, *Campanula piperi*, which some call the floral pride of the Olympics, for nowhere but on the Olympic Peninsula can Piper's Bluebell be found.

Hurricane Ridge and Deer Park roads are the only high-country areas that can, as yet, be reached by car. The Ridge road is generally open from July 1 until closed by snow in the fall. Deer Park Road, somewhat strangely because it has a summit elevation of 6,007 feet as against the Ridge elevation of 6,450 feet, is usually open by May 15.

There are those who say that of the two, Deer Park is the more accessible. This is not my experience. I have been up its eleven agonizing miles of almost continuous rugged surface and precipitous drop-offs in torrential rain and a blinding cloud-mist; under such conditions it has a fair claim to being one of the worst roads in the United States.

The same obliterating fog conditions harass those who venture up either the Deer Park or the Hurricane Ridge roads. But this adds rather than detracts from the search for alpine flowers. The uncertain journey, the ephemeral flowering of these plants in the short spring and summer weeks of high alpine summer, is but a small price to pay to see the mountains in flower.

Even a bad day brings its rewards, fleeting glimpses of strange and beautiful sights that are part of the wilderness appeal, a sense of elemental oneness that does not belong to sunlit days and cloudless skies. There is the triumph of having braved the elements, of having reached the top; the startling glimpse of a deer silhouetted on a precipitous drop-off against the rolling mist, or the leap of a tiny spotted fawn across your path; the swoop of an eagle above your head. To stand in an all-enveloping mist which blocks out all visibility; to see the mist suddenly part and the shadow of a mountain emerge and loom before you, and a shaft of sun reveal an alpine scree in swirling cloud is one of the sights of a lifetime.

A new road to Hurricane Ridge is planned for completetion by 1958. The Ridge will then he within easy reach of all. But to some the old road, the hard way, will still be the best way to take.

Part of the attraction of alpine flowers is, no doubt, due to their high country setting. To my mind the flowers of the lower altitudes are actually more beautiful, and on the Olympic Peninsula there is reward enough for those who do not want to venture into the Arctic-Alpine zones.

Almost all of the Peninsula coast-line is unspoilt, and what is known as the Olympic Ocean strip is a fifty-mile stretch of coastline which is one of the most primitive coast-lines left in the continental United States. And there is the vast Rain Forest, a strange stage-setting, washed with a tender green light, which seems to belong more to the world of make-believe than the world of Highway 101, which rings the whole surround of the Peninsula's forest and mountain land.

Once, along the Quinault River way into the Rain Forest, I stopped to watch men fishing for cut-throat salmon. One paused to pass the time of day. "You can go where no one has yet ever been," he nodded his head towards the forest, "not even the Indian." He continued, "It's unrecorded, and it's beautiful country."

My feet sank deep into the cushioning moss wherever I walked. Moss that was an arm's length in thickness clothed the trunks of hoary oaks, moss hung in long festoons from the branches. My hands and arms sank into moss as I pulled myself up and across enormous fallen logs.

There is something somber, a density of sound in the words "coniferous timber"; something savage in the word "primeval." But there is no gloom in this virgin forest, rather a happiness of mood, a sylvan beauty where the shafts of sunlight penetrate down to the open glades.

The trees are so immense, the moss so golden brown and golden green that the predominating color of the forest seems more golden brown than evergreen. You stumble as you walk, looking up at the trees above you, and down at the miniature forest of ground cover at your feet. In late July, the Canada dogwood's tiny clusters of reddening bunchberries are bright among the ferns and moss; a single porcelain-blue berry is like a jewel between each pair of Queen's cup leaves. Speckled berries mark the withered blooms of the wild lily-of-the-valley. The green, yellow, and scarlet berries of *Streptopus streptopoides* dangle on their curiously twisted stalk, which gives the plant its botanical tongue-twisting name. Tiny berries make coral sprays of birdsfoot bramble; the blue and red huckleberries, and the flat raspberry-like berries of thimble berry and yellow salmon berry are thick in fruit.

My footfall made no sound as I walked over that miniature forest beneath these enormous trees. But the forest was not silent. It was full of sound. The wind would sigh among the branches softly, and rub one broken branch against another with a dry, rasping rub. There was the rustle of life among the fallen leaves.

This is the kingdom of the Douglas fir, the undisputed king of the northwestern forests. Here is the stronghold of

their titantic might—the monarch fir among them is one
which measures a little over 17 feet in diameter, and soars
some 221 feet high. As I stood among these forests giants, I
sensed the timeless continuity about me. Along the fallen
trunks the seedlings of future giants were growing as miniature forests, staking out their ancient succession on ground
which the centuries would rot away.

24 ❧ Off the Map

ℬIRD CREEK MEADOWS, which are alpine meadows just under the summit of Mount Adams, Washington, were one of my goals. When in San Francisco I had asked Don Kelly, Editor of *Pacific Discovery,* for suggestions on getting into that country, and he had suggested I write to Miss Ella Clark who had spent a summer fire-watching in the area.

I wrote to her, with a map and William O. Douglas' book *Of Men and Mountains* beside me, asking her many questions, explaining it was Douglas' book that had made me want to see Bird Creek Meadows. Her reply gave me more details of places and plants than I had asked for. In directing me from Portland, along the north bank of the Columbia River, to turn north from Bingen and White Salmon to Trout Lake, she suggested I stop by to see Ray Filloon. He was a retired Forest Ranger, and once official photographer for the Forest Service in that district. She said he had a summer cabin on the White Salmon River.

About one thing she miscalculated. She took it for granted I had a car. How was I going to reach Bird Creek Meadows? How was I going to see Ray Filloon? How was I going to follow her directions along the unpaved and narrow roads northward from Trout Lake? "Your map may not show a road from Trout Lake to Randle," she wrote optimistically, "but it is there—and the trip is beautiful."

By the time the snow was melting in the mountains, and the slopes were bursting into flower, I was in Seattle, and not in Portland. Bird Creek Meadows, without a car, was now farther away; to get there I would have to go a long way by bus, and somehow get help for the rest of the way. I nibbled my pen as I sat looking out over Puget Sound from the house where I was staying on Queen Anne Hill. Would I? Should I? I wrote to Ray Filloon.

At the end of July, a week after I had his reply, I was up and over the Snoqualmie Pass, going east by bus across the sagebrush country of eastern Washington. Down in the valley the hay was cut, the oats unharvested. Beyond the sagebrush-covered hills of the frowning Ellensburg Canyon, the country changed abruptly again: there were peach orchards, acres of truck garden crops, asparagus, rhubarb, and strawberry fields, and then vast wheat and hopfields.

All through the broad Yakima Valley there was the smell of new-mown hay. Then the distant hills came nearer until they narrowed and rose cliff-like in deep shade on either side of the road. And the sage crept back, covering the hills with a faint purple-grey mist; there were miles of sagebrush, endless sagebrush it seemed.

The light had almost gone as we went along the Colum-

bia River highway between Goldendale and Bingen. Mount
Rainier, Mount Adams, and Mount St. Helens stood up in
enormous black silhouette, poster-like outlines with no detail visible. Below us the broad Columbia River caught the
last of the light, winding its way as a wide light ribbon
through the darkening gorge.

A truck driver sitting beside me pointed out the Indian
fishing reservation at Celilio Falls. I could just see the water
breaking over the rocks in the wide pool of the river. Away
in the distance, beyond the white peak of Mt. St. Helen's, a
faint plume of gray haze drifted across the horizon.

"You see that haze?" the truck driver said, "It's the smoke
of forest fires. They are bad this year, they've stopped logging in the forests. It's so dry."

"And isn't Mount Hood beautiful?" I exclaimed.

He hesitated. "Yes, I suppose it is, but I never think of it
as beautiful; it's part of everyday, part of Portland where I
live. It's just there."

Obviously he felt he had failed to point out everything
that might be of interest to a stranger. He had remembered
Ceilio Falls and the smoke haze from the fires. Then he
craned forward.

"You see that star up there?" I nodded. "It's the first star
to come out each evening, so we call it the Evening Star."

It was my turn to hesitate. "Yes," I replied, "it is lovely,
so you call it the Evening Star." I saw his wonder at my
slow reply; if Mount Hood had been remarkable to me, why
wasn't the Evening Star remarkable too? How should he
know that the same star rose in the evening sky the world
over?

Ray Filloon had promised to meet me and he kept his
word, dressed as he said he would be, in forest green. He

was big, wind-etched, grayed, a fatherly Gibralter of the forest. We drove up to the Filloon's cabin on the White Salmon river, turning north to Trout Lake. I had no map, I had no car, but I was going the way Ella Clark had told me to go.

Almost as soon as we arrived I helped Ray with his edge-of-night chores. I sprinkled the salt mixed with soil that he put out every night for the deer, and for the chipmunks laid out some stale hotcakes on top of the woodpile at the door. After dinner I turned in early to my bunk under the Douglas fir and the Ponderosa pine. The snows, I knew, were melting up on Bird Creek Meadows; White Salmon river was in full flood a few yards from my feet.

Next morning, after breakfast of bacon and buckwheat cakes and coffee—we made enough hotcakes for the chipmunks' supper—we packed up the lunch. We fetched beer from the small spring house hidden under the arrowwood and ocean-spray bushes, took out the rye bread, which does not dry out quickly, and Black Rock cheese. This was the local goats' milk cheese, known formerly as Guler, because it is made in a cave near Guler where the temperature differs no more than four degrees the year around, the condition identical to that in the French caves where Roquefort cheese is made.

Ray Filloon took me first to a Forest Lookout, a small, square glass-walled crow's nest at the top of a tall Ponderosa pine, which served as a firewatcher's summer home. It was a pull-up: sixty-seven steps up a vertical ladder to reach the platform eighty-seven feet above the ground. Inside, a large compass took up almost all the room, leaving only enough space for the student watcher and myself to move round, one at a time. To the north was Mount Adams, to the

west Mount St. Helens, and to the south Mount Hood rose
in dazzlingly white above the rolling green forests. Away to
the east I could see the Glenwood Valley and its checker-
board of grain and pasture land.

Afternoon found us in the wild country above the Klick-
itat River where blue pentstemon and mariposa lilies were
in flower among the ochre rocks and sandy soil. It was lonely
looking country without a sign of human habitation.

We went back, in the evening, through the open pine
forests, on our way to a lumber camp. Here the Ponderosa
pine, not so widespread as in the forests of western Washington, is one of the most stately evergreen trees east of the
Cascades. With little underbrush, the wide-spaced trees give
a park-like effect to the forests, which cover hundreds of
square miles.

I am sure that none of the roads we followed were marked
on any map. Even Ray Falloon hesitated now and then as
the narrow dirt-track ended abruptly, its outline blurred
through disuse. But it mattered little to Ray; he made his
way by sense of direction and some odd landmark that a
less observant eye than his would never notice.

Quantities of pearly everlasting grew there with the tall
yellow mullein, the mauve asters and goldenrod. Once we
stopped to look at a mass of pink spirea and goldenrod outlined against the snow-clad summit of Mount Adams. Everywhere ocean spray tumbled its laden foaming branches over
the rocks and fallen logs.

That evening, over dinner with Elmer and Effie Loffgren
at the lumber camp, we talked of Bird Creek Meadows. Ray
doubted whether the snow at their altitude would have
melted sufficiently. Although it was an early year, two weeks
ahead of the normal flowering season, he said it was yet too

early to find flowers, and altogether foolish to try. But Ray's heart could not allow him to go so high up the mountain, which was probably why he was so discouraging. Effie said she was willing to take me, that we should be lucky if only we made a try, and the plan was made to go up to the Meadows the following morning. That day was to prove the longest and one of the most arduous days I ever spent in the Northwest.

Ray wanted to camp that night beside Bird Creek, an hour's driving distance from the lumber camp, and small Billie Loffgren and I accompanied him. Billie chose a level bit of ground beneath a red cedar for my sleeping bag, a yard or two from the creek. We slept soundly and woke early. At 4 A.M. we were up and busy, cooking our bacon and scrambling eggs by the car headlights. It was bitterly cold; Billie and I shivered. Ray was cold too, but he had enough discipline neither to complain nor shiver.

Effie was ready by the time we got back to the lumber camp. Ray was still dubious and discouraging about tackling the meadows. Only three days ago, he said, a car had stuck in the snow on the forest road below. I think he wanted terribly to come along, and I wish he had, for he is now dead.

Effie and I set off in her car, going up the narrow dirt-track road, past open glades of pine forest, past the place where the other car had stuck, slipping and sliding on the last lap. Somehow Effie just managed to persuade the car up the last grueling ascent, and we were at the end of the road, within a stone's throw of the Meadows beneath the south side of Mount Adams. And we were in luck.

Above us the rounded snow-capped dome glistened in the morning sun. About two thousand feet lower than Mount Rainier, Mount Adams is the third highest peak in the Cas-

cade Range, and appears a friendly mountain, more accessible and intimate. Away to the west Mount St. Helens
floated in the cloudless sky. It was a peerless morning, and
although still early the sun was already hot.

At our feet, spreading upwards to the snowline, was a
kaleidoscope of blue and red and yellow—countless blue
lupine banners among the scarlet paintbrush and buttercups.
The small woolly grey-flowered heads of pussytoes, *Anten-
naria*, grew with the red paintbrush, *Casteilleja miniata*.
There were brilliant wide swaths of the scarlet paintbrush,
Castilleja crispula, and the fine-haired petals of white cat's
ears, *Calochortus albus*.

Everywhere the streams were leaping and cascading down
from rock to rock, from ledge to ledge, in the flood-tide of
the melting snow, until in the lower meadows they moved
more slowly in wide encircling loops of water before they
hurried on again, working down the steep slopes beyond.

In contrast to the riot of color on the upper slopes, there
was a northern fraility, a delicacy among those miniature
water-meadows. There the moss and quiet-flowering elkslip
marigold fringed the margin of the streams, making islands
of fragile bloom.

We wandered across those unharvested lawns, from the
eastern slope to the south, southwest and back again. There
were stray clumps of gentian, sometimes great masses of rose-
red mimulus besides the jostling waters; quantities of white
and red heather covered the rocky boulders.

Only time and the mosquitoes plague us. By mid-day we
were due to join the loggers, to go into the Yakima Indian
Reservation Forest and watch them falling and loading the
timber. But even if time had not driven us away the mosquitoes certainly would have done so. They come as the

snow melts, and they settled on our faces and even our eyelids, drawing blood from our cheeks, hands and legs.

Still we lingered, to the last moment. How was I going to remember this flower field at my feet? Would the colors stay as bright as I saw them now, against the snow and under the late summer sun: blue lupin, rose-red to scarlet paintbrush, and golden cinquefoil? Would I forever see the mimulus and the heather, the rocky slopes broken into a series of rock and water gardens, as beautiful as any mountain gods could devise? Effie was waiting; I had to go.

An hour later we were racing along the wide roads. These belonged to the lumber company, were controlled by their own traffic laws, and posted for the unwary trespasser, "Danger, Keep Out." The trucks had the right of way at all times. They traveled sometimes on the right and sometimes on the left of the road, always at high speed, carrying enormous loads which equaled three full rail-trucks of timber.

Elmer Loffgren was in the front car. We stopped now and then for him to radio back to base, report our own position, and learn if a truck was on its way. If one were coming we would wait for it to go by, leaving the car, scrambling up the embankment to see it come roaring past, throwing up a great smoke screen of dust behind.

We could get out of the way of the trucks but we could not escape the dust. It rose in billowing clouds behind Elmer's car, and behind us. It seeped in through the closed windows, finding a way through every crack. Finally we gave up any attempt to protect ourselves. I covered my camera with my jacket as best I could. When we left the cars we were covered with a thick light-brown powder from head to foot.

In the forest we stood deep in dust; even a bird alighting

near us on the ground sent up a puff of dust as it touched
down. The loggers were wearing respirators as they loaded
the trucks with clockwork precision. Tractors hauled the
great fallen Ponderosa pines alongside and the cranes moved
like the arms of praying mantis, lifting the timber from the
ground in one mighty embrace. The wheels churned the
earth into a dark brown-grey powdered dust.

Elmer wanted us to watch a tree being felled. Our feet
were sand deep in dust as we followed him along the forest
road. Dust trickled down into our shoes; our faces were
brown and our hair stiff with dust.

The men were sawing at the base of a mighty Ponderosa
pine. We stood and watched them until a shudder went
through the upper branches of the tree. Soon the whole
tree swayed from top to base, and recovered. Suddenly it became a horrible scene to watch, but we stayed.

"It's going . . . now," Elmer cried. Again the tree swayed,
and again it rallied, making one last desperate stand. Then
it swayed again—for the last time—and gathering momentum
crashed with an appalling catastrophic crash.

There was a deep unfathomable silence, as though even
the loggers were appalled at what they had done. The sun
would never touch those topmost boughs again; the squir-
rels and the birds would forsake the tree, the great Ponderosa pine which had taken so many years to reach such
stature was now dead. The sight sickened me.

After dinner at the camp, and two successive baths to
clean away the dust, I caught the 3 A.M. overnight bus to
Yakima. From there I started the journey back over the
Chinook Pass, and it was 11 P.M. when I got back to Queen
Anne Hill in Seattle. I stood a moment looking out over the
City and the Sound, seeing the lights reflected along the

water. I glanced at the postmarks on my letters. And suddenly I could look no more. I had another bath, and tumbled into bed, too tired at first to sleep.

"Your map may not show a road from Trout Lake but it is there—and the trip is beautiful." I had put out the hotcakes for the chipmunks, and slept beside the Salmon River. I had heard the Chinook wind rustle the sage, as Douglas heard it; I had tasted the shepherd's doughbread. There had been lupins and paintbrush, marsh marigold and mimulus . . . clouds of dust . . . the splintering crash of a falling tree . . . Bird Creek Meadows . . . lupins and paintbrush. It was a long time ago, but far away I had walked across the Meadows . . . "Your map may not show a road . . . but it is there."

25 ❧ The Mountain That Was God

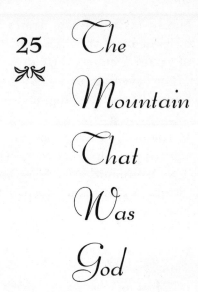

CAPTAIN GEORGE VANCOUVER of the English ship *Discovery* was the first white man to record seeing The Mountain. "A very high mountain covered with snow," he wrote prosaically, "which, after my friend Rear Admiral Rainier, I distinguished by the name Mount Rainier."

I wish he had not named it for his friend.

To the Indian it was Tacoma or Tahoma, The Mountain That Was God. To the people of western Washington it is something only a little less than a god, and something much more than a mountain. It is *The Mountain,* the presiding genius of America's Far Northwest.

How can the white man, any better than the Indian, comprehend the sheer immensity of the vast, broken, snow-covered mass though he describes it by measurements of such exactitude? How can he convey the presence of The Mountain by saying in bare figures that it covers a hundrd square miles at base, and rises almost from sea level to an altitude of 14,408 feet, or nearly three miles high?

One evening, as we lay becalmed in a skiff far out on Seattle's Lake Washington, we looked toward The Mountain. The evening was serene and still after a day of bright and brittle heat. Not a breath of wind moved the sail, not a current rippled the blue water. Immediately to the south of us, The Mountain, clear from base to summit, towered above, unique, solitary and compellingly beautiful against the evening sky.

"No one has ever really described it yet, you know. People use the same inadequate words every time they try," someone said.

"Most of them are negative words, too, aren't they?" I asked. "Indistinguishable and unsubstantial; colorless and formless; mysterious and disembodied, lost in mist and cloud. Yet, now, at this moment, it is clear-cut and dominating."

"Maybe it just can't be described as a mountain," was the answer. "When you live beside it for a time you look for it always. It's part of our lives. Even when we cannot see it, we know that it is there." Seattle-born, the speaker had grown up in the realm of Mount Rainier.

We were silent then, and I sat in the small boat thinking how Seattle had completely baffled me the first few weeks. For all the beauty of her setting there was a nonchalance, a curiously impersonal air about the city.

Only in the Farmer's Market along the waterfront on Pike Place had I felt a different atmosphere. I would go there in my lunch hour, walking first along the long line of open stalls facing the street, and piled with fruit and vegetables, and bunches of fennel tied to the posts. I would walk back past the fishermen's stalls that lined the Sound, where there was salmon and Hood Canal shrimp, and fish of every description. Finally, I would walk down the gangways over the water, and look across to the Cascade Mountains as I had my sandwich. The market was a friendly place, lively and entertaining, with an air of the farm, the river, and the sea about it.

Early one morning Harry Higman took me in his canoe across a waterway he knows better, probably, than anyone else, and which he has described in his book *Union Bay: The Life of a City Marsh.* The loosestrife dyed the narrow waterways with the reflection of its rosy-purple bloom. The red berries of enchanter's nightshade twined among the reeds and yellow flags, and the white and yellow pond lilies were floating islands of green studded with flowers.

It was the opening day of Seattle's Sea Fair, and a cavalcade of boats was passing across the Marsh out to Lake Washington beyond. We had passed safe and assuredly between the boats from one side of the marsh to another, and had pulled in to a backwater near the beaver's lodge where we might watch the birds.

"Where else do you know of a beaver's lodge within a city's limit?" Harry Higman asked.

I was not expected to answer; nor would I know. But, oddly enough, it seemed perfectly natural that the beaver was there.

Harry Higman caught hold of a blackberry spray, pulling the canoe closer to the bank so that I could reach more of the big ripe berries.

"This Pudget Sound country," he looked about us, "it's got about as much as anyone could wish—forests, fresh and

salt water, and the mountains. Seattle is in reach of it all,"
he waved his arm, "all this wonderful country."

Then he spoke of the mountain. "It is the same dominating symbol to us of the Northwest as Fujiyama is to Japan.
No matter where you turn or what may hold your gaze, the
magnetism of that peak will always draw you back. Everything else becomes subordinate to its grandeur."

That morning down on the marsh, which was still the
haunt of the bittern and the beaver, I began to understand.
Now, this evening on Lake Washington, I felt I understood.

The heart of Seattle was not in her streets. Her people
looked outward across the water to the mountains, to that
far-offness, that untouchedness of the last frontier. Wasn't
Seattle still the last outpost, the springboard to Alaska, the
nearest flying point to the Orient? Wasn't it always towards
the unending distance that Seattle looked?

The men who built the city on the hills above their inland
sea had great tenacity of purpose. Did they not say that
Puget Sound was big enough to harbor all the navies of the
world; that it was an inlet of the Pacific Ocean lost among
great mountains? From the mountains they drew their
strength, and it was towards the mountains that they always
looked.

Seattle people are mountain-minded. *The Mountain* is
part of their lives.

The sun set behind the jagged walls of the Olympic Mountains. As the faint purple shadows lengthened and deepened
across the high snow fields, a golden radiance faded upward
across the sky. Away to the east, far back among the Cascades, the white summit of Glacier Peak caught the afterglow. Wild duck circled overhead, and came down to the
water. The warm resin fragrance of pine came to us from

the rafts of floating logs along the lakeside. Vega, the star of the northern summer sky, was already a brilliant glitter directly above us.

The boats were now going home all along that inland sea. Everyone waved in greeting as they passed. Lights flashed. The stars came out. The color drained from the water.

It was at this moment what seemed a phantom ship came by. She was tall-masted. Her rigging was warm cinnamon as the bark of the madrone, her hull pale aquamarine. A hand waved as she sped by, swift and slender, beautiful as any boat could be. And she was gone. Could it have been *Discovery?*

Instinctively we looked up then at The Mountain. It too had disappeared, and the long violet-shadowed northern twilight faded into night.

I was content. Tomorrow I was going up to The Mountain to follow .Tolmie who had been the first to climb the lower slopes, and the first to bring back from there a bunch of flowers; to see what John Muir had described as the richest subalpine garden he had ever known.

I woke next morning knowing that evening promise would be fulfilled. The day was clear and sunlit. Before the sun was high we were on our way.

The Mountain did not disappoint; all that I had read and imagined was there. A climax of flowers covered the slopes from one snowbound horizon to the other. Between the hummocked bosses of red and white mountain heathers, the ground was thickset with blue lupins, scarlet paintbrush, and the bright golden cinquefoil. The seed heads of the western anenome were like the ranks of ghostly busbies, which English guardsmen wear, among the white-flowered mountain dock. Drifts of rose-red mimulus bordered the streams, leaping and falling from rock to rock, hurrying with the weight of water from the fast-melting snows above them.

I looked up at The Mountain and back to the pinnacled crest of the Tatoosh Range across the valley. What far-off memory should I have of days such as these, my mountain days? Should I always remember the sight of this wild garden at my feet? How could I stamp such things in my mind?

I remembered then what John Muir had said, that days such as these would enrich all his life, that they would not exist only as mere pictures but would saturate themselves into every part of his body and live with him always. And I knew I no longer had need to question. As long as color had any meaning for me, as long as memory would serve, all would be mine. There was no end to such a day.

At last we turned to go. There was nothing to say except the trite, the obvious superlatives. I thought of what an Austrian said about these flower fields, regretting that he could not pick the flowers, that children could not gather them as the children of Vienna gather the wild flowers in the woods to sell in the city streets. And he missed the sight and sounds of human habitation in the mountains, the bark of a dog and the sounds of cowbells.

I had heard cowbells in Colorado and the Napa Valley in California. Surely, I thought, there must be cowbells somewhere among these alpine meadows, but I heard none. A day or so later I read a news story, of men who year after year had gone hunting and logging in the Blue Mountains of Eastern Oregon, and who had come back to tell of a far-away tinkling, a ghostly bell ringing near the little village of Kamela. The men thought they were hearing things, for no one could trace the sound. Finally, when lumberjacks one

day brought down a mighty Ponderosa pine to make a right
of way, they found a bronze cattle bell, tied by a shriv-
eled leather thong, among the branches of the fallen tree.
"Saignelegier—Chiantel— Fondeur. 1878" were the words
just barely distinguishable on the worn-thin clapper. The
people of Kamela guessed then that some pioneer had tied
the cowbell to a sapling when he and the pine were young.

So I told my companions of my mountain day the story
of the Bell of Kamela and what the Austrian had said, as
we drove down for dinner at "Ohop Bob's." As we waited
for Bob to serve us his fried chicken and berry pie, the
same menu he has prepared every day the last thirty years,
we went out to the open porch of his simple white-pillared
restaurant house to look down across the valley and to The
Mountain at the valley's head. The snow on the great peak
was crimson with the afterglow. In the fading light we
could see the checkered floor of the valley, pale squares
where the hay had just been cut and gathered, green pastureland where the cows were going out for the night's grazing
after milking.

"Listen!" It was Thane, the boy with us, who heard them
first. With his feathered cap awry, bright-eyed and listening,
Thane held up his hand to silence us. The quiet, regular
tinkling of cowbells, many cowbells, came up to us from the
valley.

We went into dinner with the cowbells ringing in our
ears. The farmer, Bob told us, had brought the bells with
him from Switzerland. "Ohop," he volunteered, "is the
Indian word for pleasant: Ohop Valley, Pleasant Valley."

It is hardly surprising that The Mountain colors are my
best memories of Seattle. I had seen it from afar and from
close at hand; from the sagebrush plains of eastern Washing-

ton; from across the waters of Puget Sound in Canada's Victoria; from the berry farms of the Puyallup Valley and from the Oylmpic Peninsula. Day after day it had been there on the horizon of my sight and mind. Most often I had seen The Mountain from a garden which sloped steeply down in a green sweep of lawn to Lake Washington.

There was nothing, you would say, that could possibly link this garden with either the Farmer's Market or the beaver's lodge—unless it were the Indian arrowhead which had been found there. Yet each, in its own language, had given me the feel of Seattle. As a stranger, I had been reluctant to accord the city her due; I had felt it an impersonal city. But before I left it seemed that what the gardener of this Seattle garden said was true: "In a sense you've come home, haven't you?" he said.

I stood with my back against the rock walling below the terrace, remembering the rock had been brought as ballast from New Orleans.

"Stranger?" said the gardener, "You're not a stranger, you're an old familiar."

My memory stirred. Whether or not it was coincidence, the other time I heard those words was in New Orleans. Suddenly the riddle of the city was solved. Seattle was wedded to The Mountain as New Orleans was wedded to the Mississippi River.

I looked towards the far-offness of the last frontier; it was beautiful beyond compare. Neither over-colorful nor over-obvious, neither brilliant nor sophisticated, but rather of a wistful northern beauty, of soft and tender light.

"Here is the beauty and stark grandeur of a North that has no harshness." As I read those words, I closed the book which had been given me. I had lived beside The Mountain.

I had put my foot upon its flowering hem. I knew now that The Mountain means many things to many men.

To the traveler it means, in a sense, the end of the road. He may make his way north across the continent and take the mountain passes from the dry sagelands of eastern Washington; or he may come south and up the fabulous West Coast, a thousand miles or more of extravagantly spectacular scenery. Whichever road he takes, and when at last he looks toward The Mountain from across the waters of Puget Sound, he will know that this is the supreme sight of the road.

26 ❦ The Miracle of Color

$\mathcal{A}$s I turned eastward to complete my journey full-circle the landmarks were wide-spaced and, because my time-table was set, my stops were comparatively few. Re-crossing the Continental Divide after leaving copper-mining Butte in Montana, I marked the milestone in my mind by the sage-brush and goldenrod growing on the summit of Pipestone Pass.

Southern Montana was wide to infinity. Massive buttes, squared off as though by mathematical precision, rose up abruptly from the plains. Herds of Hereford cattle grazed the sagebrush, and the bee farmers had set out their colonies of hives for the sage-honey gathering bees.

It was the country of the Crow Indians and Big-horned Sheep, the Land of the Ranger Riders, and the "Smoke-jumpers" who parachute down from planes to fight forest

fires. The Yellowstone flowed into the mighty Missouri, their
river banks bordered with willow and silver maple trees.
Sometimes on the upland plains there were mile-long acres of
wheat; then the sagebrush, the seemingly endless sagebrush,
crept back again.

The bus passengers talked but little. Maybe it was the
long stretches of unvaried landscape which drowsed them;
maybe they were simply taciturn by habit. Only one little
man spoke his comments out loud, from time to time, in
bursts of conversation. Natural hay, he declared, was better
for cattle than alfalfa, more long-lasting. His tanned companion, who made up for him in size and silence, nodded in
agreement. Occasionally he made a monosyllabic reply, treat-
ing the little fellow with the same tolerance an old horse
would a fly, shaking the words off with a jerk of his head.

Southern Minnesota was a three-color landscape of blue
lakes and green grass, with acres and acres of yellow sunflowers. Monotonous country to some, perhaps, but it has its
own placid beauty, and the color reminded me of the long
green and yellow border in the Capitol gardens at Olympia.

In the corn-belt country of Iowa, north and south, east
and west, the great mile-wide squares and oblongs of green
corn flecked the gently rolling hills with tasselled heads. At
one ranch, where the Hereford cattle were fattened for the
Chicago market, I stayed long enough to learn the cattle-
men's two-step, a dextrous quickstep method of getting the
muck off the soles of your shoes after a walk across the cattle
yards.

The night of a short stay in a rambling house at Winnetka,
an outlying district of Chicago, for the first time in my life
I listened with intense enjoyment to the sound of heavy
raindrops beating down through the trees in steady accom-

paniment to the Katydids' rasping chorus. For one whole year I had not heard the sound of rain and though I could have done without the Katydids, they were familiar and foretold my return from the West back to the East, to the America I had first known.

One day, traveling downtown on Michigan Boulevard, along Chicago's Million Dollar Mile on vast Lake Michigan, I remarked to my companion on the sea-green water of the lake breaking white along the shore. She turned to me, smiling her approval at my notice of this Windy City patch of beauty.

"There's a green in Wedgwood china just like it, isn't there?" she asked, and then, more directly, "You *are* English, aren't you?" She went on: "Our's is a dirty old city, a railroad town, the home of the stockyards, but if you love it you love it to death."

In spite of the once bitterly anti-British daily newspaper, the Chicago *Tribune,* I found Chicago the most spontaneously friendly of all American cities. Policemen, storekeepers, restaurant waiters, taxi men all went out of their way to help me for no other reason than my English accent. One policeman in the quick-paced Loop district took my arm and walked half a block to put me on my way, asking as we went what I thought of America in general, and of Chicago in particular.

Chicago has no reputation for beauty, and few approach it the best way—along the North Shore Road with the distant view of the skyscraper-skyline ahead. But those who do can hardly deny the magnificence of Michigan Boulevard, with the tall buildings on the city side and the park-like areas of green lawns and shrubs bordering mighty Lake Michigan. The Boulevard can fairly be likened, at night, to a tree-lined,

dazzlingly lit Paris boulevard. Michigan Boulevard is one of
the great streets of the world.

At Ithaca in New York state, I stayed with friends who
took me to see the grand old man of American horticulture,
the late Dr. Liberty Hyde Bailey. He was then ninety-three
years old, frail in body, but perfectly clear in mind. He
spoke in beautiful measured prose, as a student rather than
an authority. He loved the English countryside; he loved
asters and goldenrod. As we talked, his memory began
reaching far back, to the days of his youth, to stories his
father had told, which he now in his turn told again.

His father had left Vermont with his belongings tied up
in two bundles and hung on the stock he wore over his
shoulder. He had crossed the Green Mountains and made
his way across the Mid-West to Mud City. That name seemed
the touchstone of history, for Mud City is now Chicago, and
Dr. Bailey himself was but a few years younger than the
Northwest's great cities of Portland and Seattle. Two generations spanned the founding and maturing of the American West.

All across the continent I had hurried, this continent
that was a wilderness when old England was old in terms of
centuries. My time-table was set by the fall color dates of
the New England calendar. Would I arrive at Casey's home,
the farmhouse at Gilmanton in New Hampshire, old as
America reckons in generations, in time to see the autumn
color at its height? Casey was the Casey of what now seemed
like my long-ago days at Williamsburg.

When I did arrive all was hidden in mist; the weather
had been bad for days. And so it stayed. I would go out in
the mist and climb over grey stone walls where the wild
clematis trailed its sprays of soft grey seed-heads. I would

go up through the orchard where a few bright red Mackin-
tosh apples—Robert Frost's apples—still hung on the bare
trees, but most were windfalls in the grass. I followed the
stream up through the woods, came back across meadows
where only the withered stems of Michaelmas daisies and
goldenrod remained, except here and there a stray standard
of gold was left standing beside the tattered petals of a
once mauve aster. Only a last pale lemon-yellow evening
primrose opened in the mist.

Lying in bed at night in that old farmhouse, I listened
to the brook chattering its way down the hill, and wondered
if the mist might clear before I left. And then one morning,
as I leaned out of the window, I saw it shift from the wooded
slopes above the brook. The sun came out as I watched,
and there was blue sky, at last.

One limb of a sugar maple was a scarlet banner among
the bright emerald unturned leaves; another maple was
mottled red and yellow, another was solid red against the
autumn sky. This was the promised day, another mountain
day of color, leaf-color such as I had never seen, even in my
first Pennsylvanian fall.

There was still some green, and the same sunlit gold I
had first seen in the Norway maple. Here it was the gold and
the reddened leaf together that was such a miracle. Nor does
red describe the whole wide color range which the red and
sugar maple reveal, for it is red that runs from the first
crimson flush to vermillion through to scarlet, to brilliant
flaming scarlet which consumes itself, at the last, to rich
turkey-red, deep blood-red, and finally to wine-red or mur-
rey-red.

Only higher, in the White Mountains, did red yield to
gold. We looked up at the Indian face of rock, which no

hand of man had sculptured. How many moons, how many autumns had The Old Man of the Mountain seen?

Around the lake the trees were entirely gold, so that their reflection covered the water with a pale patina of autumn color. It was almost a relief, after the gorgeous color symphony, to look on the quiet yellowing overtones the trees cast on the water.

Casey was not at home, but her voice came back to us over the telephone wires as we sat that evening in front of the wood fire. "Have you been along the stream to find the beaver's dam? Did you climb up the ski trail, past what the children call the Forty Acre Woods? Did they drive you past the pond where we swim, and up Belknap, Gunstock, and Piper?"

"Color," I answered. "I don't know what else to tell you, Casey. The beaver's dam, yes; and Forty Acre Woods, but it's the color. Today was the peak day of fall color, eighty degrees of summer sun and the sky clear October blue. It's the red, the vermillion, the scarlet. I'm saturated with color."

Boston was my last port of call; home of the fantastic Ware Collection of Blaschka Glass Models of Plants in the Botanical Museum of Harvard University; of the Massachu-setts Horticultural Society, and of the Arnold Arboretum, one of the greatest collections of hardy shrubs and trees.

Dr. Don Wyman, the Arboretum's Horticulturist, made time to take me a quick tour round. It was Dr. Wyman who had given me, on one of his visits to West Grove, my early garden measuring rod. Corn, he had said, should be planted when the oak leaf was as large as a squirrel's ear. This told me, in part, of corn's pride of place in the American vege-table garden; it also showed me a comparatively larger scale of reckoning than I was used to: my old English gardener used to tell me to wait to plant peas until the hawthorn leaf was as large as a mouse's ear.

Dr. Wyman also gave me other comparative figures now. He had been to England that summer, and told me that Kew Gardens employed one hundred and fifty men on some three hundred acres as against the Arnold Arboretum's thirteen men on slightly less acreage. "We have to be on the ball for machines," he added, but granted that Kew maintains rock and formal gardens which necessitate much detailed work. Also, the Arnold Arboretum has five thousand woody plants, Kew ten thousand. Dr. Wyman believed that Golden Gate Park in San Francisco contains a far greater number of woody plants than the Arnold Arboretum.

I think Dr. Wyman had been shocked at the lack of maps and records in English horticultural centers generally; certainly he had been astonished to find no display of hedge material. But hedges are so much a part of the English garden and of the English landscape that, in reality, all England is a hedge display, and I should have been surprised if Kew or any other public garden had exhibited any hedge-material collection. As Dr. Wyman himself remarked, "most decent shrubs would make a hedge." He had a particular liking for hedges; they had been the subject of his first book, and the Arnold Arboretum display contains one hundred and fifteen varieties.

Few hawthorns remained from the original vast and valuable collection. They were victims to scale, red spider, and other diseases, and the public had shown comparatively little interest in these trees. But if there was now no room for hawthorns or buddleias, there was space enough for the wonderful collection of crab-apples, lilacs, and philadelphus,

and for the viburnums, many of which were berrying beautifully for my visit.

In the Arboretum I added one more goldenrod to my
small knowledge of that immense tribe, the white goldenrod,
Solidago bicolor. There was also another shrub, once an
oldtime favorite of English cottage gardens which is now
but rarely seen, the Buffalo currant, *Ribes odoratum*, native
to the Great Plains, and loved for its fragrant yellow
flowers.

"English gardeners, you know, maintain that American
natives are difficult to grow," Dr. Wyman said as he saw
me off. "But look at what they've done in improving the
strains of some of them, asters and lupins and others. And
we, oddly enough, have trouble with these Anglicized
strains, for they do not re-adapt themselves to cultivation
back here very easily." He laughed. "Oh, over in England
there is so much more than we have, so much more, but
then they've been at it longer, haven't they?"

27

The Love of Gardening

I SAT in the Library of Horticultural Hall, home of the Massachusetts Horticultural Society. Now that my three-year journey around the perimeter of the continent was completed, I could no longer postpone my answer to the question, "What do you think of our American gardens?"

I sharpened a pencil, fidgeted. What could I say? Three years, I thought, is a long time to spend looking at gardens, I ought to be able to say something. Yet no one knew better than I did that I had seen only a fraction of America's gardens, and not even all her representative ones. I had not seen the desert bloom, and in many other places I had not seen the gardens at the right time of year. At best I had had only a bird's eye view.

However, looking back today at the notes I made at the end of my first journey around the continent, looking back

after six added years, I know that the summing up has not
changed. The old phrase of comparison between the American and English garden has grown faint in my mind. Over
the miles and the years I have learned that America possesses an extraordinary diversity of gardens, great and small,
wild and tamed.

To compare America and England gardenwise is not only
unfair but absurd. America as a whole is not so garden-
minded as England, which probably has more gardens, more
home gardeners than any other country of the world. To
England gardening is as painting is to France or skiing to
Switzerland. About ten million out of forty-two million
English are gardeners; America's gardening population is
probably no more than five million among a total population of one hundred and sixty million. Make no mistake,
however, half as many gardens as England is a lot of gardens,
and America is less than half England's age.

Gardening is one of the oldest of the arts; it is also one
of the most ephemeral. It has followed the same pattern
of development in every civilization. Plants have been
grown first of necessity, for food and healing; then for trade
at home and overseas, and only lastly have they been grown
for decoration.

It is worthwhile to understand what contributed to the
making of the English garden, since it is the type garden
which has mostly influenced the making of the American
garden.

The English garden as it is known today has taken centuries to reach its present form, a modified blend of various
European influences, particularly the French, the Italian,
and the Dutch. Out of the maze of intricate parterres and
the fantastic absurdities of topiary, two modified features

remain as an integral part of their design: the lawn—that most simple of all parterres, and the hedge—the most simple form of topiary art.

The garden of the English country houses, closely knit both with the house and the surrounding countryside, has reached a certain perfection in garden art. So too the cottage garden, with its careless orderliness, has its own unique place in garden history, and expresses the stability and love of the countryside which are integral parts of the British character.

The history of gardening in every country is finally shaped by climate, by the country itself, and by national temperament. And the climate of America, mentally and physically, is different from that of Europe; the natural landscape, the national temperment are different. It follows, therefore, that gardening plays a different part in the life of Britain than in the life of America.

It is true that America generally is not as flower-conscious as Holland where once they sank entire fortunes to buy a rare new tulip bulb, nor is she proportionally so garden-minded as Great Britain. But America is not yet nearly so closely settled as Europe, nor has she generally speaking a gardening climate. And although people enjoy working their own gardens more and more, I believe that the American woman prefers, if she has to make a choice, having hired help for the garden rather than in the house, whereas the English housewife prefers it the other way round, and chooses her hired help in the house rather than in the garden. The practice of having someone design, plant, and maintain the garden is still more widespread in America than in England, where home owners prefer to create and maintain their gardens themselves.

The English-type garden has probably had the greatest influence on American design. In the West, however, gardens show the marked influence of the Spanish patio, and northward from San Francisco there is often a hint of the Japanese garden. But during the last ten years or so there has also been a marked change in American gardening. Designers have discarded much traditional European influence; they have modified and re-adapted the English-Spanish type of layout to suit their climate and their need. The American Garden has emerged.

This new style of individual American Garden was developed, it is said, first on the West Coast, and since the war has spread throughout the United States. It aims at harmonizing the house with the garden in such a way as to conform with American living, using it in the dual capacity of outdoor living room for entertainment and as garden proper where its owners may enjoy their plants the year round. Its farthest development is the outdoor room which has a roof, fireplace, and one wall, and is equipped with a barbecue and bar facilities. Often it is dramatically lit, and serves both as a house wear-and-tear saver and as a glamorous setting for parties.

Oriental architecture, the Spanish patio, the English garden have all made their contribution to this development. And America has one great advantage over all other countries to aid her in her chosen design. The contemporary western architecture and new type garden can only be entirely successful by the use of heat and outdoor lighting systems. Radiant heat under the outdoor terrace has made outdoor living possible at longer times during the day and through the year than was ever possible before, as well as in climates where previously it was entirely impractical. The American house and garden have been adapted to the climate in a wider sense than any other country has yet been able to achieve or to afford.

If I were asked if there was one single feature of American gardens as a whole which had caught my attention, I would unhesitatingly say the lack of hedges. But I do not mean by this that there are no hedges in gardens; on the contrary there are many and as people live closer together in built-up areas and need a certain degree of privacy, they are increasingly being used.

William Cobbett could not understand why America did not possess the English hedge. "She has," he declared, "English gew-gaws, English Play-Actors, English cards and English Dice and Billiards: English fooleries and English vices enough in all conscience; and why not *English Hedges,* instead of post-and-rail and board fences? If, instead of these sterile-looking and cheerless enclosures the gardens and meadows and fields, in the neighbourhood of New York and other cities . . . and, as America owes to Europe her *Wheat,* why be ashamed to add fences to the debt?"

Why indeed? There is, I think, a very good reason for not doing so. You may tell a man by his border, so it is said, as you walk along the street. The use of the hedge in England reveals the English love of privacy and non-interference. As one garden writer said recently, to the Englishman the hedging of his plot is a pious custom. He may love his neighbor as himself, but his hedge is a rampart against prying eyes and a screen to blot out that which would offend his own. "It is so much the guardian and solace of his domestic soul that in its absence he is unhappy." And I would add that he also regards a hedge as the finest background to his flower borders and as a framework to his garden as a whole—and in this respect I do not think he errs.

But to an American a hedge is often a superfluity. More, it can be regarded as a sign of unsociability. I remember once explaining the English love of hedges to a Garden Club, saying that the first thing the owner of a new garden does is to make an enclosing hedge around him. Shocked murmurs followed my remarks.

No, the lack of hedges in widespread areas reveals the American character as much as their presence in English gardens reveals the British character. It reveals the gregarious streak in the American character, and also shows something more. It shows the community-mindedness, the good citizenship in districts where the gardens of an entire avenue may appear as one. Above all it shows the open-hearted sharing-generosity by which Americans are known and recognized the world over.

Garden sightseers, whether they are citizens or overseas visitors, and in particular those who make whirl-wind lecture tours, are apt to know only the well-groomed gardens of Garden Club presidents, the public gardens, and other "show-places." But to understand wholly you must go through the side streets of the cities and the country towns, to outlying estates and isolated homesteads, there to see the cultivated flower, often a jumbled mass of bloom beside the tasselled corn. And you must go even further, far beyond the picket fence, to see the eastern asters beside the golden-rod; the western lupins beside the poppies; to see the prairie alight with bloom and the mountains thick with alpine flowers. You must go over the whole vast territory which is larger than western Europe to know that not all of Europe has wild gardens such as Americans know and take for granted as a part of the grandeur of their continent.

"The love of gardening," as Gertrude Jekyll wrote, "is a seed that once sown never dies, but always grows and grows to an enduring and ever-increasing happiness." She might have added that a love of gardening is not the sole prerogative of any one country or people. Gardens the world over thrive on the interchange of garden ideas and plant material. And how much poorer the English gardener might be without those American treasures the pioneer plantsmen "sent home" so many years ago; how disappointing it would be if American gardens were entirely similar to those of England.

It is time now for me to go out into my own garden, one acre of land that had been neglected for two or three years when my Pennsylvania-born husband and I bought the place. For these parts it is an unusual garden, and although we are its new owners it holds much association for us.

We have to thank the original owner, "an Easterner" who planted the pink and white Eastern dogwood, the Southern magnolias and the sweet bay beside the door, the Concord grapevines and the big sweet shrub bushes. We think of the Southern gardens when we look at the four ancient oaks draped with streamers of gray moss. Seeing them above the camellia bushes we are reminded, impudent as it may sound, of a corner of Magnolia garden. When the scent of the bean-fields comes to me, when we hear the sound of the wild doves, when we see the Hereford cattle graze across the pastureland, we are reminded of Pennsylvania and England. When we look up across the wooded foothills to Mount St. Helena, four thousand feet or so above us, we remember

Robert Louis Stevenson who wrote his *Silverado Squatters* on the mountain slope during a summer's stay.

Sometimes I wonder where I am. Then I remember. The golden poppies have furled their petals. The evening air blows cold. The garden needs water for we are now in the first of the six rainless summer months. And I know that I am home, in Northern California.

APPENDIX

I have been asked, from time to time, to make a list, state by state, of America's most sightworthy gardens. I have neither the years left in my life nor the money in my purse sufficient to undertake the appraisal that would be essential to such a task. America is too big, and has far too many gardens.

Then, who am I to sit myself up as judge? A fine garden is a work of art which each of us sees with different eyes. The garden that gives you pleasure is a fine garden to you indeed, regardless of how I or any other might view it. To the true gardener, his garden is the finest in the land, or someday it will be!

Over any work of art, even the "experts" may and often do disagree. To the lover of the prairie, that is the great garden; he who loves the rose may discard the most glorious iris.

How to set about garden sightseeing? The place to begin is in your own state. Fine private gardens are not always open to visitors, but many are, and when and where is not hard to find out. The garden editor of your newspaper can start you off on the right track—a garden editor is often the best guide in locating the president or secretary of the garden clubs. I, coming as a stranger, found that my own love of gardens was an open sesame wherever in America I let that love be known; gardeners speak an international language.

But I have made a list. It does not pretend to be either comprehensive or final; largely it is limited to the great "show places" that any one who has the desire and time may visit and enjoy with a minimum of trouble, and which welcome the public. It includes also some of the great natural areas, the wild gardens, that belong to the people of America, free for all to enjoy.

No, my list is not complete—I shall be charged with glaring omissions. There is no mention of the countless hundreds of beautiful private gardens, nor of nurserymen's grounds, some of which provide magnificent floral spectacles. Yet it *is* complete in one and a very real sense. You may, probably have, seen at least some of my chosen elite; but until you have seen them *all*, each in proper season, you have not seen America!

BOTANICAL GARDENS AND ARBORETUMS

THE ARNOLD ARBORETUM, Boston, Mass.: located in Jamaica Plains about five miles from the center of the city. A great arboretum which has earned the title "America's Greatest Garden," containing acres of rare trees and shrubs from many parts of the world, including splendid flowering collections of forsythias, azaleas, oriental cherries, magnolias, crab apples, rhododendrons and lilac, etc. Most popular visiting time is from early April until mid June, but it is a place of year-round beauty and interest.

ASH LAWN, Charlottesville, Virginia: home of President James Monroe. The old-time garden, with a fine view over the valley to Monticello, has some of the best boxwood in the country. It is a small garden but redolent of Old Virginia.

THE BROOKLYN BOTANIC GARDEN, Brooklyn, New York, is a famous institution, with its roses and azaleas, perennials and other plants, and the Japanese Gardens. Here also the large greenhouses containing plantings of commercial value, tea, coffee, etc., is of special interest.

THE BOYCE THOMPSON SOUTHWESTERN ARBORETUM, Superior, Arizona, contains a great collection of desert plants from all over the world, in addition to the natural flora of the state. Also a testing ground for eucylaptus over the Western states.

EL ALAMO, San Antonio, Texas. The one time Spanish Governor's Palace garden, a finely planted Patio Garden well worth seeing in regard to the American adaptation of the patio, and for its fountain at the center of the courtyard.

THE FAIRCHILD TROPICAL GARDEN, at Coral Gables, Florida, is one of the great botanical gardens of the world. Covering 83 acres, it contains tropical trees and plants from almost every tropical area.

THE FORT WORTH BOTANIC GARDEN, Fort Worth, Texas, is beautifully planted with some 2,500 labeled plants, and includes a water garden, a rose garden, and a garden of native plants.

INTERNATIONAL PEACE GARDENS, North Dakota, in fertile Turtle Mountain Valley, astride the U.S.-Canadian border. Here 2,220 acres were set aside in 1929 as "a symbol of everlasting peace between the two countries." Wild life is abundant, and area a great rendezvous of song birds. Formal gardens have been built and are being extended. Yearly, each July, the gardens are rededicated to the cause of Canadian-American peace.

THE MISSOURI BOTANICAL GARDEN, St. Louis, Missouri, covering 75 acres, is one of the outstanding botanical gardens of the country. Famous for the orchid, cacti and succulent collections under glass, and for its Aquatic Gardens and tropical lilies.

THE MORTON ARBORETUM, Lisle, Illinois, is an 800-acre arboretum planted with a great number of rare trees and shrubs, many of which were introduced by Dr. Ernest H. ("Chinese") Wilson. Also contains many native specimens.

THE NEW YORK BOTANICAL GARDEN in Bronx Park, New York City, has a very large rock garden; in addition plantings of many varieties of bulbs, a rose garden and natural areas. In the Library a magnificent collection of fossil plants may be seen, flowers and leaves preserved through the centuries in stone but which once grew where New York now stands.

ORTON PLANTATION, near Wilmington, North Carolina, a fine estate, with its antebellum house and southern garden overlooking the Cape Fear River. Open public year round.

THE PORTLAND INTERNATIONAL ROSE TEST GARDEN, Portland, Oregon. As befits Portland, the City of Roses, this is one of the finest public rose gardens in the country, and magnificently placed in Washington Park, high on a bluff overlooking the city.

THE RANCHO SANTA ANA BOTANIC GARDEN, Claremont, California, devoted to botanical and horticultural research of the California flora, and a mecca for specialists.

THE SANTA BARBARA BOTANIC GARDEN, Santa Barbara, California. This collection of native California flowers, trees and flowering shrubs is superbly situated in a canyon above sea level. It is arranged into such typical areas as the Arroyo, Canyon, Desert, Foothill and Woodland, and forms a wonderful wildflower display.

STRYBING ARBORETUM, Golden Gate Park, San Francisco, California, contains important collections of plants from many parts of the world. Grouped geographically, the arboretum has an especially fine representation of the New Zealand and Australian flora. One outstanding exhibit is the famous *Magnolia campbelli,* the rose-pink magnolia which usually blooms the second week in February, bearing flowers up to 8 or 10 inches in diameter.

UNIVERSITY OF WASHINGTON ARBORETUM, Seattle, Washington, has fine collections of flowering cherries, camellias, azaleas and rhododendrons. In spring it is especially sightworthy, the western dogwood making cascades of white bloom among the evergreen trees.

VALLEY FORGE, near Philadelphia, Pennsylvania. The great historical site contains what is probably the largest planting of eastern dogwood trees in the country, planted as a memorial to Washington's soldiers in the hard winter of 1777–1778. It is estimated that upwards of 600,000 go to see the dogwood bloom each year.

PUBLIC GARDENS AND "SHOW PLACES"

THE ARTHUR HOYT SCOTT HORTICULTURAL FOUNDATION, Swarthmore, Pennsylvania. This arboretum displays plant material which can be easily grown by the home-gardener of average means, and has accordingly been termed The People's Garden. The spring display of flowering trees and shrubs is particularly beautiful. There are many plant collections including the lilac and tree peony plantings.

BELLINGRATH GARDENS, 20 miles out of Mobile, Alabama, a 60-acre planting of formal and informal gardens, presenting a succession of color
from February through to November. The camellia collection, numbering some 4,000 plants, is one of the finest. The azaleas are counted
as around 200,000, and there are vast plantings of roses, gardenias and
annuals and perennials. The Gardens should be approached from
Mobile, along the road known as The Azalea Trail.

BREEZE HILL, Harrisburg, Pennsylvania. Garden of the late Dr. J. Horace
McFarland, master printer and famous rosarian. The garden contains
a wide collection of plants, and in addition to its All-America Rose
Test Garden, there is a relatively small but exceptionally designed
rose garden of great appeal.

CAPITOL GARDENS, Olympia, Washington. In the opinion of many, the
gardens included in the 50 acres surrounding the Capitol Buildings
are the finest gardens of their type in the country. They include magnificent herbaceous and annual flower borders, and a Sunken Border
massed with bloom, which comes to its peak toward the end of July
and continues in full color into the late summer. The gardens also
boast a fine avenue of Japanese flowering cherries, very reminiscent
of the flowering cherries along the Potomac in Washington, D.C.

CAPISTRANO MISSION GARDEN, Capistrano, California, an old-time Spanish
mission garden gay with flowers during most months in the year.

THE CLOISTERS MUSEUM, Fort Tryon Park, New York City. The park
itself has beautiful plantings, including a heather garden. But the
Museum possesses a small herb garden which contains four medlar
trees, a fruit once widely used in Europe as a preserve, but little known
in the U.S. The Museum also stages an extraordinarly beautiful but
small garden under the glass roof of the Guilham Cloister.

CYPRESS GARDEN, 24 miles north of Charleston, South Carolina, is open
to the public from December 1 to May 1. Massive plantings of flowers
spread throughout the swamps. The bald cypress trees are especially
impressive.

FAIRMONT PARK, Philadelphia, Pennsylvania. Not only one of the largest
parks in the country, but is rich in its varieties of trees and superlative
driveways.

GOLDEN GATE PARK, San Francisco, California, is a great pleasure ground
as well as a great garden. Now a green heart of the city, a garden
where almost every country in the world is represented by some form
of plant life, the Park is perhaps a gardener's finest achievement against
odds. Less than 100 years ago it was a waste of sand dunes, a place
people said where a garden could not be made. Predominantly green,
with its trees and grass, it displays wonderful shows of color in one
part or another of its vast acreage the year round. February is best
for the golden-headed acacias; April for the cherry trees in the Japanese
Tea Garden; and May for the magnificent rhododendrons.

GOVERNOR'S PALACE GARDEN, Williamsburg, Virginia. Noteworthy as one of the two exact replicas of the large place eighteenth-century gardens in existence. Reconstructed and beautiful, with such famous features as a mount and a maze, the latter modelled exactly on that of Hampton Court, England. NOTE: In Williamsburg also several restored and reconstructed small-lot eighteenth-century gardens.

HERSHEY ROSE GARDEN, Hershey, Pennsylvania, is a 21-acre Rose Garden containing thousands of rose plants in over 800 varieties. Hershey might claim to have the finest planting of that great single yellow rose, Mermaid; it is used there not as a climber but as a wide-spreading ground cover to a central pool. Garden also contains thousands of spring flowering bulbs, annuals and other flowering shrubs and trees.

LONGWOOD GARDENS, Kennett Square, Pennsylvania. Estate of the late Pierre S. du Pont. One of the truly great gardens of America. A series of gardens, including a magnificent Fountain Garden. The summer evening, on certain occasions, Fountain Display, when the waters are multi-colored, is without rival in the U.S. The glass-houses which lead from the mammoth Conservatory are unique, and exhibit a year-round succession of bloom. Now known as the Longwood Foundation, the gardens are open to the public, as in Mr. Pierre du Pont's lifetime, the year round.

MAGNOLIA GARDENS, 15 miles from Charleston, South Carolina. World famous for the immense plantings of brilliant azaleas massed along the banks of the black-watered swamps. Height of bloom during March and April. Open to the public January 1-May 1.

MIDDLETON PLACE GARDENS, 14 miles from Charleston, South Carolina. Dating from 1741 these are the oldest landscaped gardens in America. Set amid the old deserted rice plantations, the terraced lawns lead down to the "Butterfly Lakes"; azaleas are reflected in the lake waters, and in addition to the massive oaks there are fine old camellias and a great planting of the southern magnolia.

MONTICELLO, Charlottesville, Virginia, home and gardens of Thomas Jefferson, both restored. For those who read Jefferson's GARDEN NOTEBOOK this is a place of rare interest.

MOUNT VERNON, a short distance from Washington, D.C. Home and garden of George Washington. Famous for its Boxwood Garden, its lilacs which are supposed to have been planted by George Washington, and imported from England. As far as possible Mount Vernon is very much as Washington left it.

OHME GARDENS, Wenatchee, Washington, contain one of the largest natural rock gardens in the U.S. Dubbed Garden in the Sky on account of its situation, high in the hills overlooking the orchard-covered valley where the Columbia and Wenatchee rivers meet. Low-growing and creeping plants from all over the world blanket the ground.

Wide planting of thyme, penstemon, *Phlox subulata,* and the rare *Lewisia tweedyi.*

THE ERNEST H. WILSON GARDEN, Peoria, Illinois, a memorial garden to the late Dr. Ernest H. Wilson, famous plant-hunter, one time keeper of the Arnold Arboretum. The main garden contains some 1000 plants, including a large group of regal lilies, one of Wilson's most famous introductions.

NATURAL WILD PRESERVES

GREAT SMOKEY MOUNTAINS NATIONAL PARK, half in North Carolina, half in Tennessee. Nowhere else in the country can so many varieties of plant life be found. Some 1200 different species and varieties flower each spring. The Park also contains great stands of native deciduous trees in upwards of 130 different kinds. Such beautiful native flowering shrubs as stewartia and the silverbell; redbud and azalea and mountain laurel can be seen in great profusion. Late April is the peak flowering time of many low-growing plants: May, June and July are the rhododendron months.

HUMBOLDT STATE REDWOOD PARK, 232 miles north of San Francisco, California, possesses one of the finest stands of the giant coastal Redwood trees (Sequoia sempervirens). An area also rich in the redwood's associated shrubs, flowers and ferns.

KINGS CANYON AND SEQUOIA NATIONAL PARKS, east of Fresno, California, is the land of the Giant Sequoias, the Big Trees (Sequoia gigantea), believed to be the oldest and one of the largest living things on earth, the General Sherman Bigtree is estimated to be 4000 years old. Also a wonderful wildflower area, approached through the foothill country where the chaparral-covered slopes are full of lupin and yellow bush poppies, and mountain lilac.

MOUNT RAINIER NATIONAL PARK, east of Tacoma, Washington, is one of the most spectacularly beautiful wildflower areas in North America. The acres of subalpine meadows that girt the 14,408 feet snow-capped Mt. Rainier are at their best in early July, when the avalanche fawn-lily, the western pasque flower and mountain buttercup take over the meadows from the receding snowbanks and in early August when the hillsides are covered with masses of the red and white so-called heathers. In July the less generally known flowers of the forests are most numerous. Over 700 species of flowering plants are to be found in the Park.

OLYMPIC NATIONAL PARK, on the Olympic Peninsula, Washington, is a unique wilderness, and probably has a more variable area and climate than any part of the U.S. The great Rain Forest, with the wettest winter climate in the continental U.S., contains the greatest stand of coniferous timber in the world, with the Douglas Fir as king of the forest.

By contrast the northeast side of the peninsula has the driest climate
on the west coast outside of southern California. In late July to early
September columbine, asters, paint brush, lupine and a myriad flowers
carpet the mountain slopes. This high country may be explored along
Hurricane Ridge and Deer Park.

POINT LOBOS RESERVE STATE PARK, near Carmel, California. Last natural
stand of the Monterey cypress. A relatively small ocean-girt headland
containing some 280 plant varieties in natural scenery of unusual
beauty. The whole surrounding coastal area, with its chaparral-covered
slopes and acres of lupins is outstanding.

ROCKY MOUNTAIN NATIONAL PARK, Colorado, lying across the Continental
Divide between Estes Park and Grand Lake, is a superlative area for
Colorado wild flowers and alpines. Elevation ranging from 7,800 to
14,255 feet.

SHENANDOAH NATIONAL PARK and THE BLUE RIDGE PARKWAY are areas
similar, as regards plant life, to the Great Smoky Mountains National
Park. All this rich and varied country was the favorite hunting ground
of the early plant collectors. Mid-April, the shadblow is in bloom;
galax is peculiar to the region and covers the ground with glorious
color. "My Kashmir" so John Bartram, the first American born plantsman, called the Shenandoah Valley.

TULE LAKE, one of the four major portions of the Klamath Basin National Wildlife Refuges on the Oregon and California borders. This
comparatively little known area is famous, to hunters and ornitholo-
gists, as a waterfowl paradise. Here occurs the largest concentrations
of waterfowl anywhere in the U.S. during the autumn migration. But
the area is also a rich field for a plantsman; the whole Basin abounds
with flowers. This is perhaps one of the most romantically beautiful
places a flower lover could ever see, in company with hosts of birds,
and the sight of Mt. Shasta, snow-capped, 50 miles to the southwest.